Kanako's Killer Life

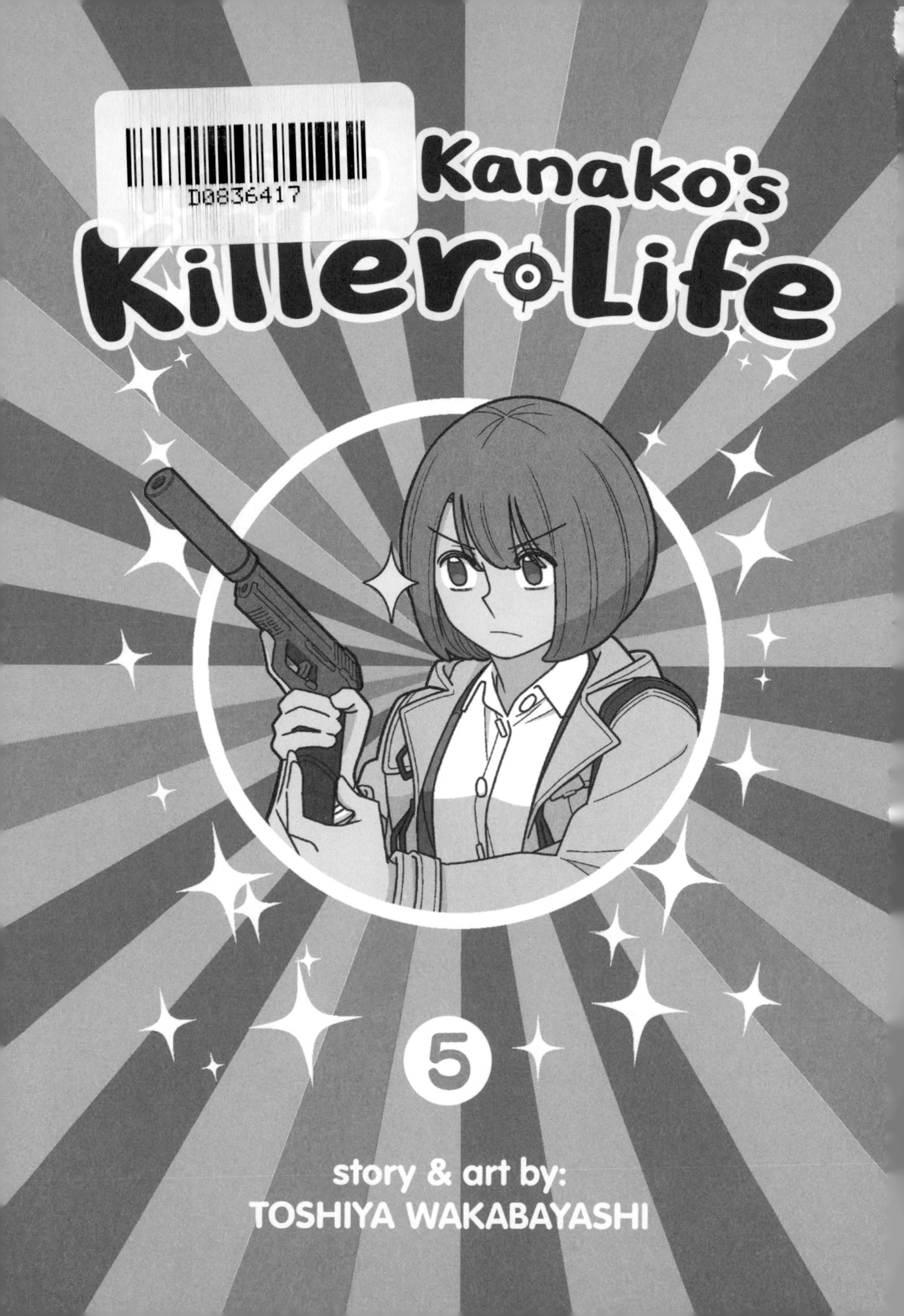

5

story & art by:
TOSHIYA WAKABAYASHI

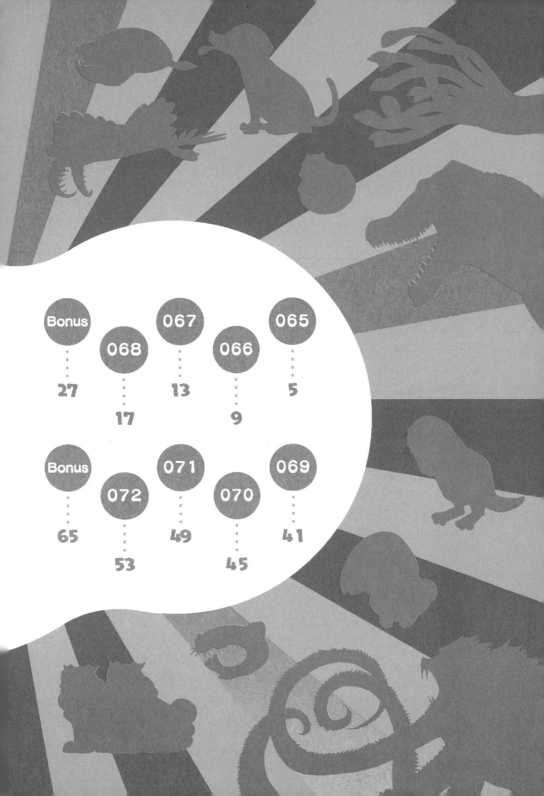

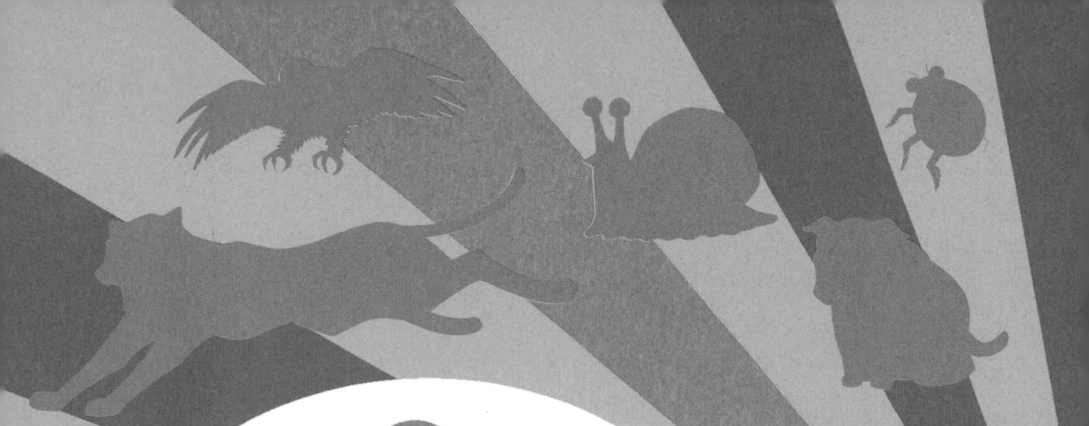

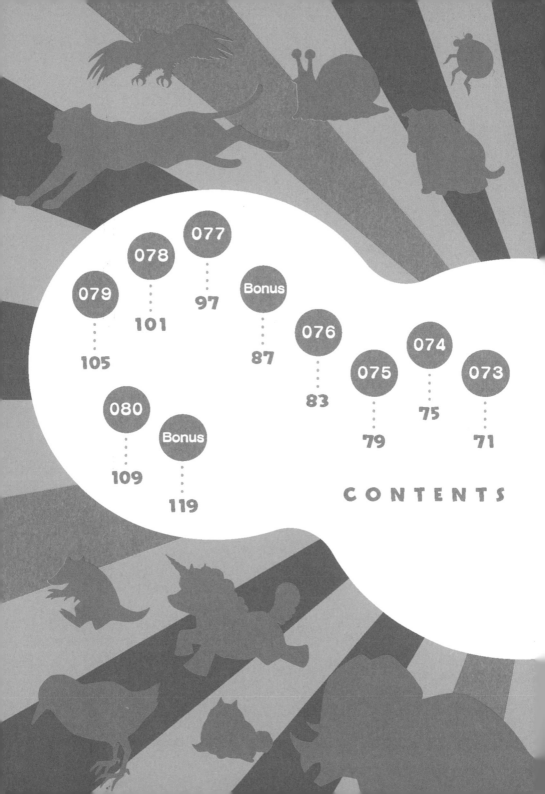

CONTENTS

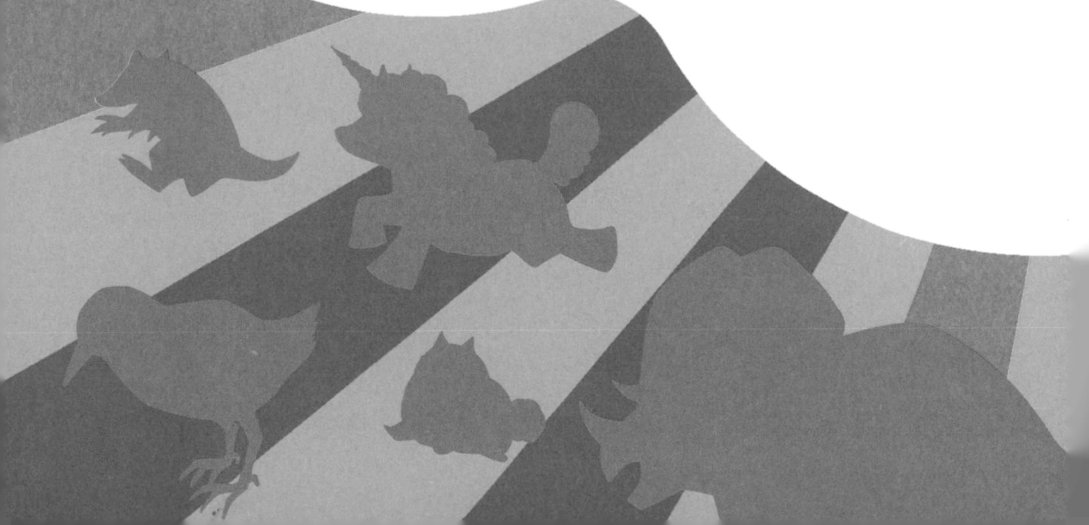

Happy Kanako's
Killer Life

I'LL
DO
IT!!

065

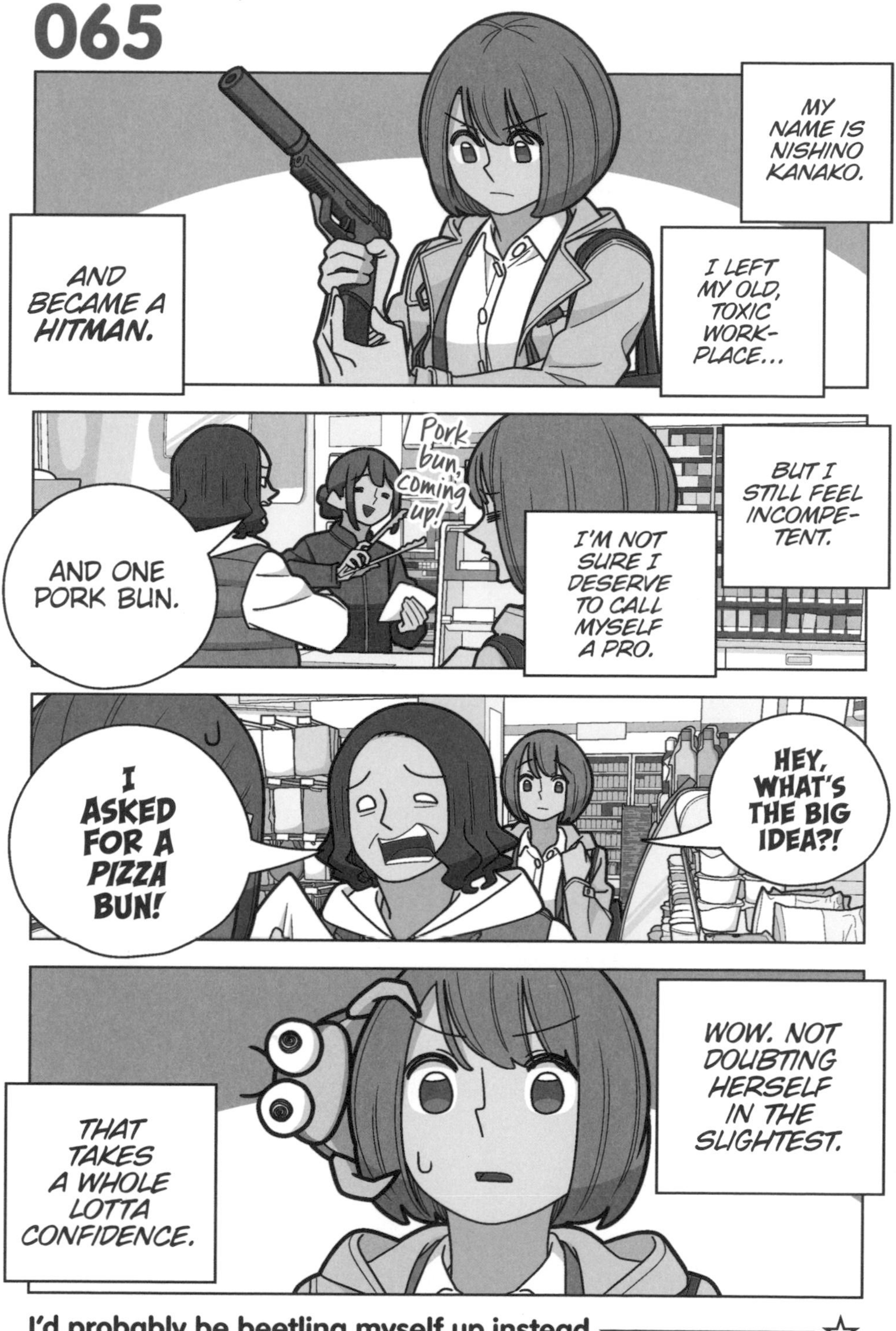
MY NAME IS NISHINO KANAKO.
I LEFT MY OLD, TOXIC WORK-PLACE...
AND BECAME A **HITMAN.**
BUT I STILL FEEL INCOMPE-TENT.
I'M NOT SURE I DESERVE TO CALL MYSELF A PRO.
Pork bun, coming up!
AND ONE PORK BUN.
HEY, WHAT'S THE BIG IDEA?!
I ASKED FOR A PIZZA BUN!
WOW. NOT DOUBTING HERSELF IN THE SLIGHTEST.
THAT TAKES A WHOLE LOTTA CONFIDENCE.

I'd probably be beetling myself up instead. ☆

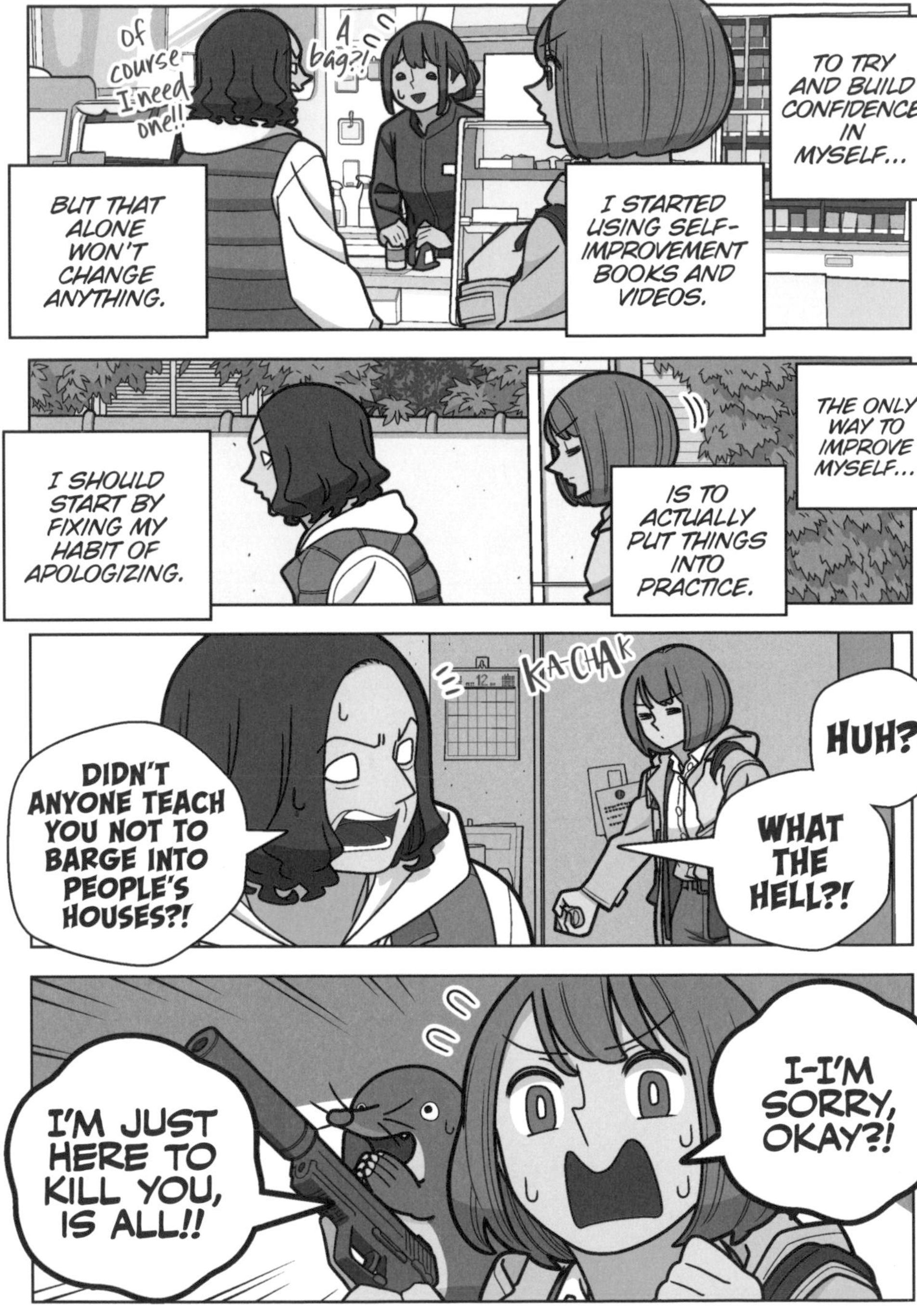
TO TRY AND BUILD CONFIDENCE IN MYSELF...
I STARTED USING SELF-IMPROVEMENT BOOKS AND VIDEOS.
A bag?!
Of course I need one!!
BUT THAT ALONE WON'T CHANGE ANYTHING.
THE ONLY WAY TO IMPROVE MYSELF...
IS TO ACTUALLY PUT THINGS INTO PRACTICE.
I SHOULD START BY FIXING MY HABIT OF APOLOGIZING.
KA-CHAK
HUH?!
WHAT THE HELL?!
DIDN'T ANYONE TEACH YOU NOT TO BARGE INTO PEOPLE'S HOUSES?!
I-I'M SORRY, OKAY?!
I'M JUST HERE TO KILL YOU, IS ALL!!

☆ Can't break the mole-d.

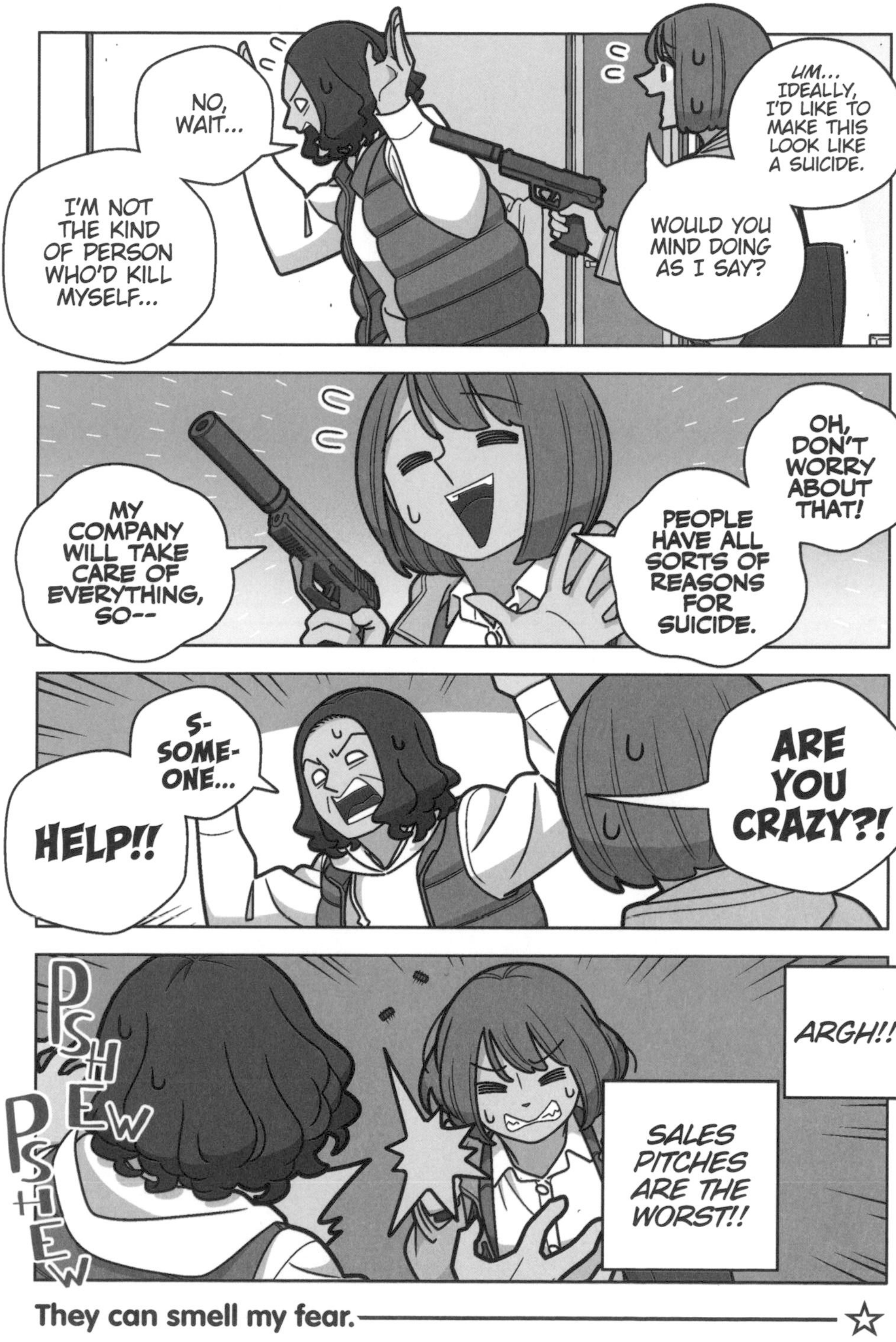
UM... IDEALLY, I'D LIKE TO MAKE THIS LOOK LIKE A SUICIDE.
WOULD YOU MIND DOING AS I SAY?
NO, WAIT...
I'M NOT THE KIND OF PERSON WHO'D KILL MYSELF...
OH, DON'T WORRY ABOUT THAT!
PEOPLE HAVE ALL SORTS OF REASONS FOR SUICIDE.
MY COMPANY WILL TAKE CARE OF EVERYTHING, SO--
ARE YOU CRAZY?!
S-SOME-ONE...
HELP!!
ARGH!!
SALES PITCHES ARE THE WORST!!
PSHEW
PSHEW

They can smell my fear. ☆

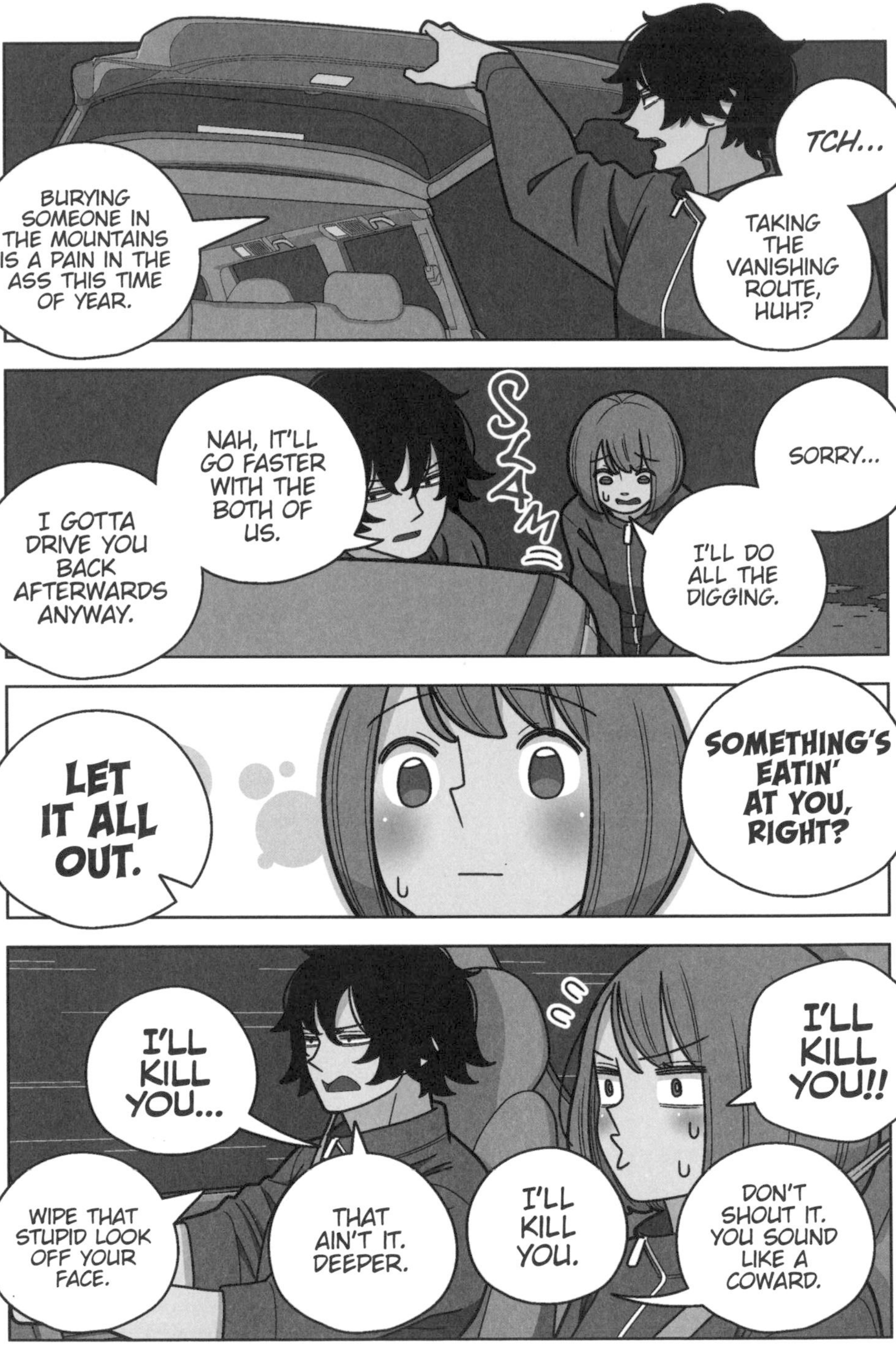
TCH...
TAKING THE VANISHING ROUTE, HUH?
BURYING SOMEONE IN THE MOUNTAINS IS A PAIN IN THE ASS THIS TIME OF YEAR.
SORRY...
I'LL DO ALL THE DIGGING.
SLAM
NAH, IT'LL GO FASTER WITH THE BOTH OF US.
I GOTTA DRIVE YOU BACK AFTERWARDS ANYWAY.
SOMETHING'S EATIN' AT YOU, RIGHT?
LET IT ALL OUT.
I'LL KILL YOU!!
DON'T SHOUT IT. YOU SOUND LIKE A COWARD.
I'LL KILL YOU.
THAT AIN'T IT. DEEPER.
I'LL KILL YOU...
WIPE THAT STUPID LOOK OFF YOUR FACE.

☆ **Baby steps.**

066

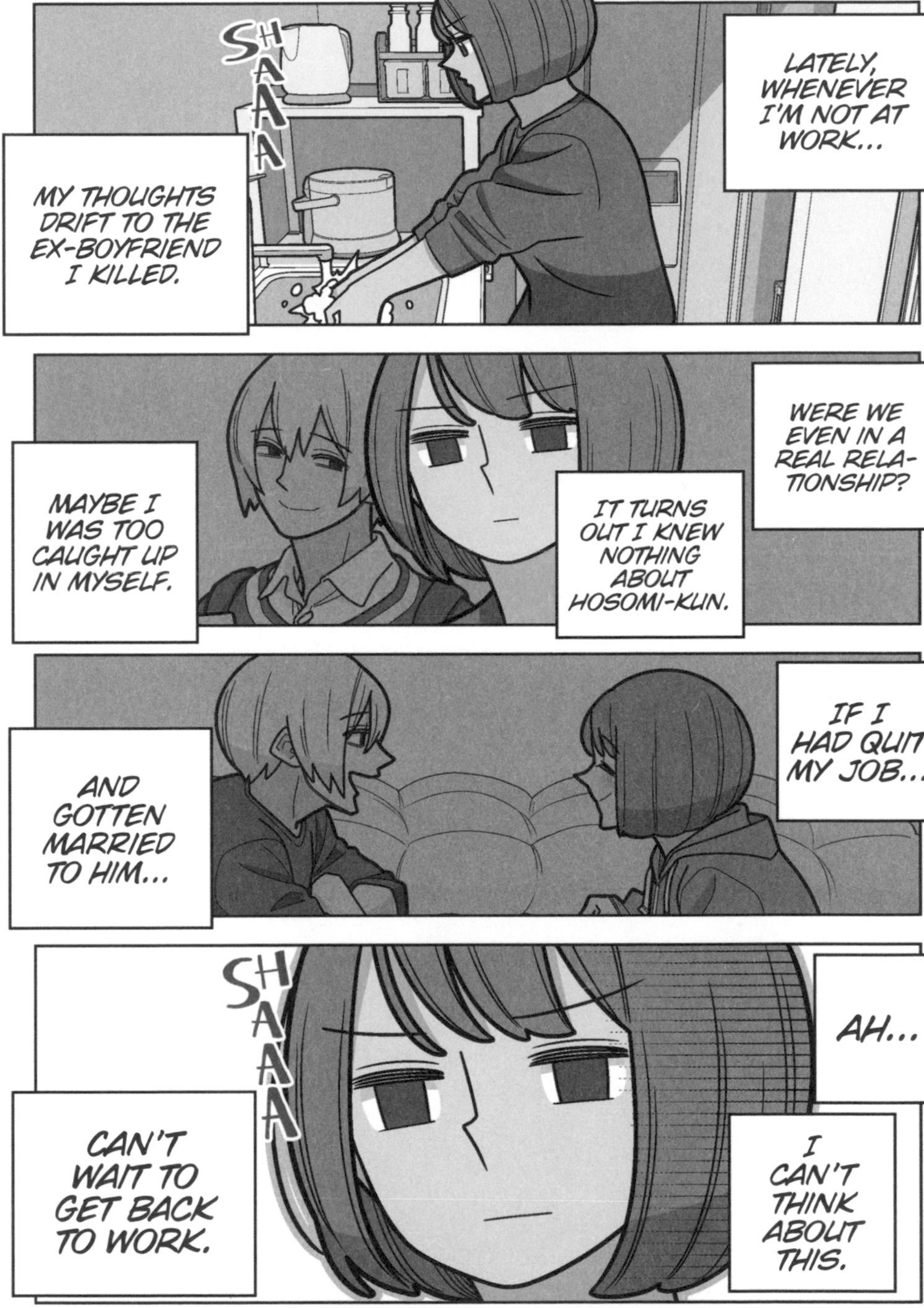
LATELY, WHENEVER I'M NOT AT WORK...
SHAAA
MY THOUGHTS DRIFT TO THE EX-BOYFRIEND I KILLED.
WERE WE EVEN IN A REAL RELATIONSHIP?
IT TURNS OUT I KNEW NOTHING ABOUT HOSOMI-KUN.
MAYBE I WAS TOO CAUGHT UP IN MYSELF.
IF I HAD QUIT MY JOB...
AND GOTTEN MARRIED TO HIM...
AH...
I CAN'T THINK ABOUT THIS.
SHAAA
CAN'T WAIT TO GET BACK TO WORK.

Why can't I wash my memories away? ☆

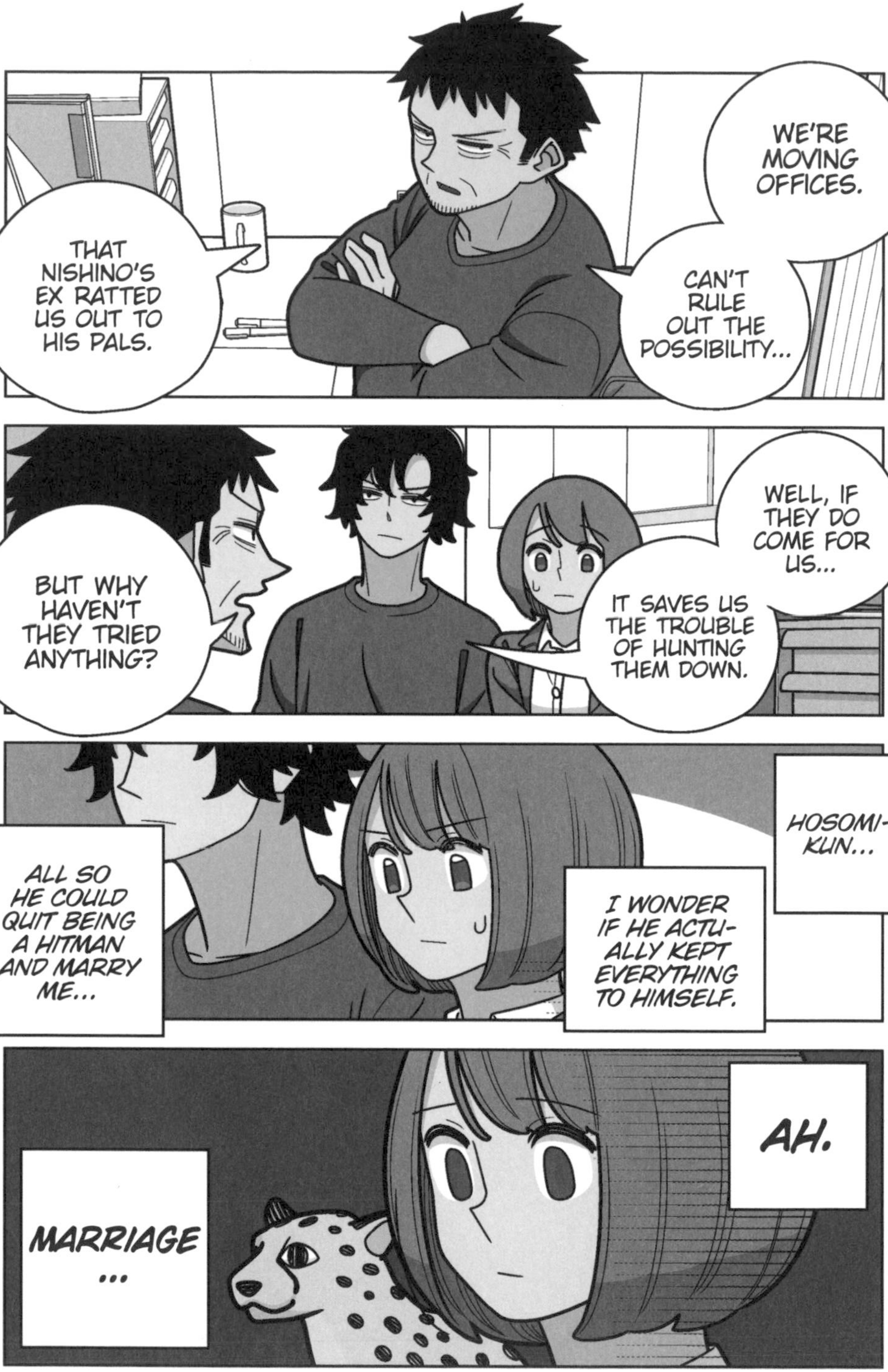
WE'RE MOVING OFFICES.
CAN'T RULE OUT THE POSSIBILITY...
THAT NISHINO'S EX RATTED US OUT TO HIS PALS.
WELL, IF THEY DO COME FOR US...
IT SAVES US THE TROUBLE OF HUNTING THEM DOWN.
BUT WHY HAVEN'T THEY TRIED ANYTHING?
HOSOMI-KUN...
I WONDER IF HE ACTUALLY KEPT EVERYTHING TO HIMSELF.
ALL SO HE COULD QUIT BEING A HITMAN AND MARRY ME...
AH.
MARRIAGE ...

☆ Cat-astrophic thoughts.

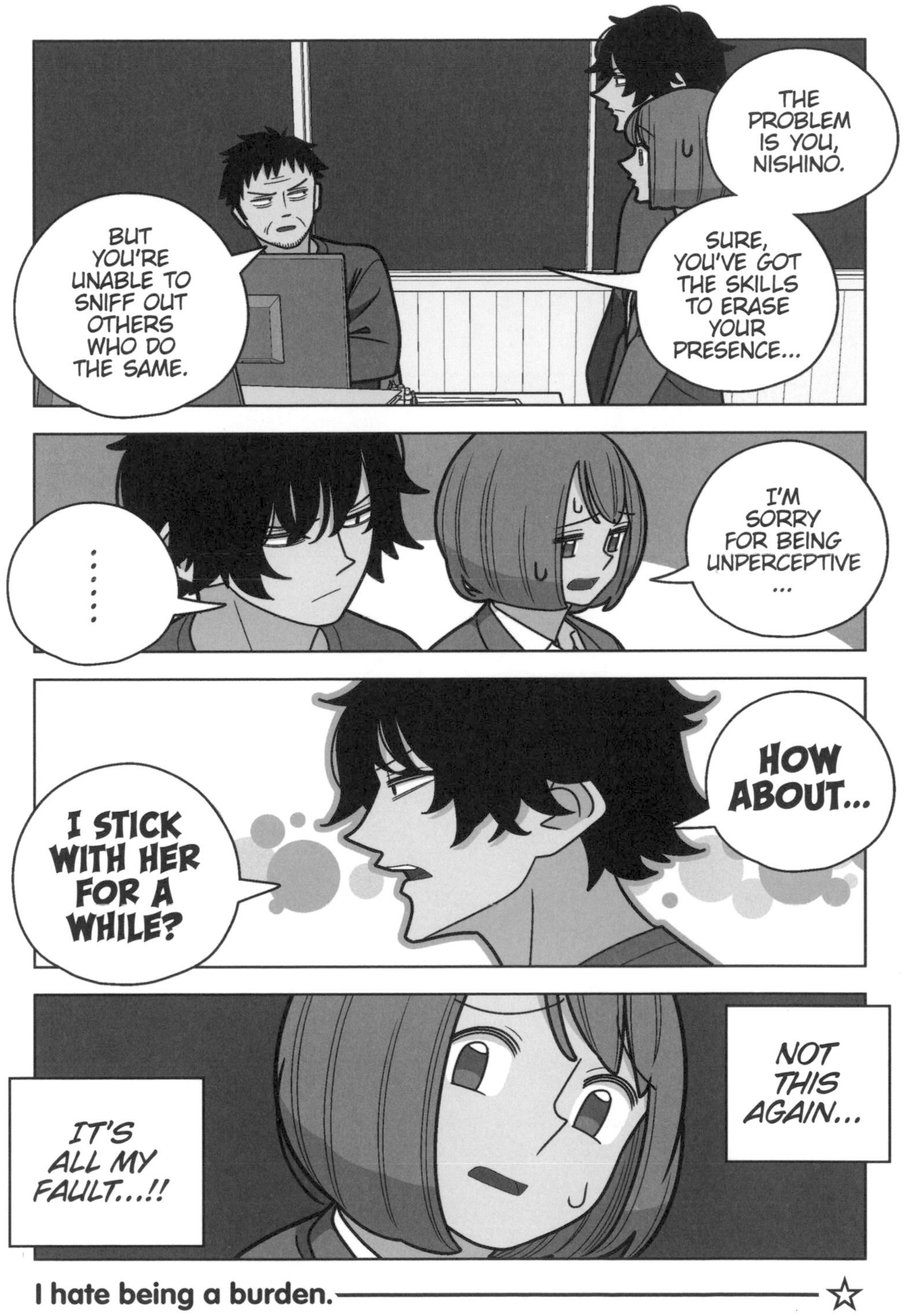
THE PROBLEM IS YOU, NISHINO.
SURE, YOU'VE GOT THE SKILLS TO ERASE YOUR PRESENCE...
BUT YOU'RE UNABLE TO SNIFF OUT OTHERS WHO DO THE SAME.
I'M SORRY FOR BEING UNPERCEPTIVE ...
......
HOW ABOUT...
I STICK WITH HER FOR A WHILE?
NOT THIS AGAIN...
IT'S ALL MY FAULT...!!

I hate being a burden. ☆

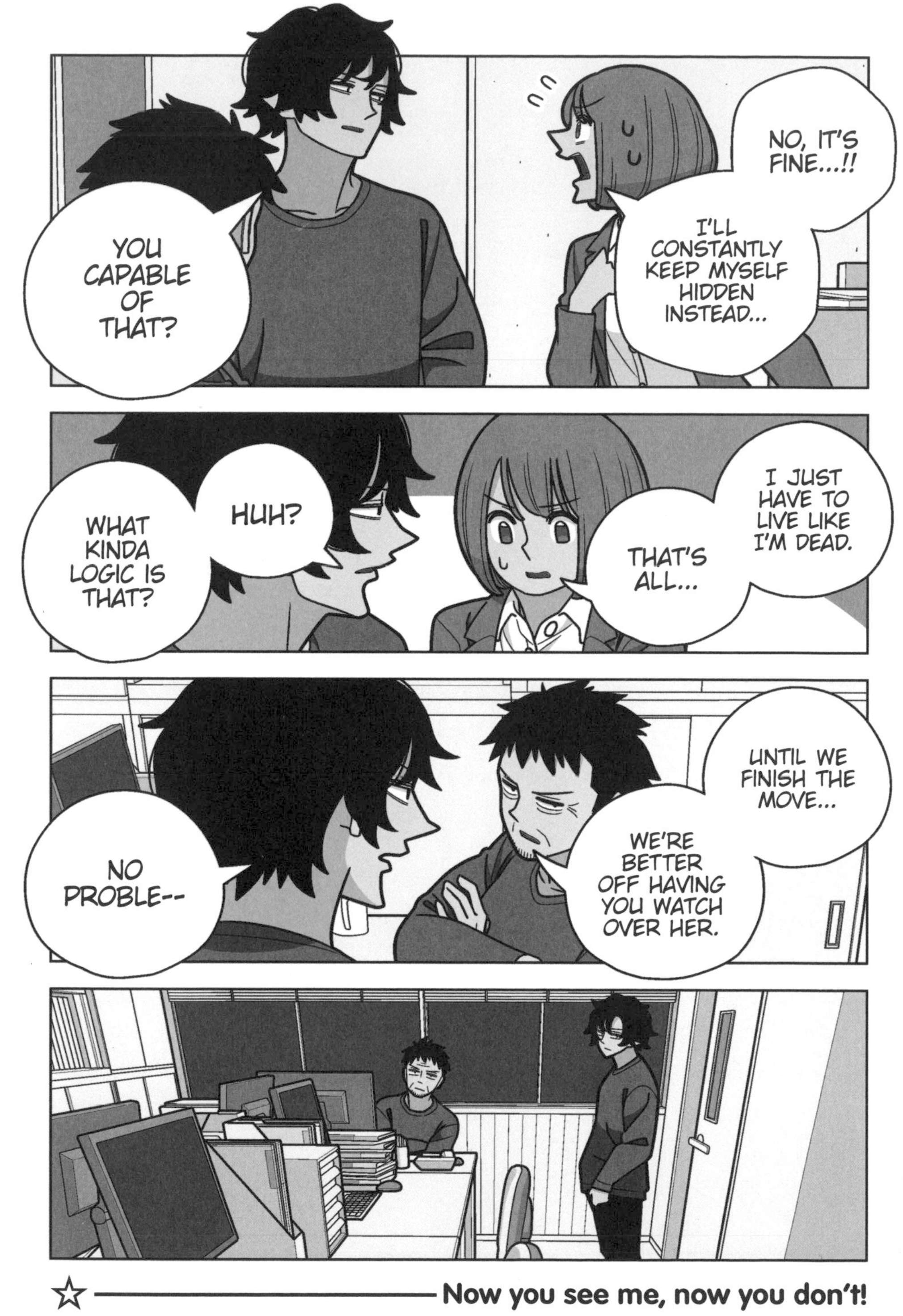
NO, IT'S FINE...!!
I'LL CONSTANTLY KEEP MYSELF HIDDEN INSTEAD...
YOU CAPABLE OF THAT?
I JUST HAVE TO LIVE LIKE I'M DEAD.
THAT'S ALL...
HUH?
WHAT KINDA LOGIC IS THAT?
UNTIL WE FINISH THE MOVE...
WE'RE BETTER OFF HAVING YOU WATCH OVER HER.
NO PROBLE--

067

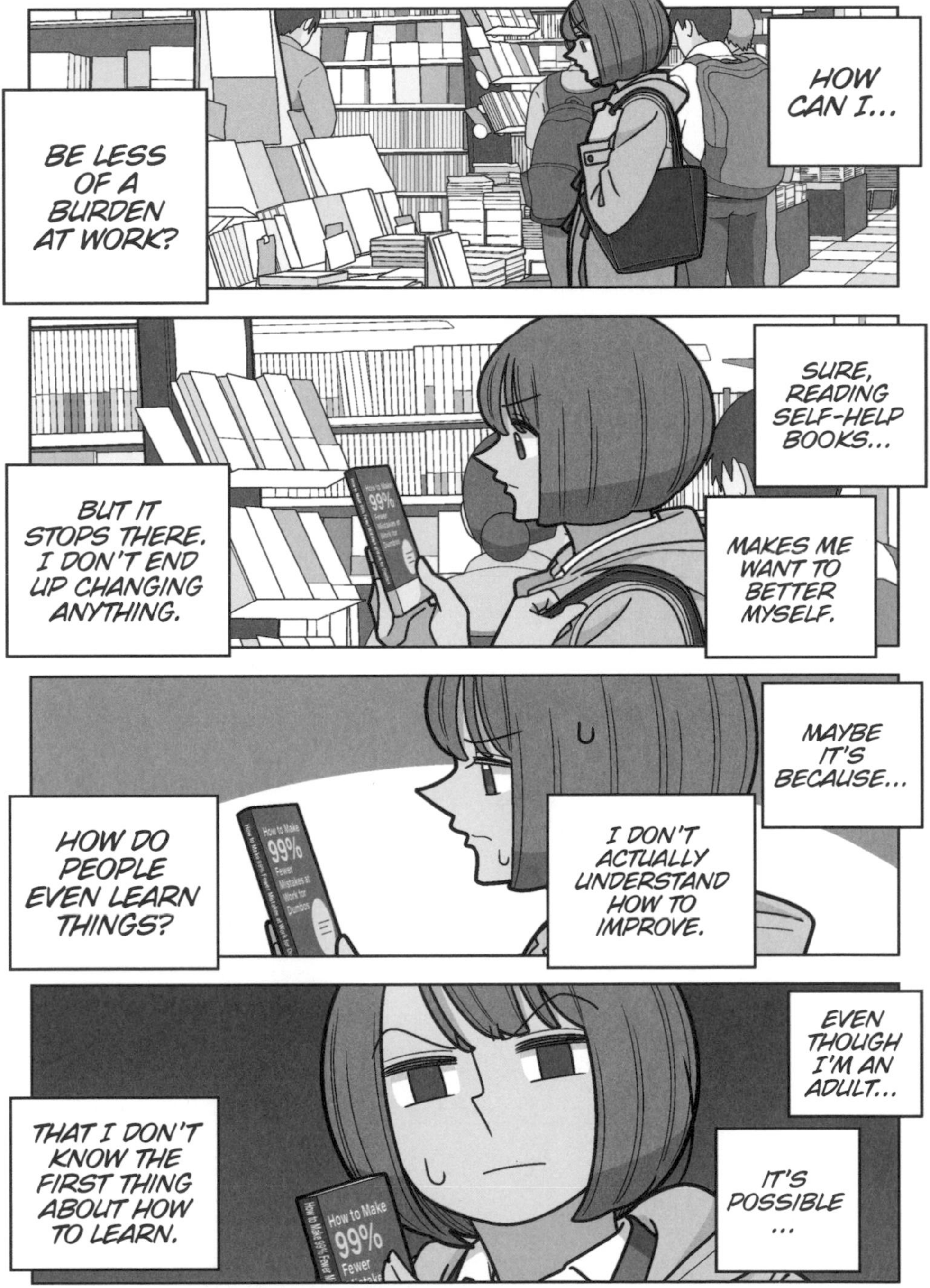
HOW CAN I...
BE LESS OF A BURDEN AT WORK?
SURE, READING SELF-HELP BOOKS...
MAKES ME WANT TO BETTER MYSELF.
BUT IT STOPS THERE. I DON'T END UP CHANGING ANYTHING.
MAYBE IT'S BECAUSE...
I DON'T ACTUALLY UNDERSTAND HOW TO IMPROVE.
How to Make 99% Fewer Mistakes at Work for Dumbos
HOW DO PEOPLE EVEN LEARN THINGS?
EVEN THOUGH I'M AN ADULT...
IT'S POSSIBLE ...
THAT I DON'T KNOW THE FIRST THING ABOUT HOW TO LEARN.

Did school teach me anything? ☆

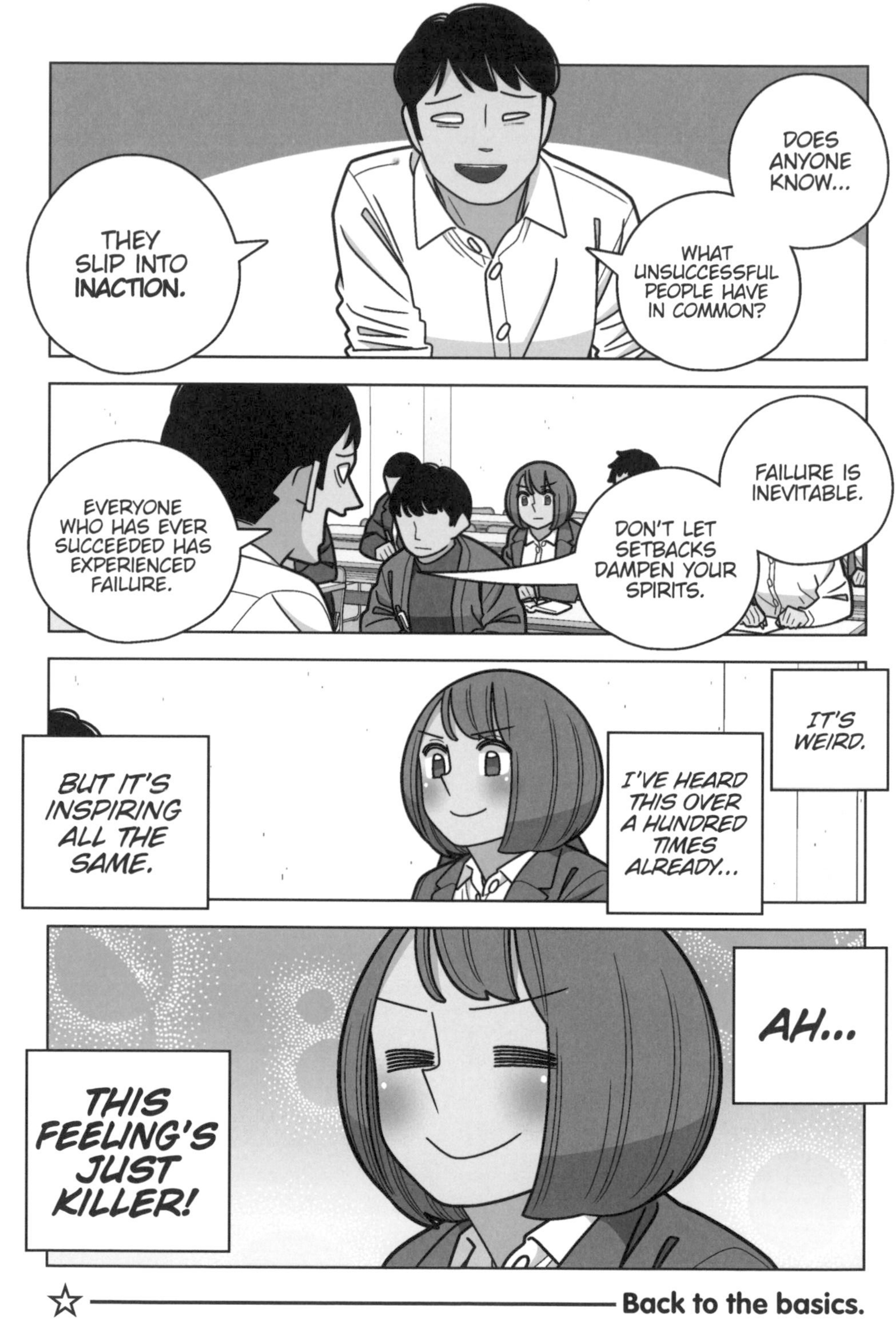
DOES ANYONE KNOW...
WHAT UNSUCCESSFUL PEOPLE HAVE IN COMMON?
THEY SLIP INTO INACTION.
FAILURE IS INEVITABLE.
DON'T LET SETBACKS DAMPEN YOUR SPIRITS.
EVERYONE WHO HAS EVER SUCCEEDED HAS EXPERIENCED FAILURE.
IT'S WEIRD.
I'VE HEARD THIS OVER A HUNDRED TIMES ALREADY...
BUT IT'S INSPIRING ALL THE SAME.
AH...
THIS FEELING'S JUST KILLER!

☆ Back to the basics.

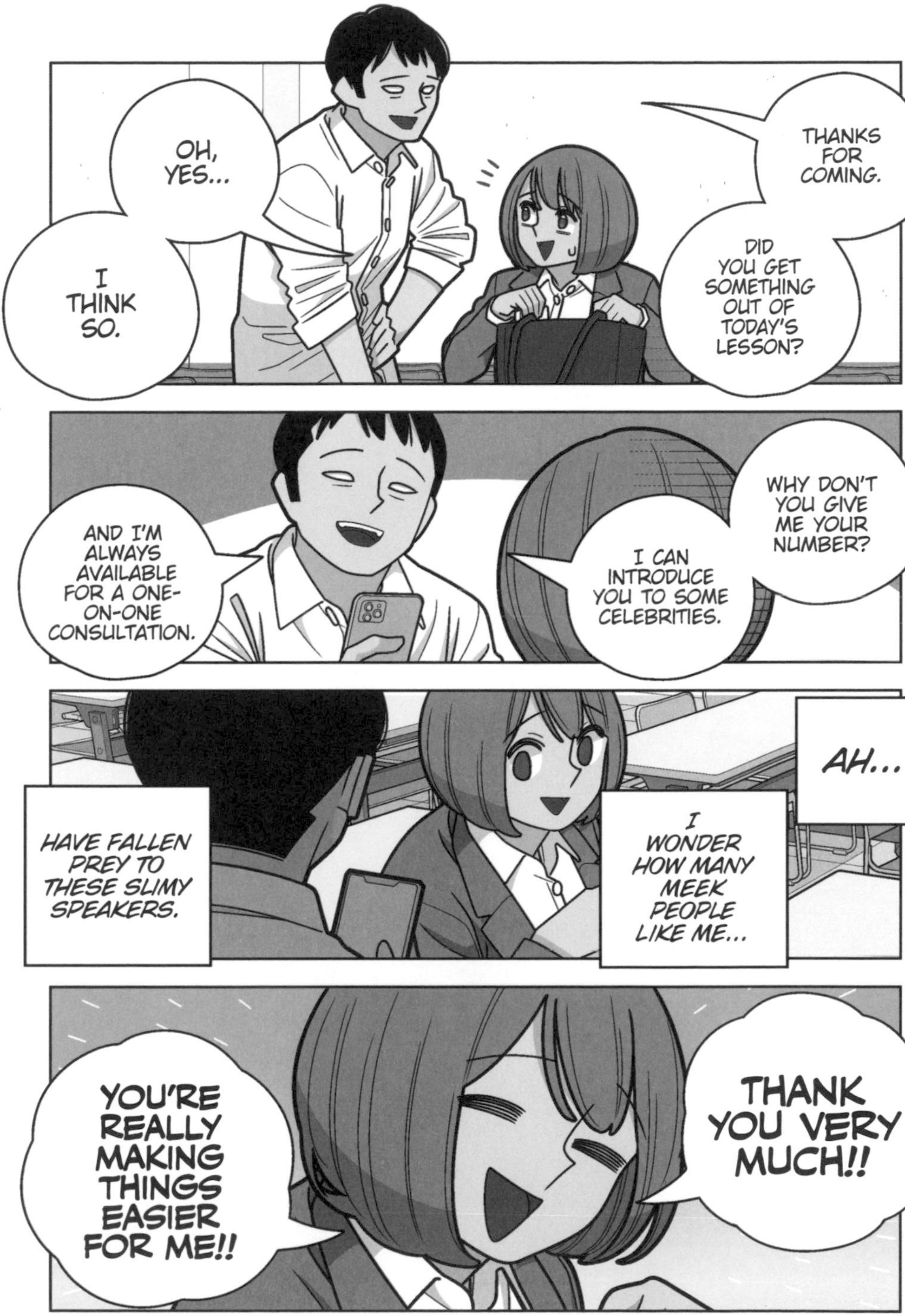
THANKS FOR COMING.
DID YOU GET SOMETHING OUT OF TODAY'S LESSON?
OH, YES...
I THINK SO.
WHY DON'T YOU GIVE ME YOUR NUMBER?
I CAN INTRODUCE YOU TO SOME CELEBRITIES.
AND I'M ALWAYS AVAILABLE FOR A ONE-ON-ONE CONSULTATION.
AH...
I WONDER HOW MANY MEEK PEOPLE LIKE ME...
HAVE FALLEN PREY TO THESE SLIMY SPEAKERS.
THANK YOU VERY MUCH!!
YOU'RE REALLY MAKING THINGS EASIER FOR ME!!

Stranger danger! ☆

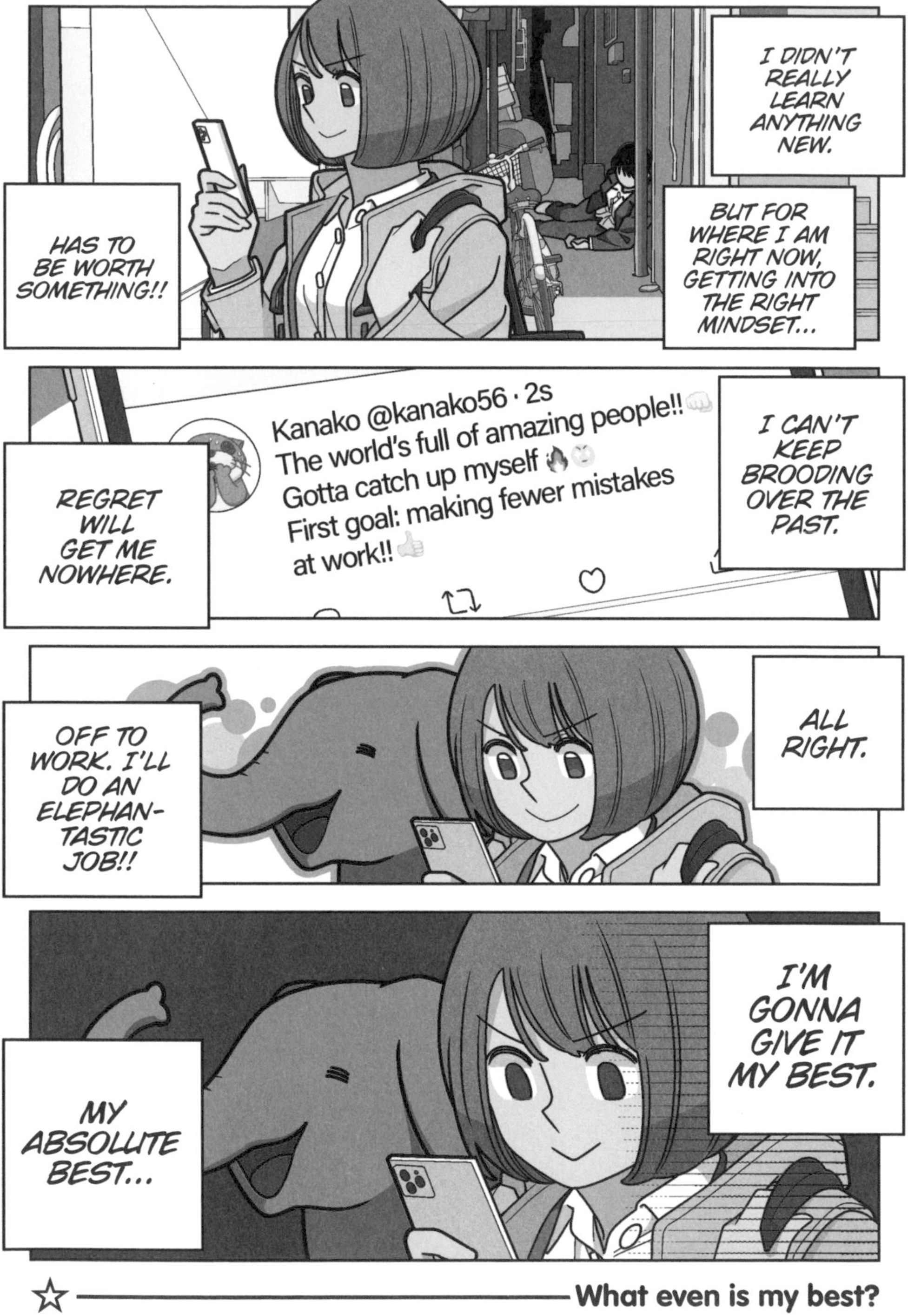
I DIDN'T REALLY LEARN ANYTHING NEW.
BUT FOR WHERE I AM RIGHT NOW, GETTING INTO THE RIGHT MINDSET...
HAS TO BE WORTH SOMETHING!!
I CAN'T KEEP BROODING OVER THE PAST.
Kanako @kanako56 · 2s
The world's full of amazing people!!
Gotta catch up myself
First goal: making fewer mistakes at work!!
REGRET WILL GET ME NOWHERE.
ALL RIGHT.
OFF TO WORK. I'LL DO AN ELEPHANTASTIC JOB!!
I'M GONNA GIVE IT MY BEST.
MY ABSOLUTE BEST...

068

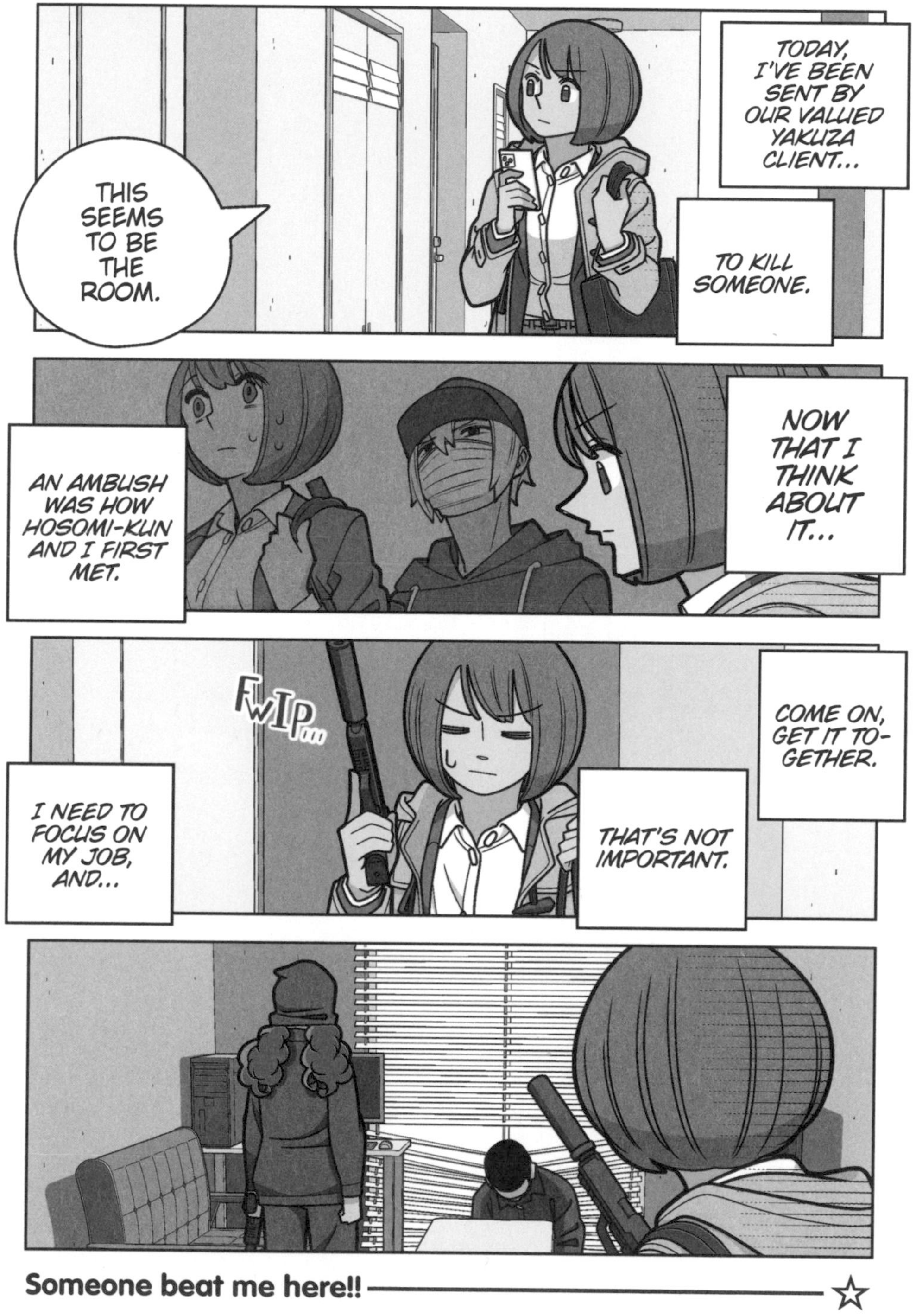
TODAY, I'VE BEEN SENT BY OUR VALUED YAKUZA CLIENT...
TO KILL SOMEONE.
THIS SEEMS TO BE THE ROOM.
NOW THAT I THINK ABOUT IT...
AN AMBUSH WAS HOW HOSOMI-KUN AND I FIRST MET.
COME ON, GET IT TO-GETHER.
THAT'S NOT IMPORTANT.
FWIP...
I NEED TO FOCUS ON MY JOB, AND...

Someone beat me here!! ☆

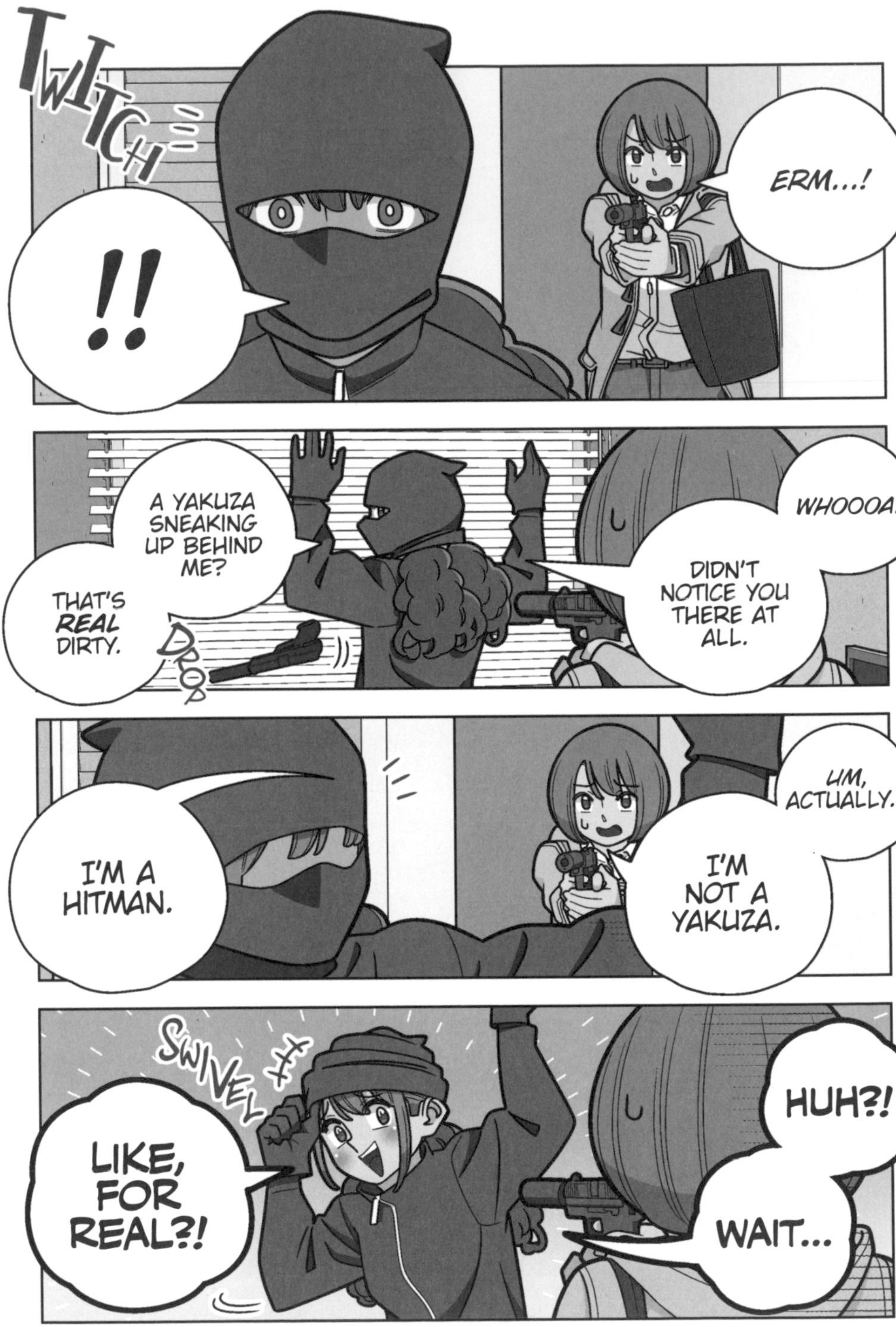
ERM...!
TWITCH
!!
WHOOOA.
DIDN'T NOTICE YOU THERE AT ALL.
A YAKUZA SNEAKING UP BEHIND ME?
THAT'S REAL DIRTY.
DROP
UM, ACTUALLY...
I'M NOT A YAKUZA.
I'M A HITMAN.
HUH?!
WAIT...
SWIVEL
LIKE, FOR REAL?!

☆——— **First time someone's ever been excited to hear that.**

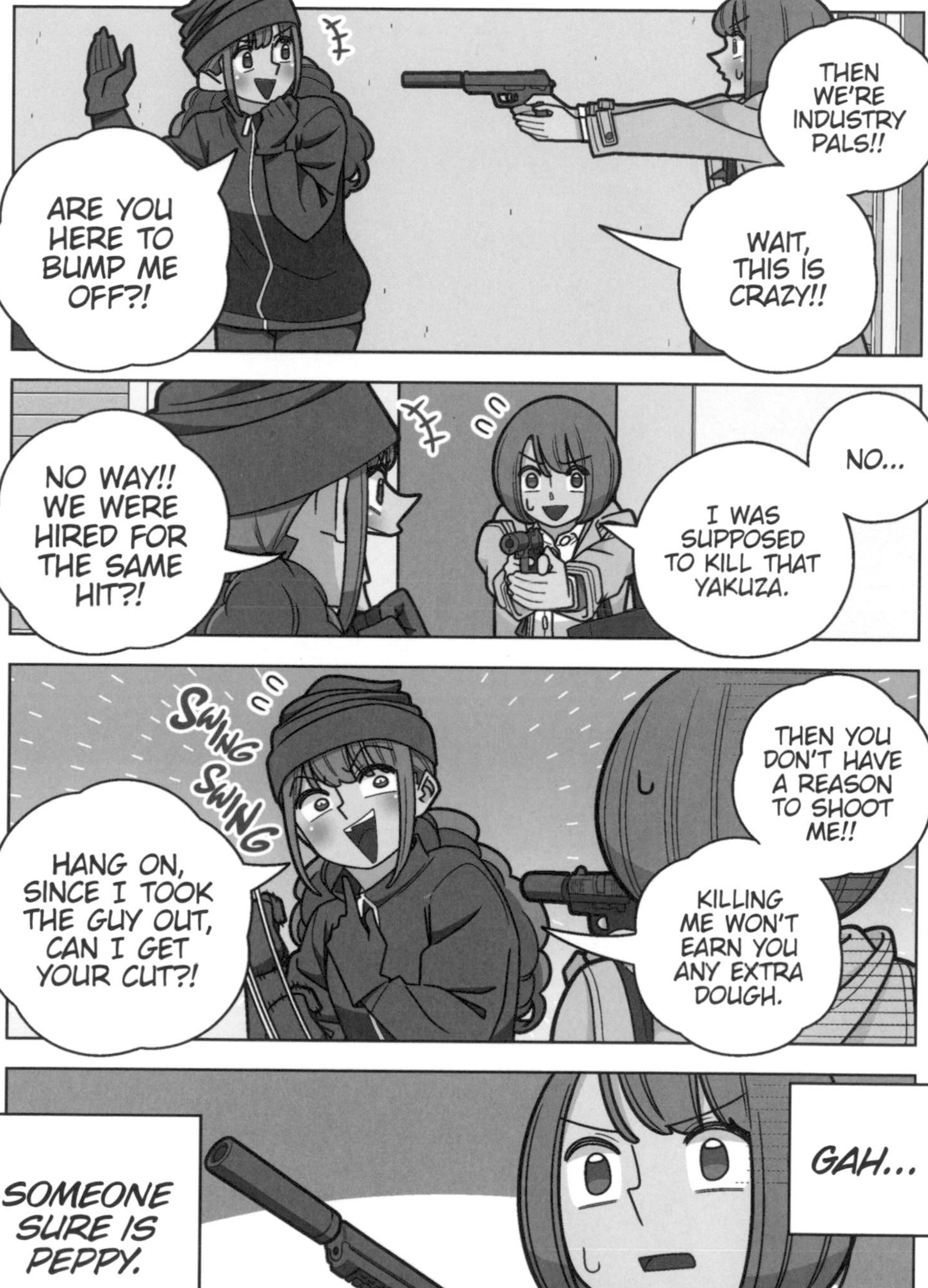
THEN WE'RE INDUSTRY PALS!!
WAIT, THIS IS CRAZY!!
ARE YOU HERE TO BUMP ME OFF?!
NO...
I WAS SUPPOSED TO KILL THAT YAKUZA.
NO WAY!! WE WERE HIRED FOR THE SAME HIT?!
THEN YOU DON'T HAVE A REASON TO SHOOT ME!!
KILLING ME WON'T EARN YOU ANY EXTRA DOUGH.
SWING SWING
HANG ON, SINCE I TOOK THE GUY OUT, CAN I GET YOUR CUT?!
GAH...
SOMEONE SURE IS PEPPY.

Social butterfly. ☆

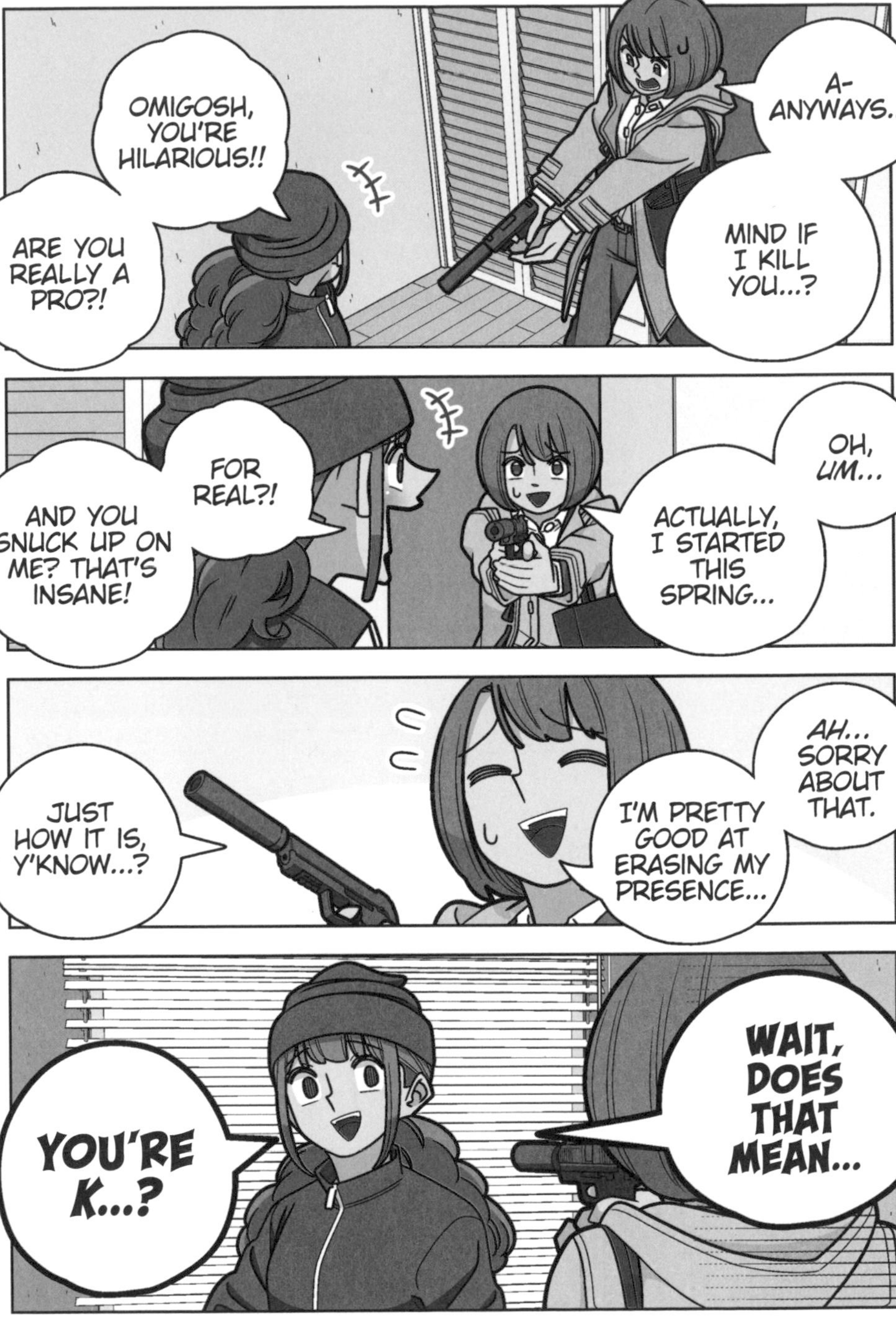
A- ANYWAYS...
MIND IF I KILL YOU...?
OMIGOSH, YOU'RE HILARIOUS!!
ARE YOU REALLY A PRO?!
OH, UM...
ACTUALLY, I STARTED THIS SPRING...
FOR REAL?!
AND YOU SNUCK UP ON ME? THAT'S INSANE!
AH... SORRY ABOUT THAT.
I'M PRETTY GOOD AT ERASING MY PRESENCE...
JUST HOW IT IS, Y'KNOW...?
WAIT, DOES THAT MEAN...
YOU'RE K...?

☆ —— **A fan.**

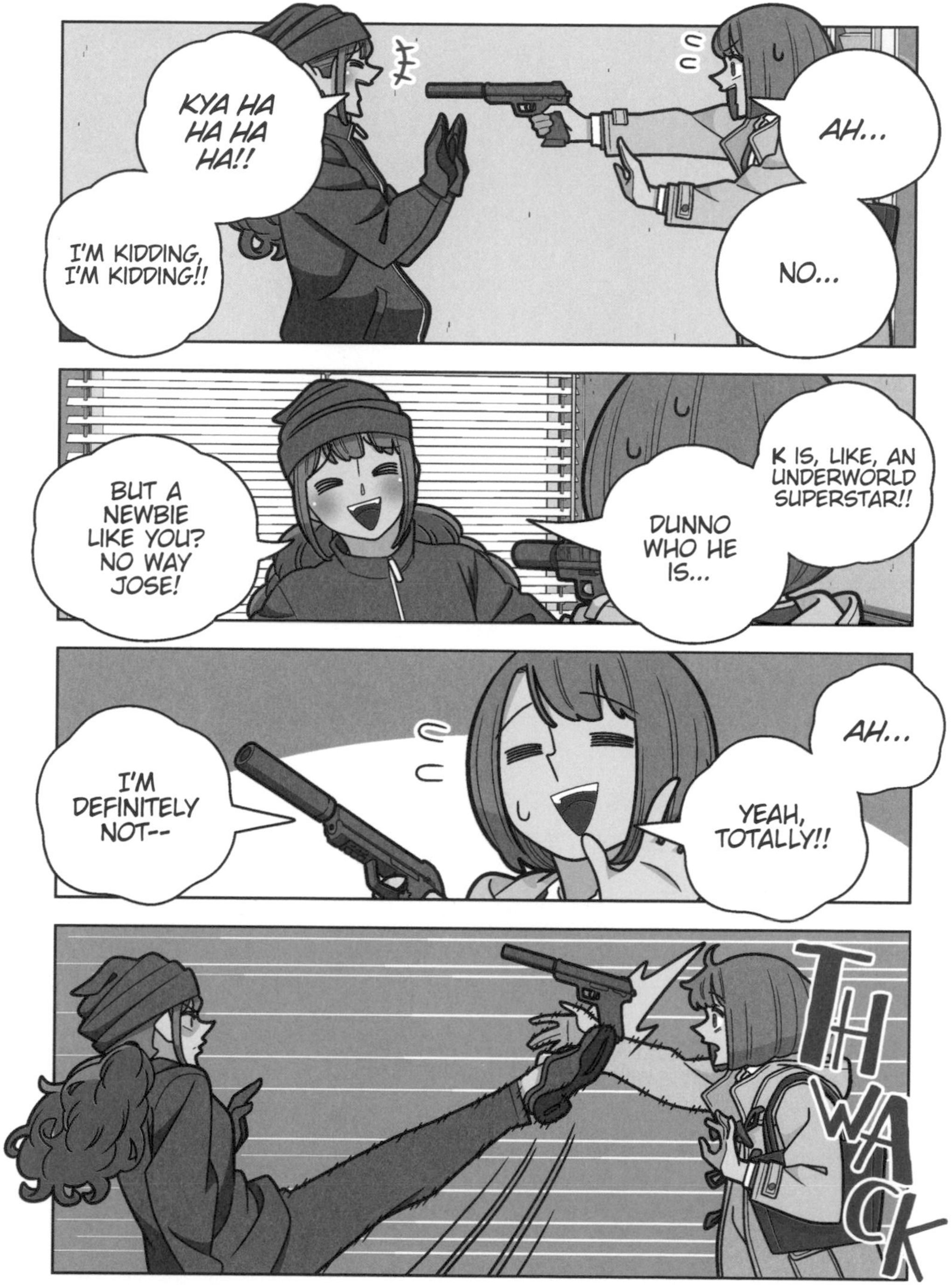
AH...
NO...
KYA HA HA HA HA!!
I'M KIDDING, I'M KIDDING!!
K IS, LIKE, AN UNDERWORLD SUPERSTAR!!
DUNNO WHO HE IS...
BUT A NEWBIE LIKE YOU? NO WAY JOSE!
AH...
YEAH, TOTALLY!!
I'M DEFINITELY NOT--
THWACK

Definitely not. ☆

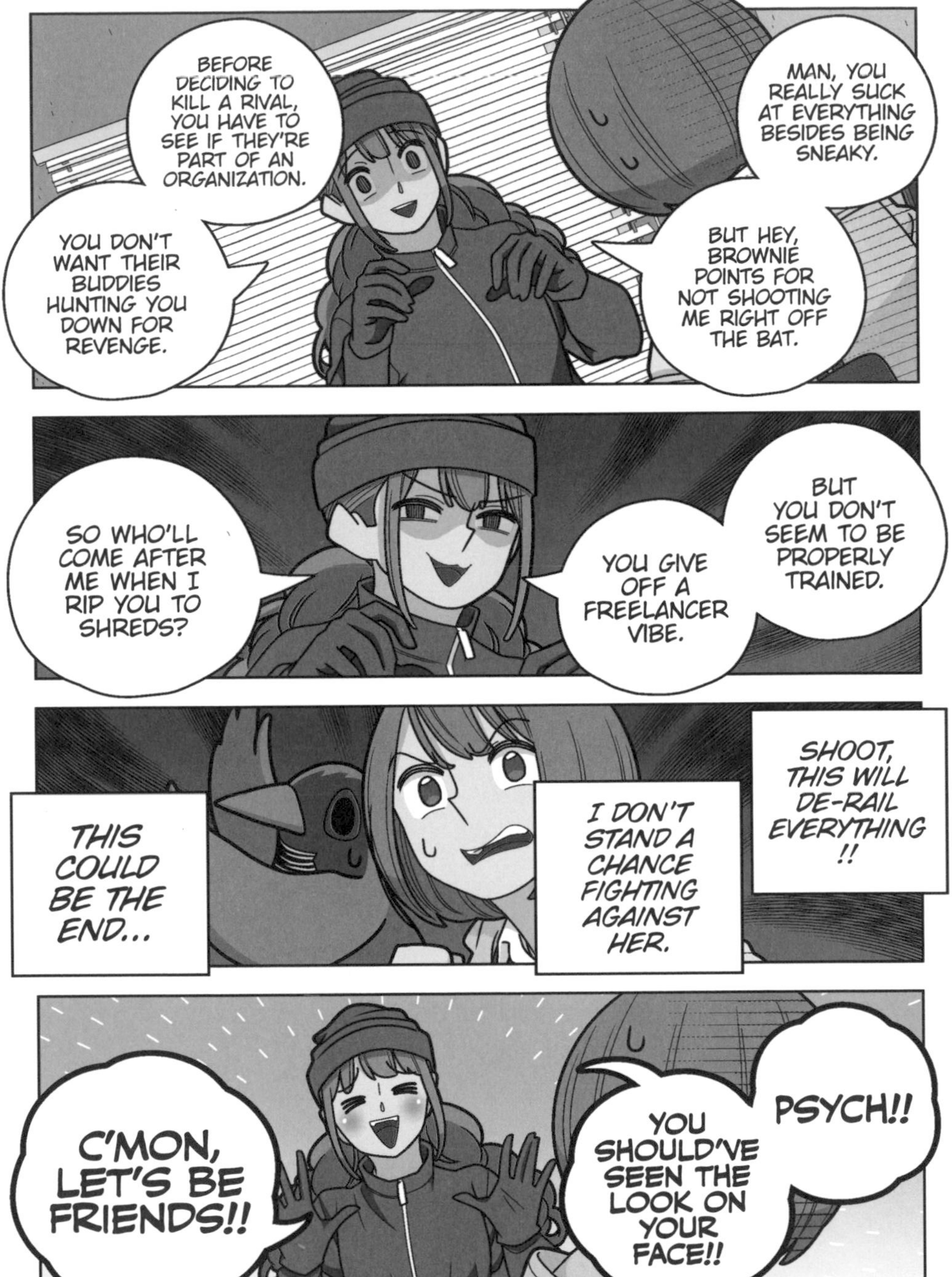
MAN, YOU REALLY SUCK AT EVERYTHING BESIDES BEING SNEAKY.
BUT HEY, BROWNIE POINTS FOR NOT SHOOTING ME RIGHT OFF THE BAT.
BEFORE DECIDING TO KILL A RIVAL, YOU HAVE TO SEE IF THEY'RE PART OF AN ORGANIZATION.
YOU DON'T WANT THEIR BUDDIES HUNTING YOU DOWN FOR REVENGE.
BUT YOU DON'T SEEM TO BE PROPERLY TRAINED.
YOU GIVE OFF A FREELANCER VIBE.
SO WHO'LL COME AFTER ME WHEN I RIP YOU TO SHREDS?
SHOOT, THIS WILL DE-RAIL EVERYTHING!!
I DON'T STAND A CHANCE FIGHTING AGAINST HER.
THIS COULD BE THE END...
PSYCH!!
YOU SHOULD'VE SEEN THE LOOK ON YOUR FACE!!
C'MON, LET'S BE FRIENDS!!

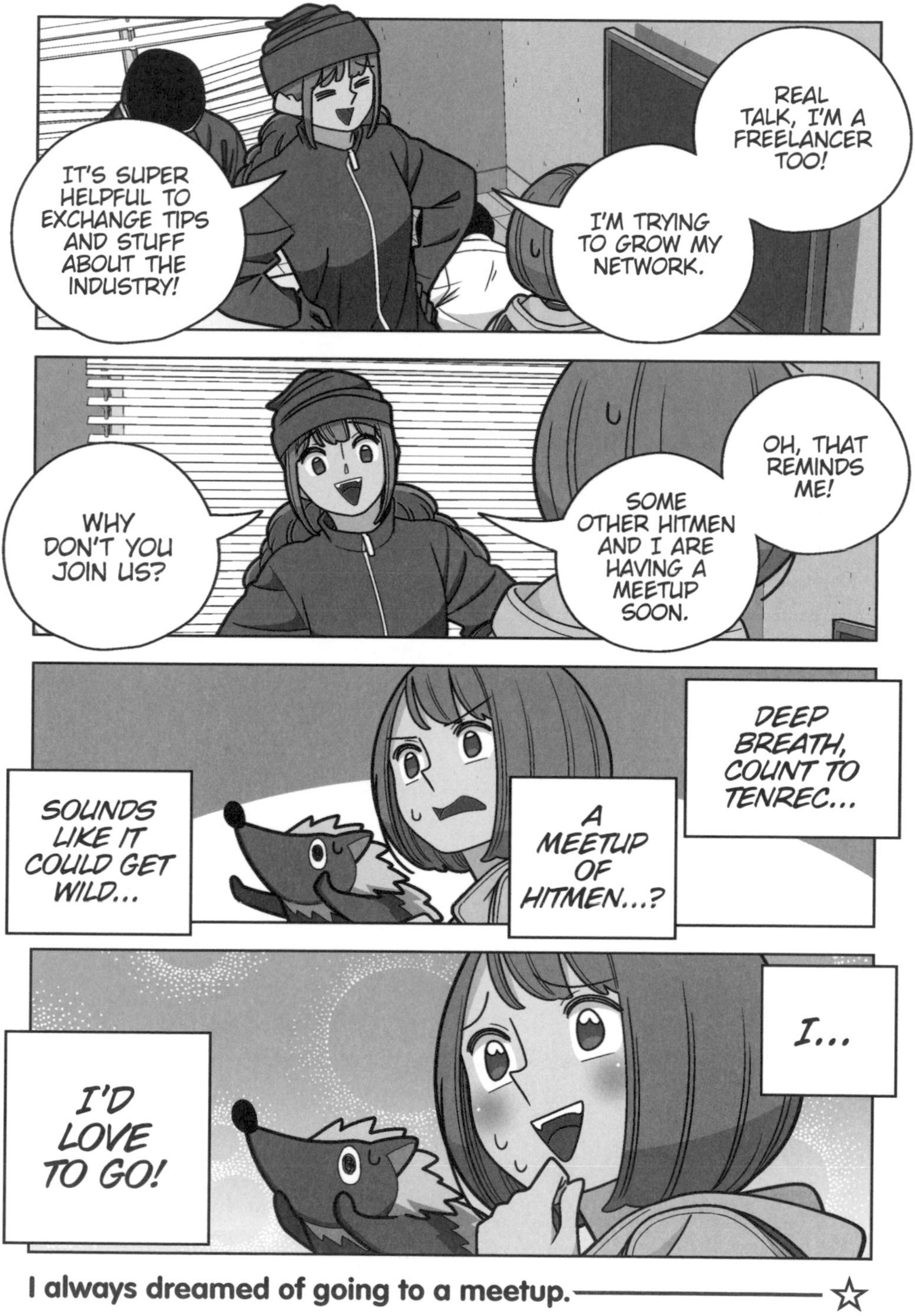
REAL TALK, I'M A FREELANCER TOO!
I'M TRYING TO GROW MY NETWORK.
IT'S SUPER HELPFUL TO EXCHANGE TIPS AND STUFF ABOUT THE INDUSTRY!
OH, THAT REMINDS ME!
SOME OTHER HITMEN AND I ARE HAVING A MEETUP SOON.
WHY DON'T YOU JOIN US?
DEEP BREATH, COUNT TO TENREC...
A MEETUP OF HITMEN...?
SOUNDS LIKE IT COULD GET WILD...
I...
I'D LOVE TO GO!

I always dreamed of going to a meetup. ——— ☆

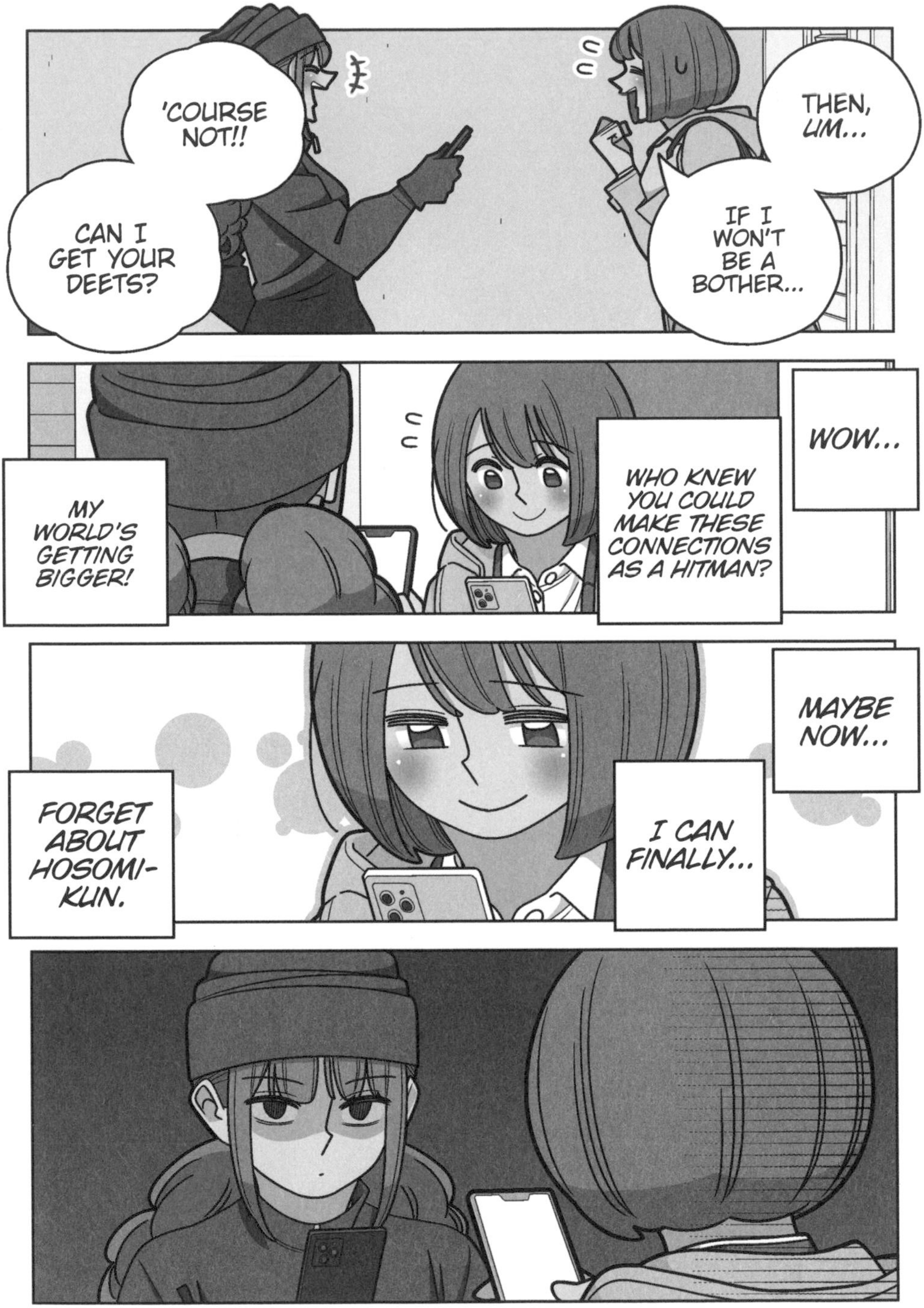
THEN, UM...
IF I WON'T BE A BOTHER...
'COURSE NOT!!
CAN I GET YOUR DEETS?
WOW...
WHO KNEW YOU COULD MAKE THESE CONNECTIONS AS A HITMAN?
MY WORLD'S GETTING BIGGER!
MAYBE NOW...
I CAN FINALLY...
FORGET ABOUT HOSOMI-KUN.

☆ —— Something wicked this way comes.

Happy Kanako's
Killer Life

Why
don't
we grab
something
to eat?

Happy Kanako's
Killer Life

BE
THERE
IN A
JIFFY!!

Bonus

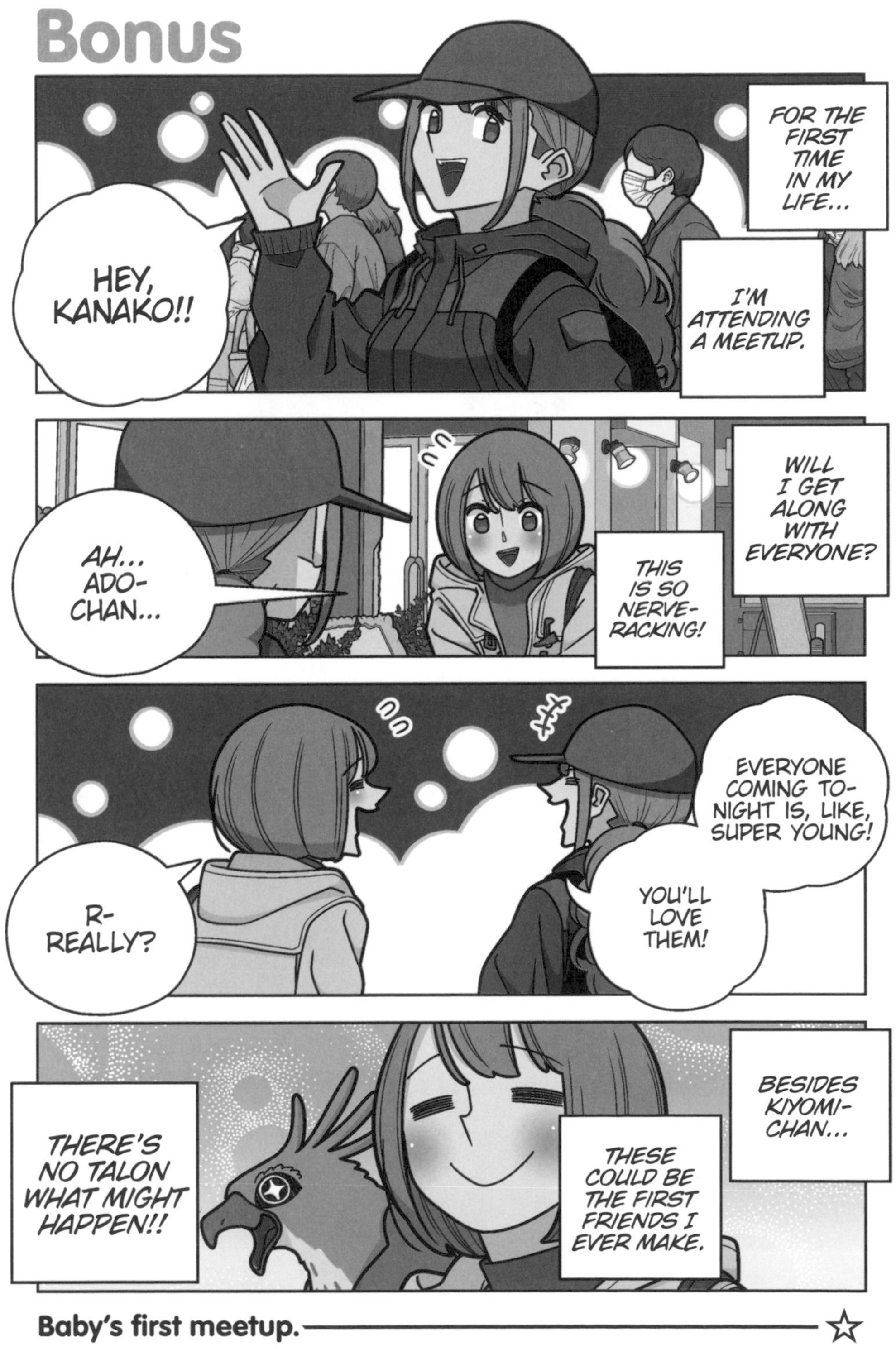
FOR THE FIRST TIME IN MY LIFE...
I'M ATTENDING A MEETUP.
HEY, KANAKO!!
WILL I GET ALONG WITH EVERYONE?
THIS IS SO NERVE-RACKING!
AH... ADO-CHAN...
EVERYONE COMING TO-NIGHT IS, LIKE, SUPER YOUNG!
YOU'LL LOVE THEM!
R-REALLY?
BESIDES KIYOMI-CHAN...
THESE COULD BE THE FIRST FRIENDS I EVER MAKE.
THERE'S NO TALON WHAT MIGHT HAPPEN!!

Baby's first meetup. ☆

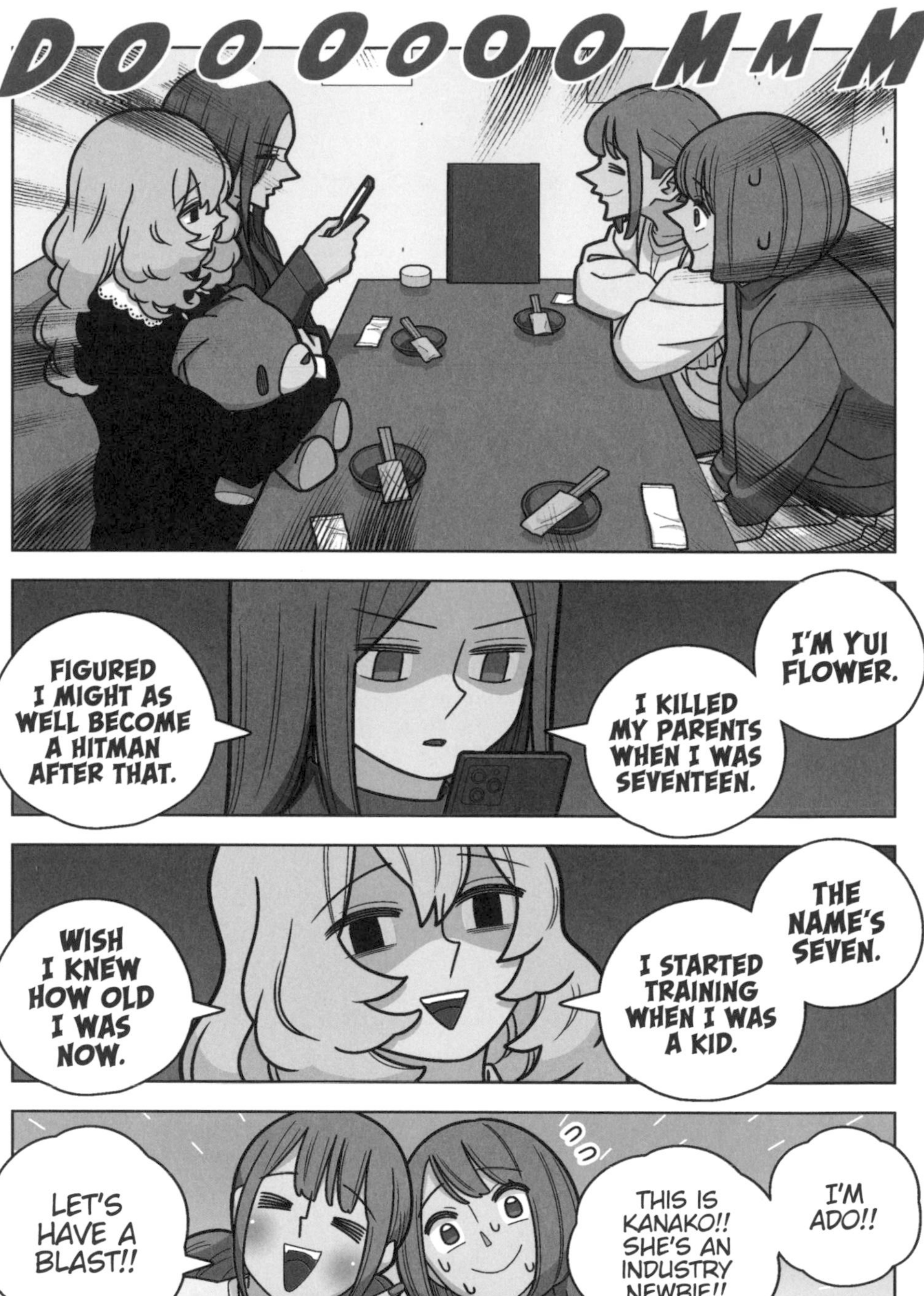
DOOOOOOMMM
I'M YUI FLOWER.
I KILLED MY PARENTS WHEN I WAS SEVENTEEN.
FIGURED I MIGHT AS WELL BECOME A HITMAN AFTER THAT.
THE NAME'S SEVEN.
I STARTED TRAINING WHEN I WAS A KID.
WISH I KNEW HOW OLD I WAS NOW.
I'M ADO!!
THIS IS KANAKO!! SHE'S AN INDUSTRY NEWBIE!!
LET'S HAVE A BLAST!!

☆ —Yaaaay!

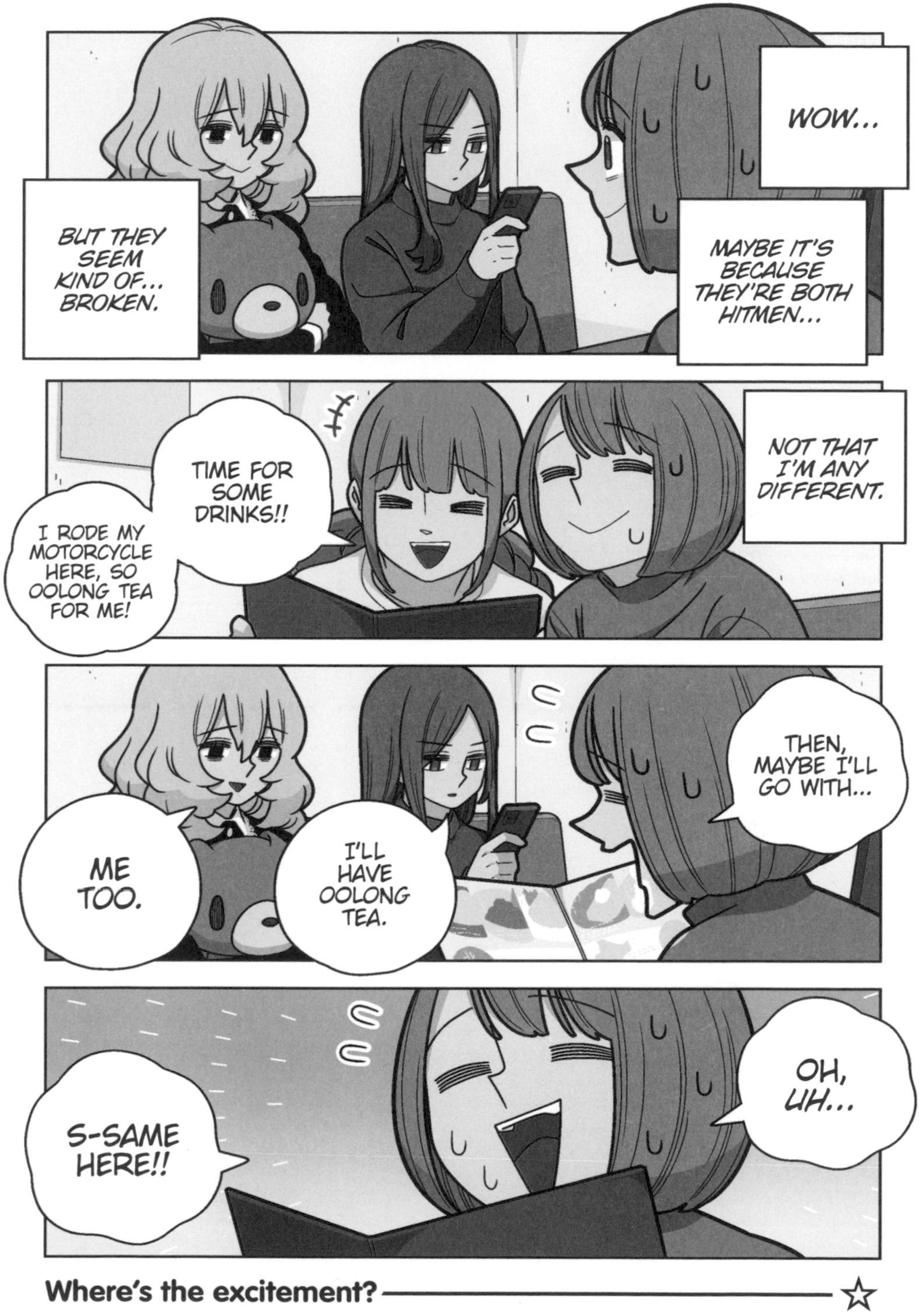
WOW...
MAYBE IT'S BECAUSE THEY'RE BOTH HITMEN...
BUT THEY SEEM KIND OF... BROKEN.
NOT THAT I'M ANY DIFFERENT.
TIME FOR SOME DRINKS!!
I RODE MY MOTORCYCLE HERE, SO OOLONG TEA FOR ME!
THEN, MAYBE I'LL GO WITH...
I'LL HAVE OOLONG TEA.
ME TOO.
OH, UH...
S-SAME HERE!!

Where's the excitement? ☆

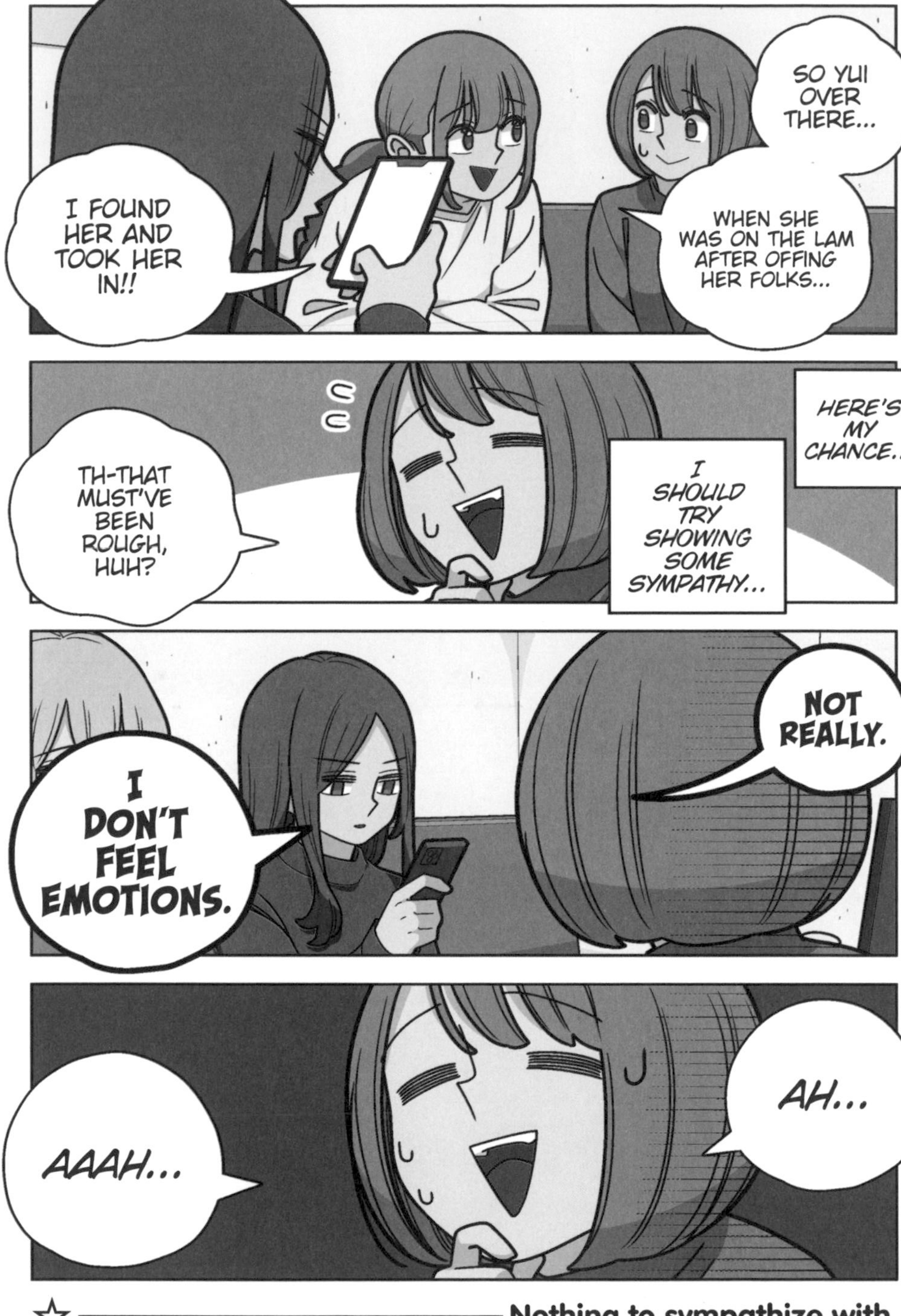
SO YUI OVER THERE...
WHEN SHE WAS ON THE LAM AFTER OFFING HER FOLKS...
I FOUND HER AND TOOK HER IN!!
HERE'S MY CHANCE...
I SHOULD TRY SHOWING SOME SYMPATHY...
TH-THAT MUST'VE BEEN ROUGH, HUH?
NOT REALLY.
I DON'T FEEL EMOTIONS.
AH...
AAAH...

☆ **Nothing to sympathize with.**

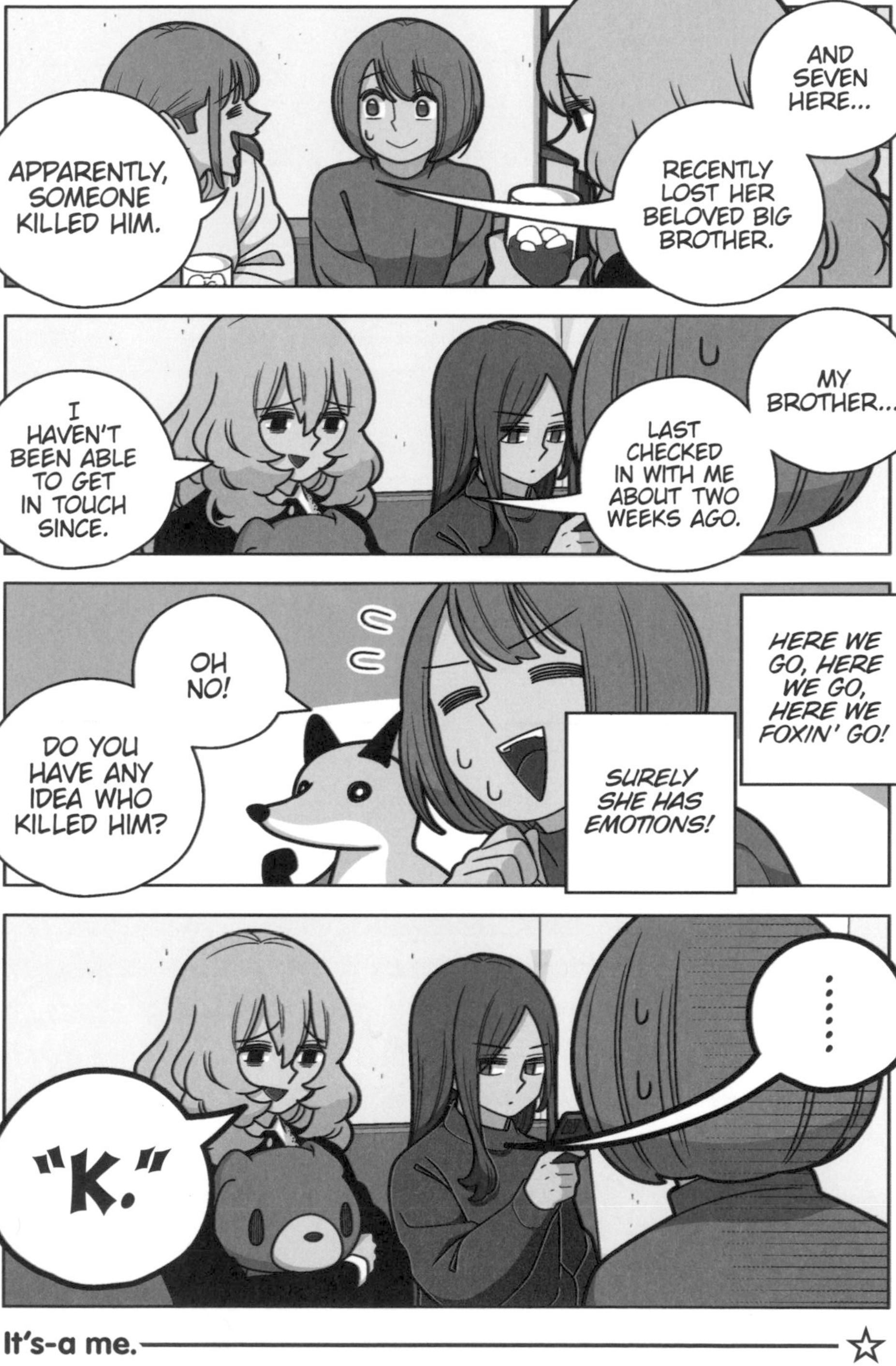
AND SEVEN HERE...
RECENTLY LOST HER BELOVED BIG BROTHER.
APPARENTLY, SOMEONE KILLED HIM.
MY BROTHER...
LAST CHECKED IN WITH ME ABOUT TWO WEEKS AGO.
I HAVEN'T BEEN ABLE TO GET IN TOUCH SINCE.
HERE WE GO, HERE WE GO, HERE WE FOXIN' GO!
SURELY SHE HAS EMOTIONS!
OH NO!
DO YOU HAVE ANY IDEA WHO KILLED HIM?
......
"K."

It's-a me. ☆

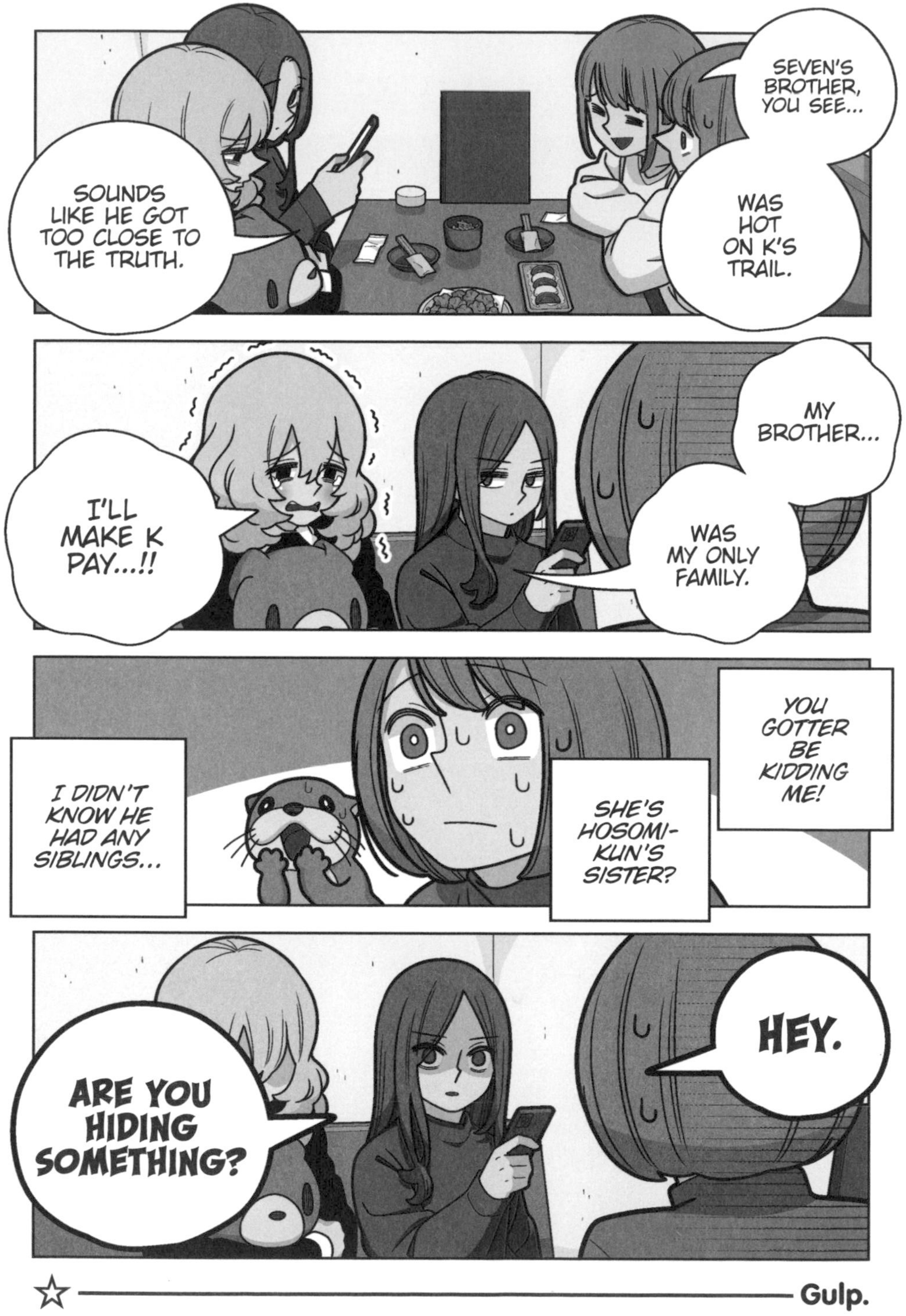
SEVEN'S BROTHER, YOU SEE...
WAS HOT ON K'S TRAIL.
SOUNDS LIKE HE GOT TOO CLOSE TO THE TRUTH.
MY BROTHER...
WAS MY ONLY FAMILY.
I'LL MAKE K PAY...!!
YOU GOTTER BE KIDDING ME!
SHE'S HOSOMI-KUN'S SISTER?
I DIDN'T KNOW HE HAD ANY SIBLINGS...
HEY.
ARE YOU HIDING SOMETHING?

☆ — **Gulp.**

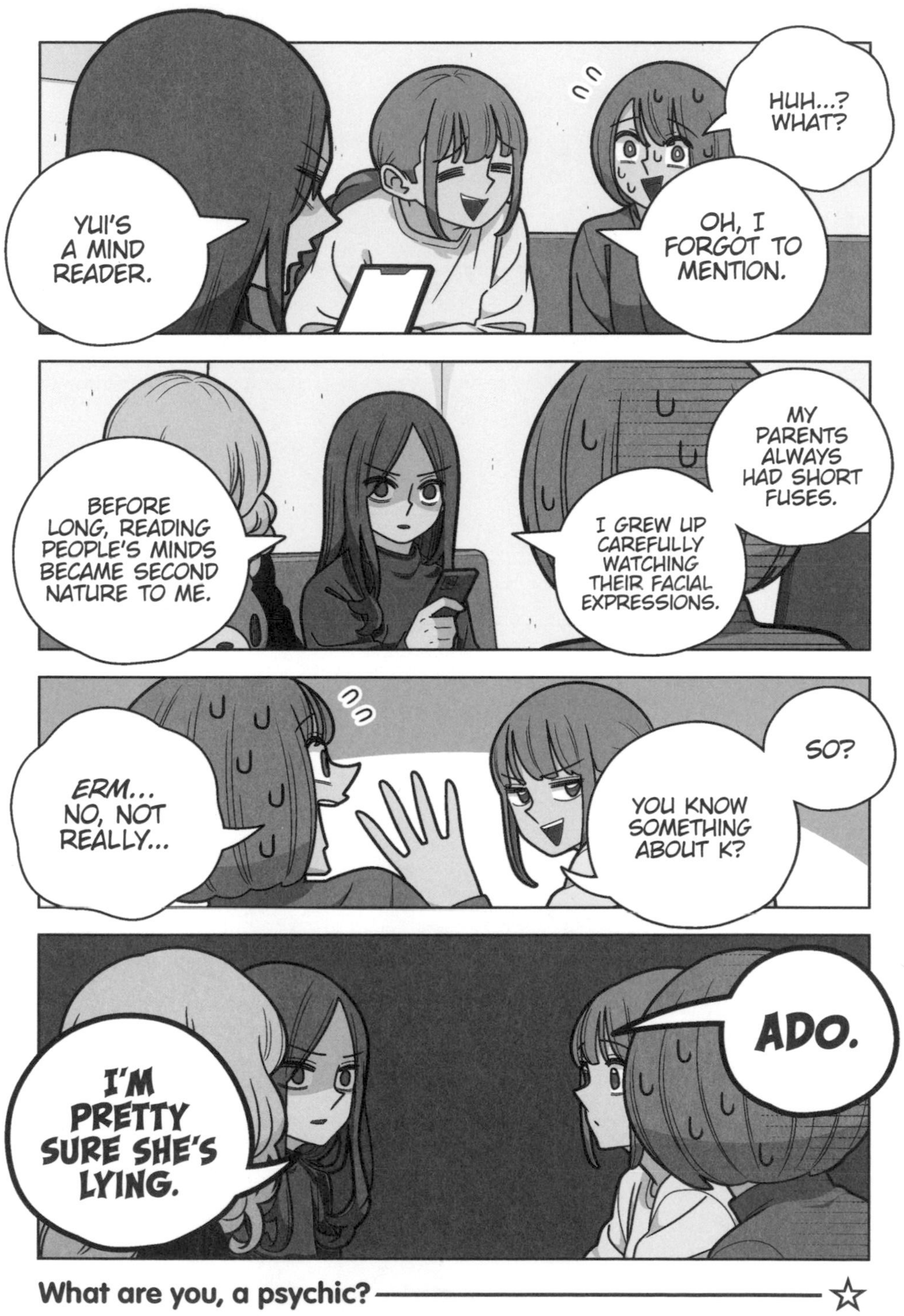
HUH...? WHAT?
OH, I FORGOT TO MENTION.
YUI'S A MIND READER.
MY PARENTS ALWAYS HAD SHORT FUSES.
I GREW UP CAREFULLY WATCHING THEIR FACIAL EXPRESSIONS.
BEFORE LONG, READING PEOPLE'S MINDS BECAME SECOND NATURE TO ME.
SO?
YOU KNOW SOMETHING ABOUT K?
ERM... NO, NOT REALLY...
ADO.
I'M PRETTY SURE SHE'S LYING.

What are you, a psychic? ☆

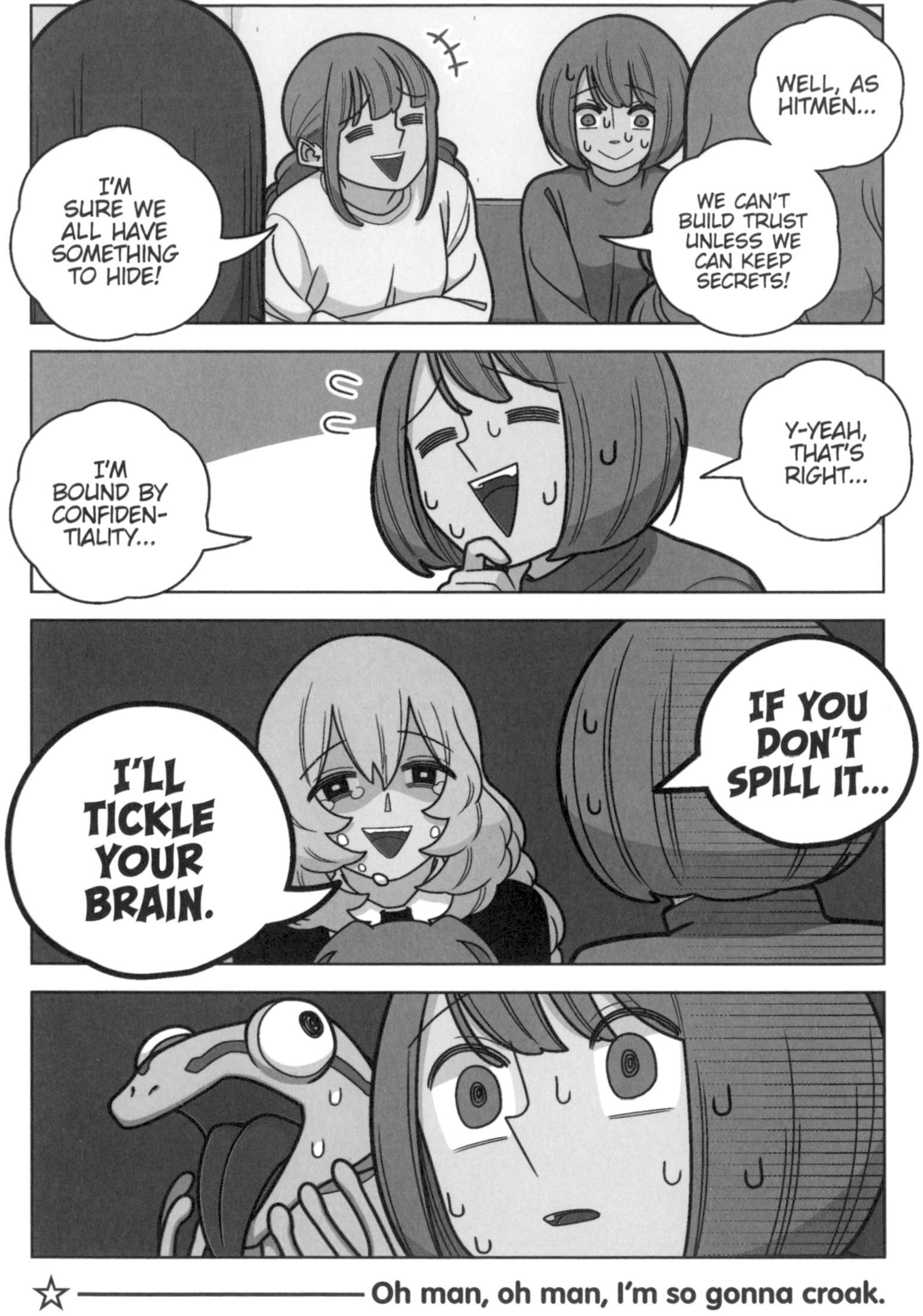
WELL, AS HITMEN...
WE CAN'T BUILD TRUST UNLESS WE CAN KEEP SECRETS!
I'M SURE WE ALL HAVE SOMETHING TO HIDE!
Y-YEAH, THAT'S RIGHT...
I'M BOUND BY CONFIDEN-TIALITY...
IF YOU DON'T SPILL IT...
I'LL TICKLE YOUR BRAIN.

☆ —— Oh man, oh man, I'm so gonna croak.

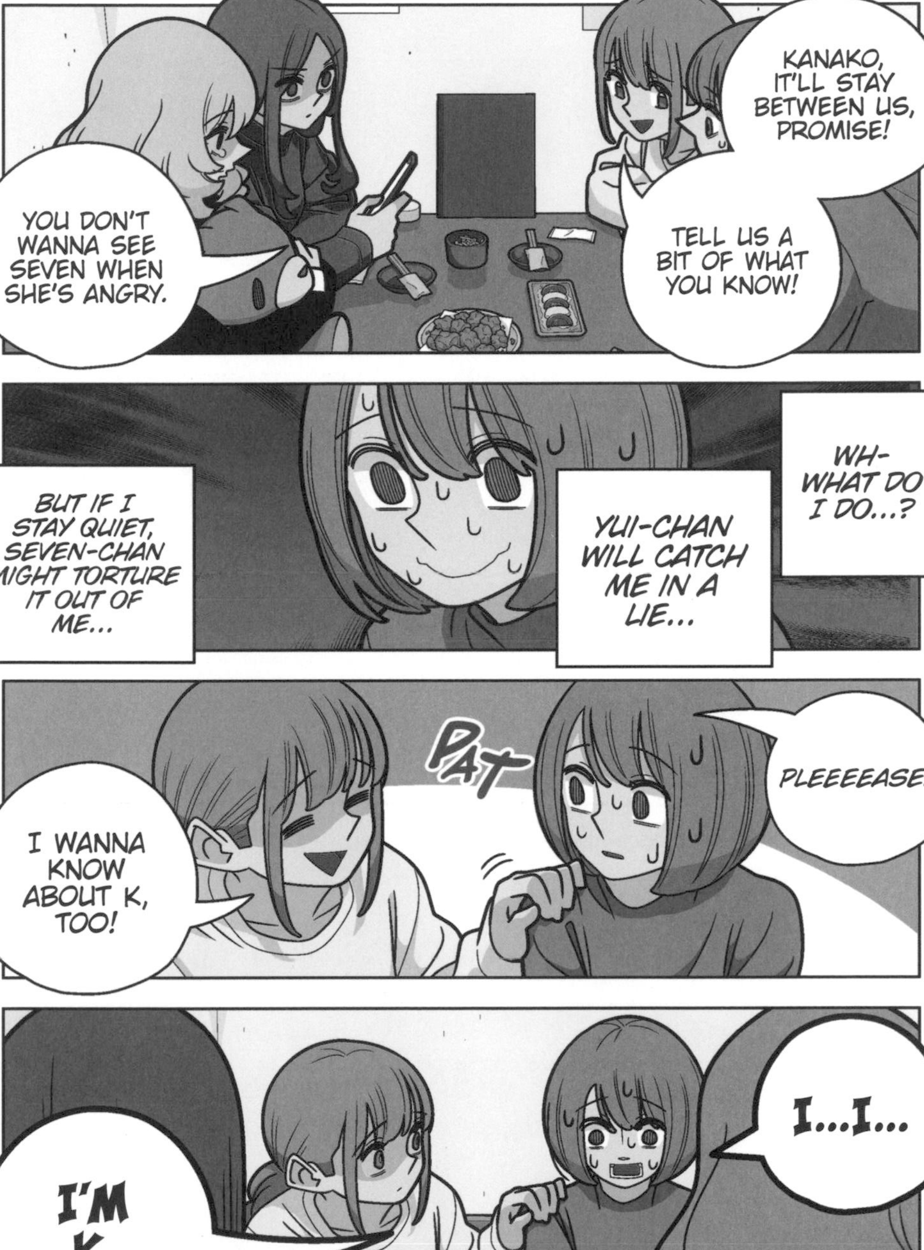
KANAKO, IT'LL STAY BETWEEN US, PROMISE!
TELL US A BIT OF WHAT YOU KNOW!
YOU DON'T WANNA SEE SEVEN WHEN SHE'S ANGRY.
WH- WHAT DO I DO...?
YUI-CHAN WILL CATCH ME IN A LIE...
BUT IF I STAY QUIET, SEVEN-CHAN MIGHT TORTURE IT OUT OF ME...
PLEEEEASE!
PAT
I WANNA KNOW ABOUT K, TOO!
I...I...
I'M K.

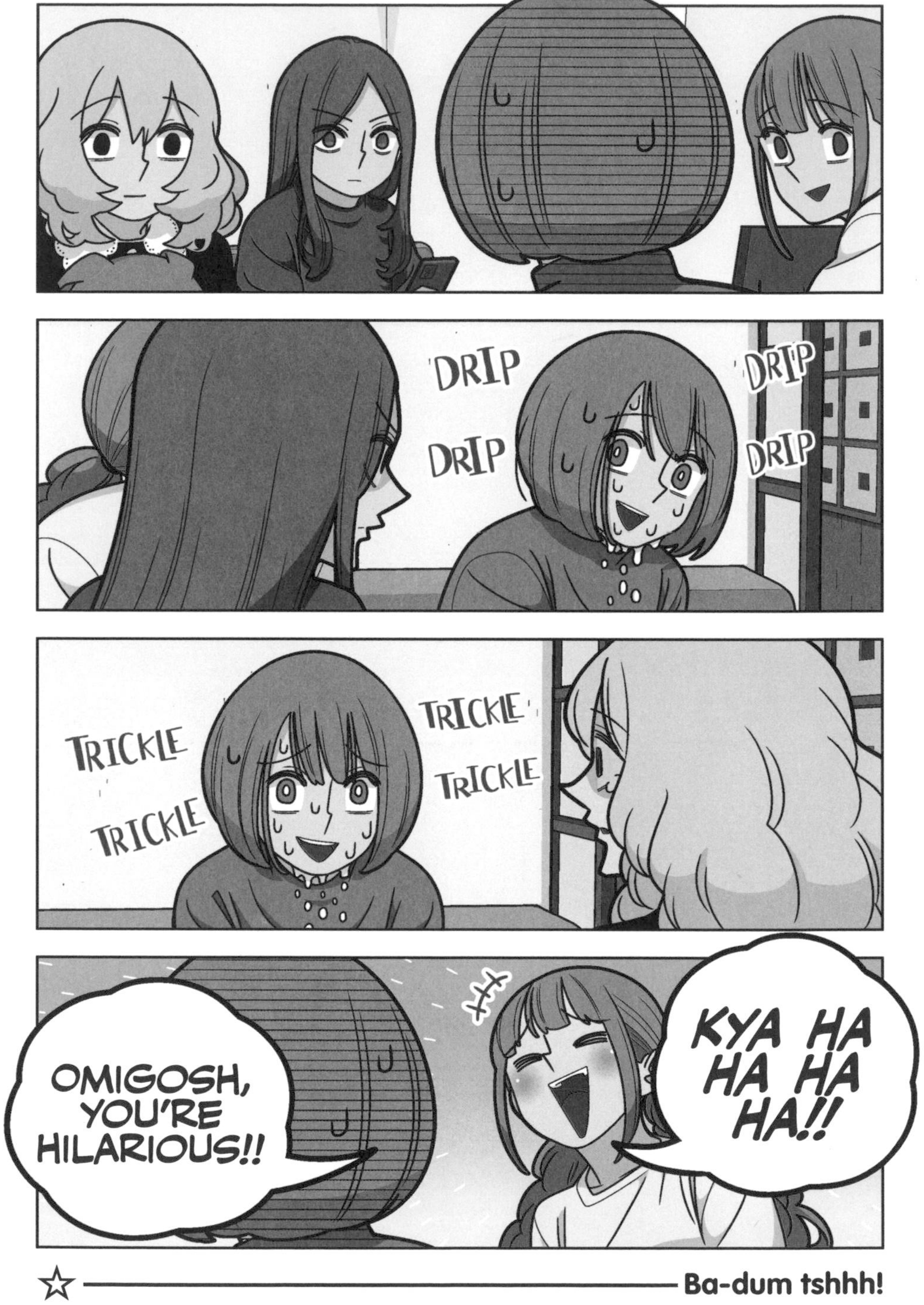
DRIP
DRIP
DRIP
DRIP
TRICKLE
TRICKLE
TRICKLE
TRICKLE
KYA HA HA HA HA HA!!
OMIGOSH, YOU'RE HILARIOUS!!

☆ Ba-dum tshhh!

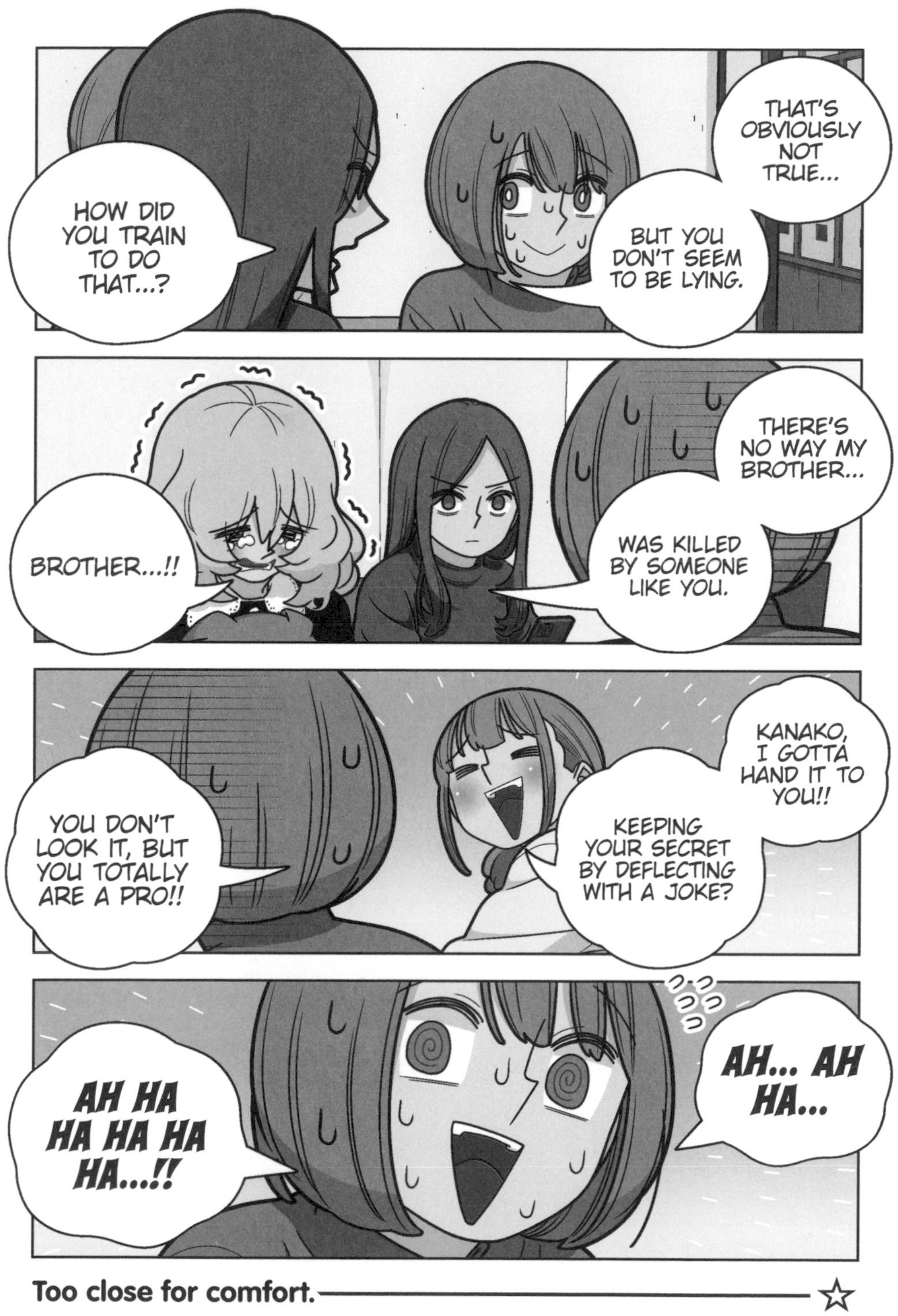
THAT'S OBVIOUSLY NOT TRUE...
BUT YOU DON'T SEEM TO BE LYING.
HOW DID YOU TRAIN TO DO THAT...?
THERE'S NO WAY MY BROTHER...
WAS KILLED BY SOMEONE LIKE YOU.
BROTHER...!!
KANAKO, I GOTTA HAND IT TO YOU!!
KEEPING YOUR SECRET BY DEFLECTING WITH A JOKE?
YOU DON'T LOOK IT, BUT YOU TOTALLY ARE A PRO!!
AH... AH HA...
AH HA HA HA HA HA...!!

Too close for comfort.———————————☆

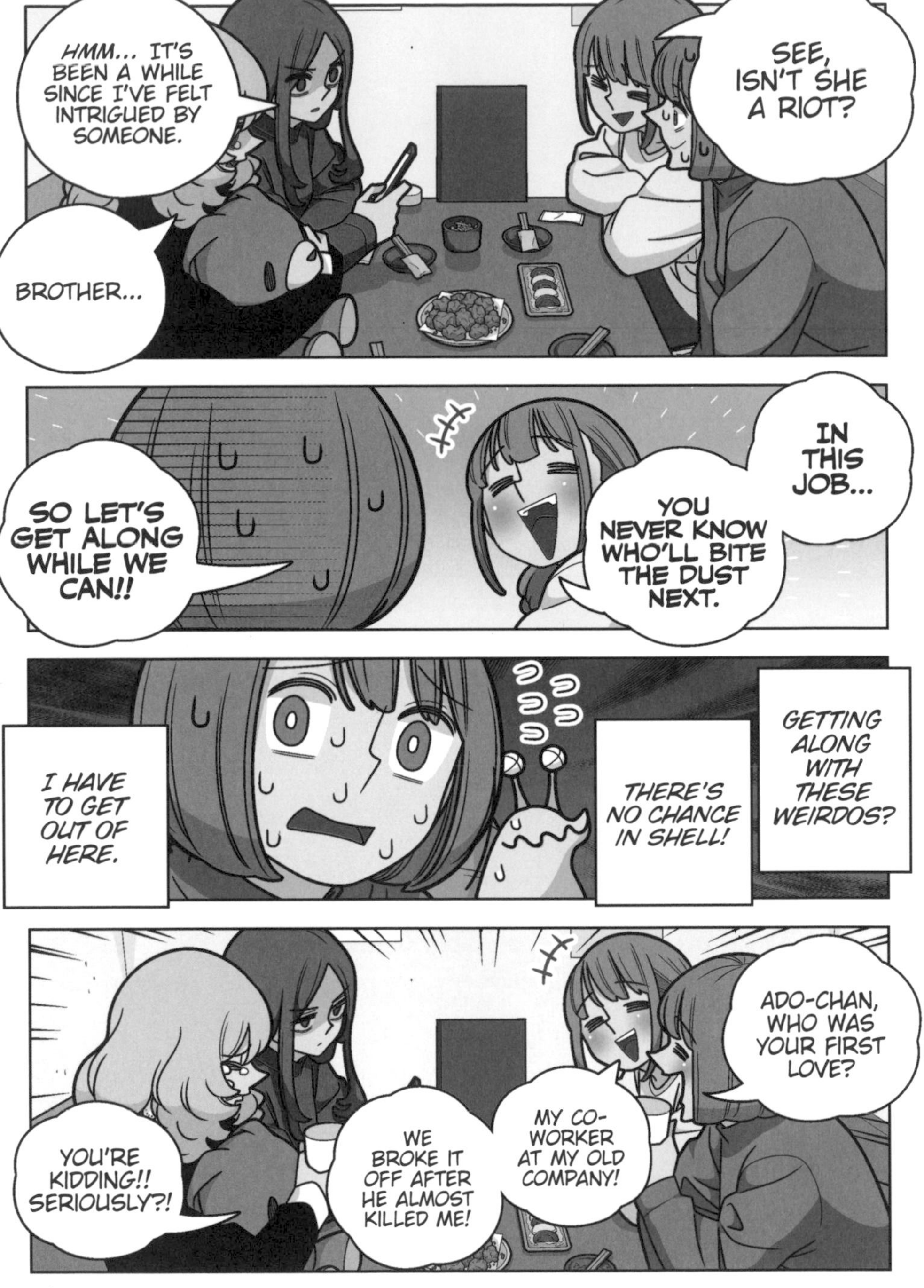
SEE, ISN'T SHE A RIOT?
HMM... IT'S BEEN A WHILE SINCE I'VE FELT INTRIGUED BY SOMEONE.
BROTHER...
IN THIS JOB...
YOU NEVER KNOW WHO'LL BITE THE DUST NEXT.
SO LET'S GET ALONG WHILE WE CAN!!
GETTING ALONG WITH THESE WEIRDOS?
THERE'S NO CHANCE IN SHELL!
I HAVE TO GET OUT OF HERE.
ADO-CHAN, WHO WAS YOUR FIRST LOVE?
MY CO-WORKER AT MY OLD COMPANY!
WE BROKE IT OFF AFTER HE ALMOST KILLED ME!
YOU'RE KIDDING!! SERIOUSLY?!

☆ Everyone's a weirdo.

Happy Kanako's
Killer Life

YOU'RE
A
NATURAL...

Happy Kanako's
Killer Life

THAT'S
THE FIRST
COMPLIMENT
I'VE GOTTEN
IN A WHILE!

069

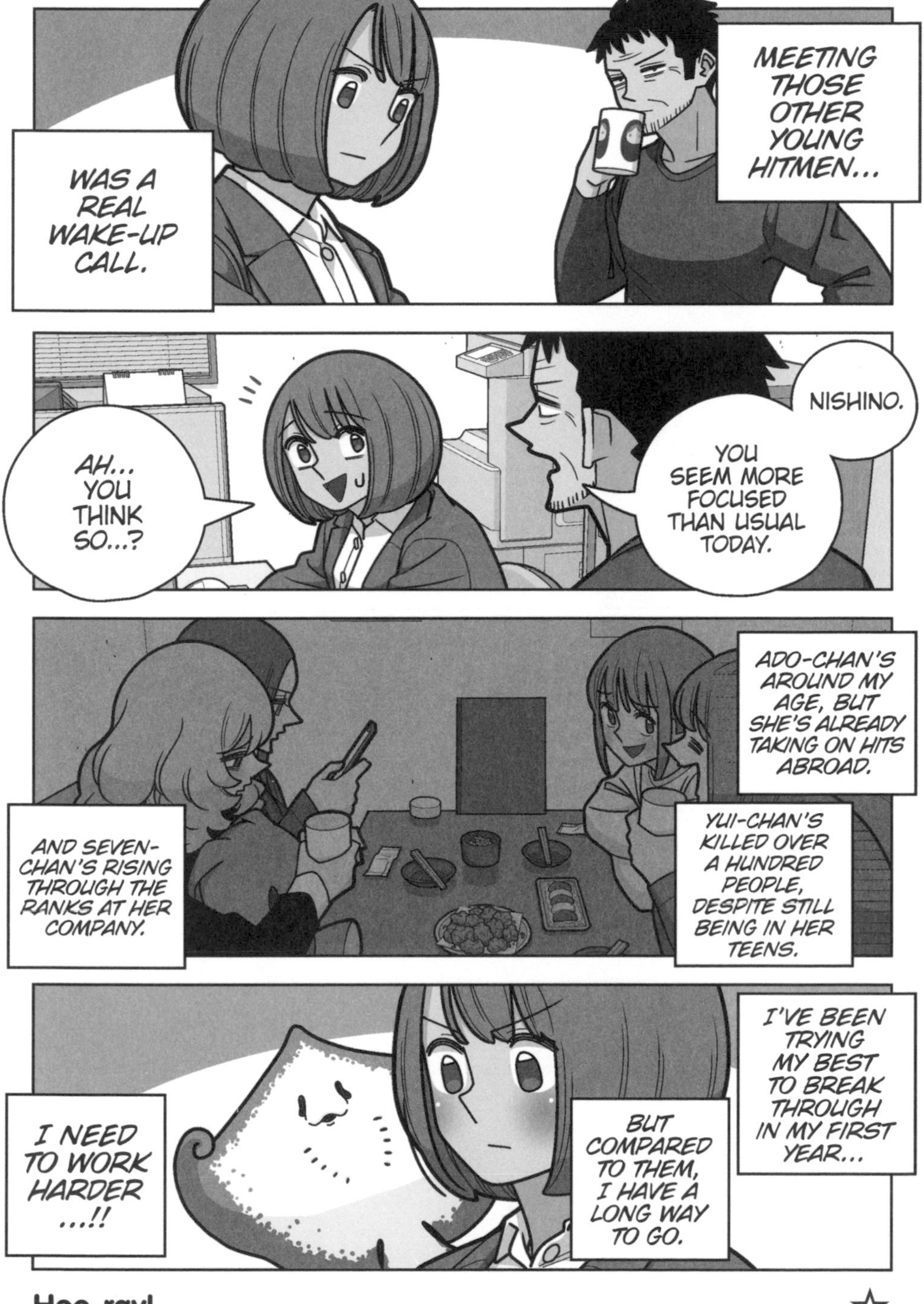
MEETING THOSE OTHER YOUNG HITMEN...
WAS A REAL WAKE-UP CALL.
NISHINO.
YOU SEEM MORE FOCUSED THAN USUAL TODAY.
AH... YOU THINK SO...?
ADO-CHAN'S AROUND MY AGE, BUT SHE'S ALREADY TAKING ON HITS ABROAD.
YUI-CHAN'S KILLED OVER A HUNDRED PEOPLE, DESPITE STILL BEING IN HER TEENS.
AND SEVEN-CHAN'S RISING THROUGH THE RANKS AT HER COMPANY.
I'VE BEEN TRYING MY BEST TO BREAK THROUGH IN MY FIRST YEAR...
BUT COMPARED TO THEM, I HAVE A LONG WAY TO GO.
I NEED TO WORK HARDER ...!!

Hoo-ray! ☆

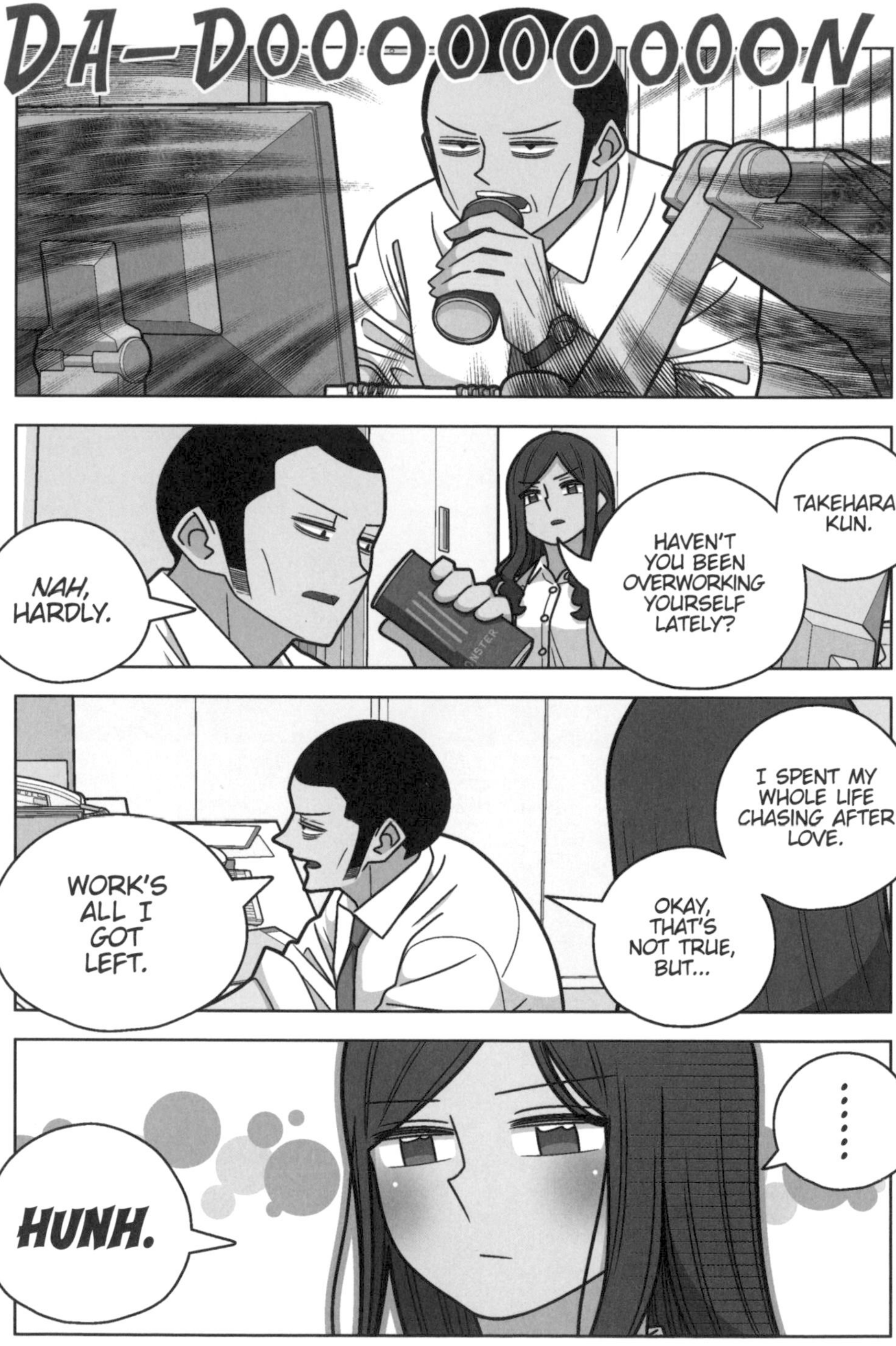
DA-DOOOOOOOOON
TAKEHARA-KUN.
HAVEN'T YOU BEEN OVERWORKING YOURSELF LATELY?
NAH, HARDLY.
I SPENT MY WHOLE LIFE CHASING AFTER LOVE.
OKAY, THAT'S NOT TRUE, BUT...
WORK'S ALL I GOT LEFT.
......
HUNH.

☆ —— **No strangers to love...**

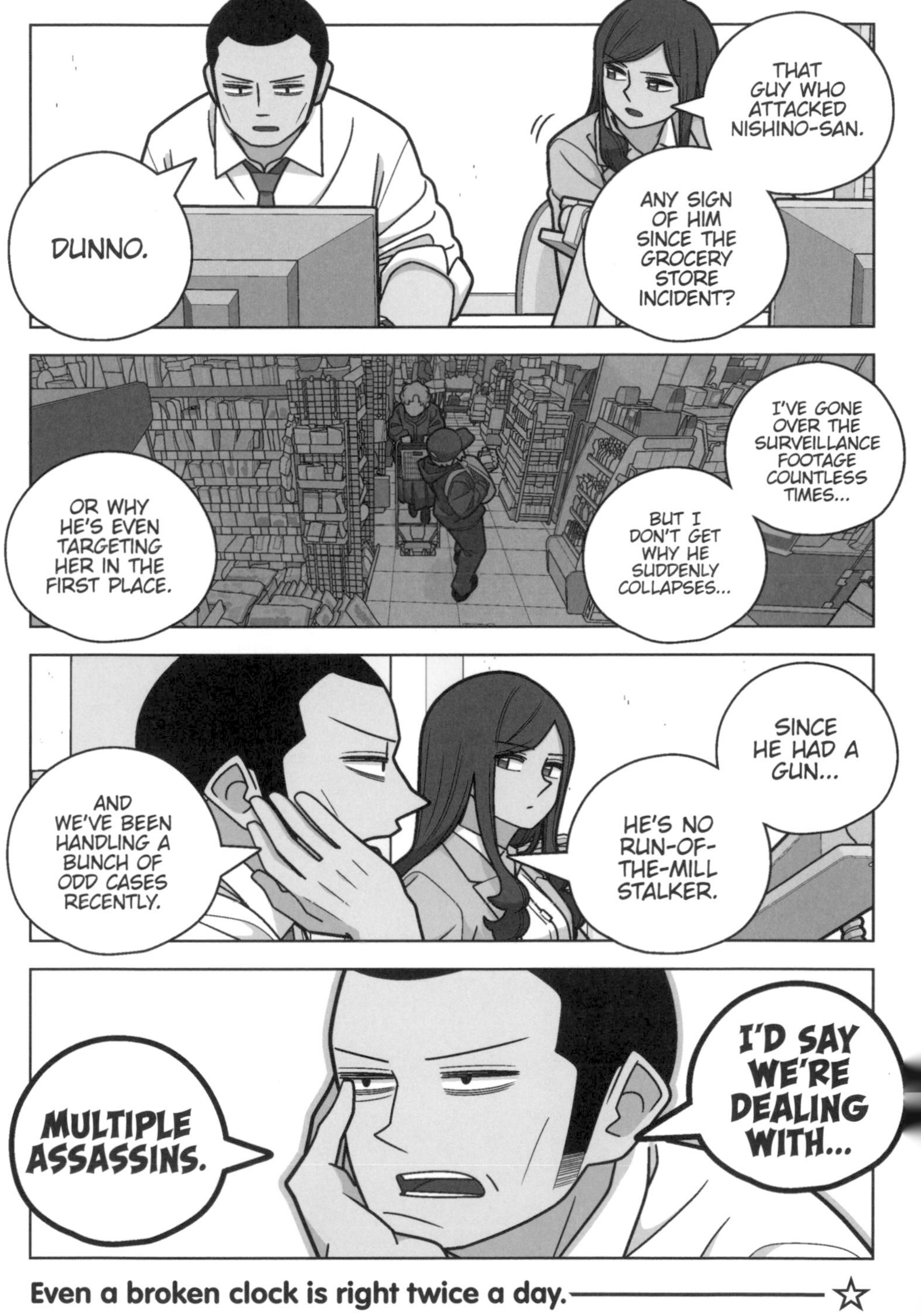
THAT GUY WHO ATTACKED NISHINO-SAN.
ANY SIGN OF HIM SINCE THE GROCERY STORE INCIDENT?
DUNNO.
I'VE GONE OVER THE SURVEILLANCE FOOTAGE COUNTLESS TIMES...
BUT I DON'T GET WHY HE SUDDENLY COLLAPSES...
OR WHY HE'S EVEN TARGETING HER IN THE FIRST PLACE.
SINCE HE HAD A GUN...
HE'S NO RUN-OF-THE-MILL STALKER.
AND WE'VE BEEN HANDLING A BUNCH OF ODD CASES RECENTLY.
I'D SAY WE'RE DEALING WITH...
MULTIPLE ASSASSINS.

Even a broken clock is right twice a day.——— ☆

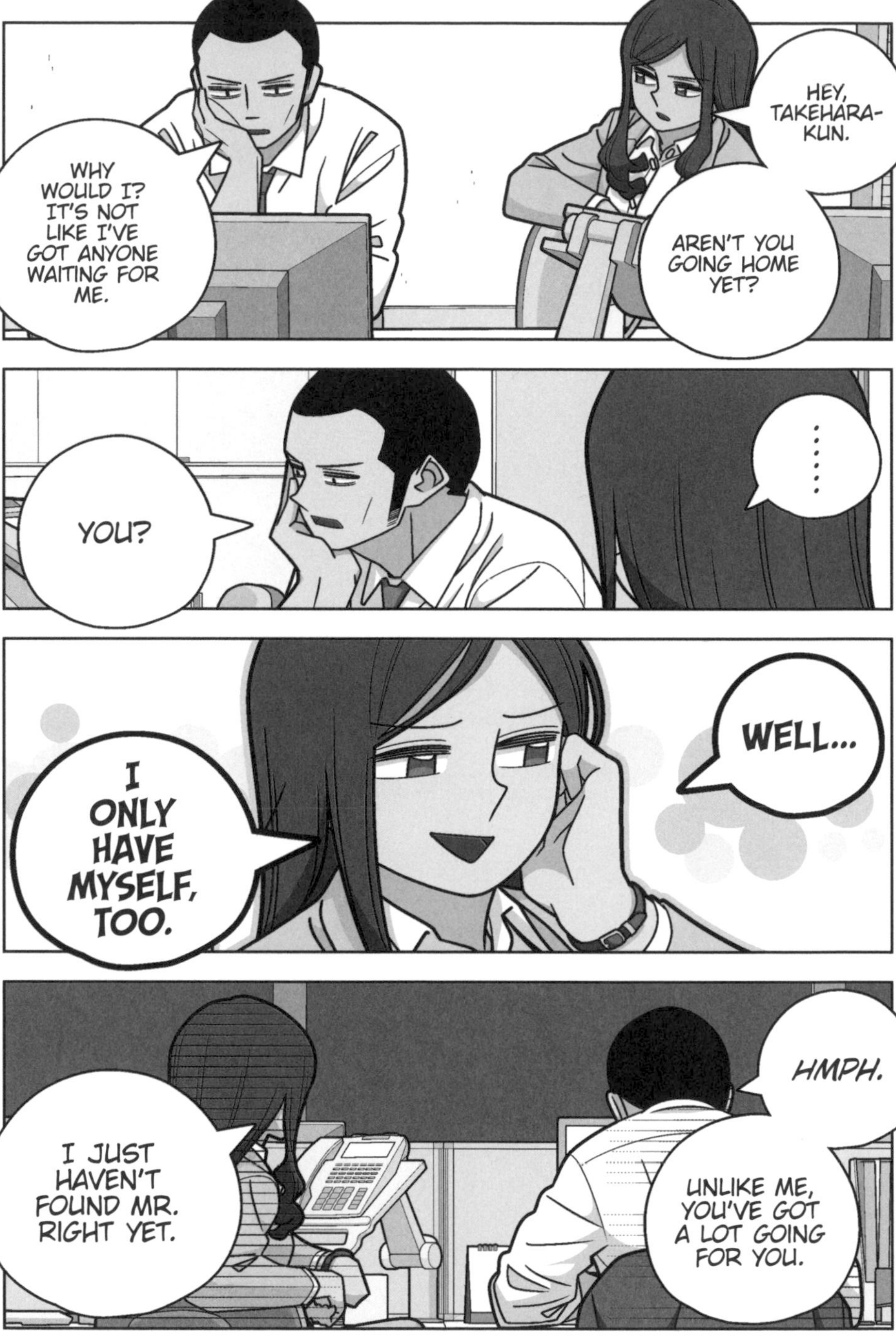
HEY, TAKEHARA-KUN.
AREN'T YOU GOING HOME YET?
WHY WOULD I? IT'S NOT LIKE I'VE GOT ANYONE WAITING FOR ME.
......
YOU?
WELL...
I ONLY HAVE MYSELF, TOO.
HMPH.
UNLIKE ME, YOU'VE GOT A LOT GOING FOR YOU.
I JUST HAVEN'T FOUND MR. RIGHT YET.

☆ —— **If only he were somewhere nearby.**

070

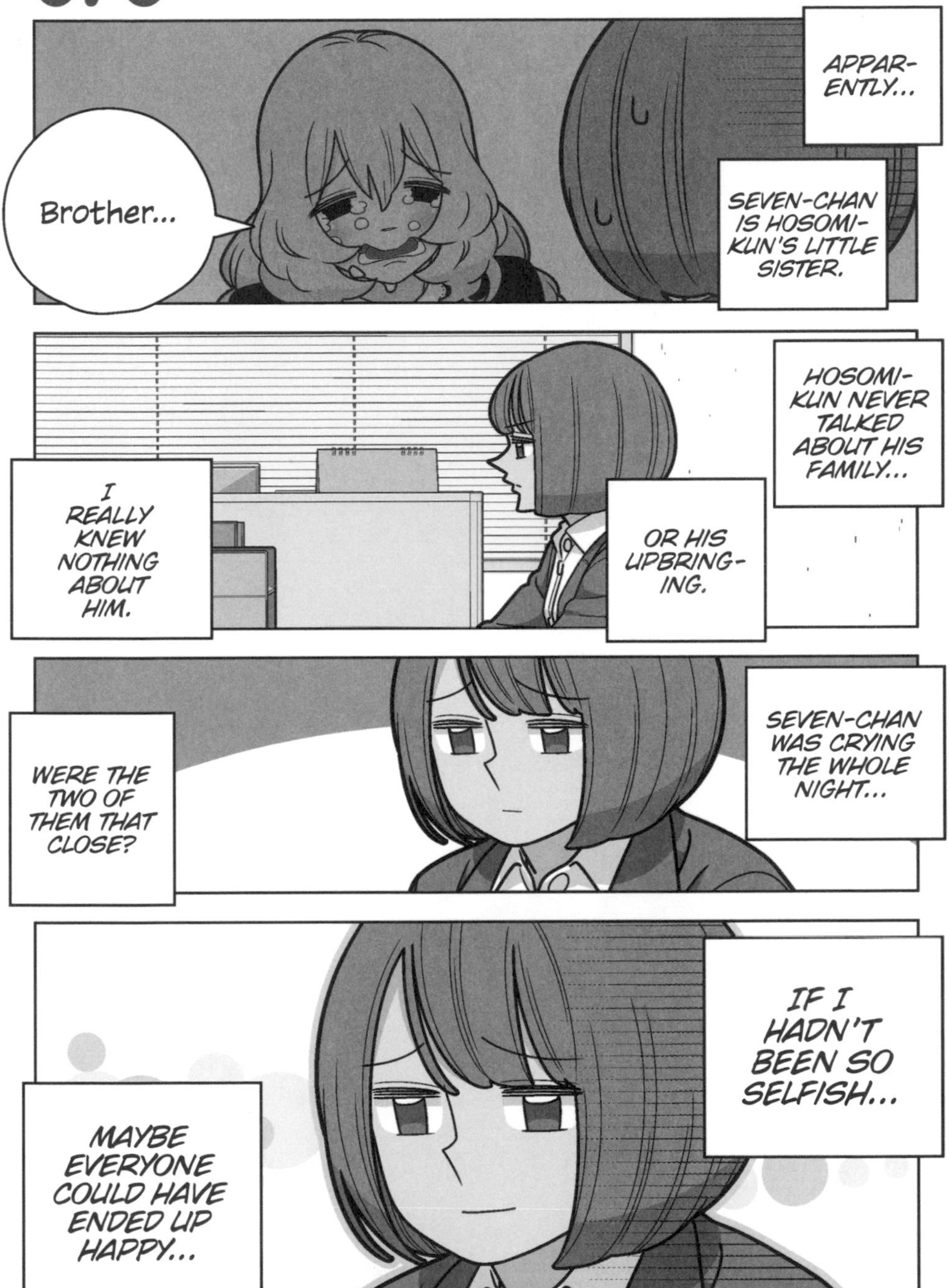
APPAR-ENTLY...
SEVEN-CHAN IS HOSOMI-KUN'S LITTLE SISTER.
Brother...
HOSOMI-KUN NEVER TALKED ABOUT HIS FAMILY...
OR HIS UPBRING-ING.
I REALLY KNEW NOTHING ABOUT HIM.
SEVEN-CHAN WAS CRYING THE WHOLE NIGHT...
WERE THE TWO OF THEM THAT CLOSE?
IF I HADN'T BEEN SO SELFISH...
MAYBE EVERYONE COULD HAVE ENDED UP HAPPY...

It's all because I chose my own happiness... ☆

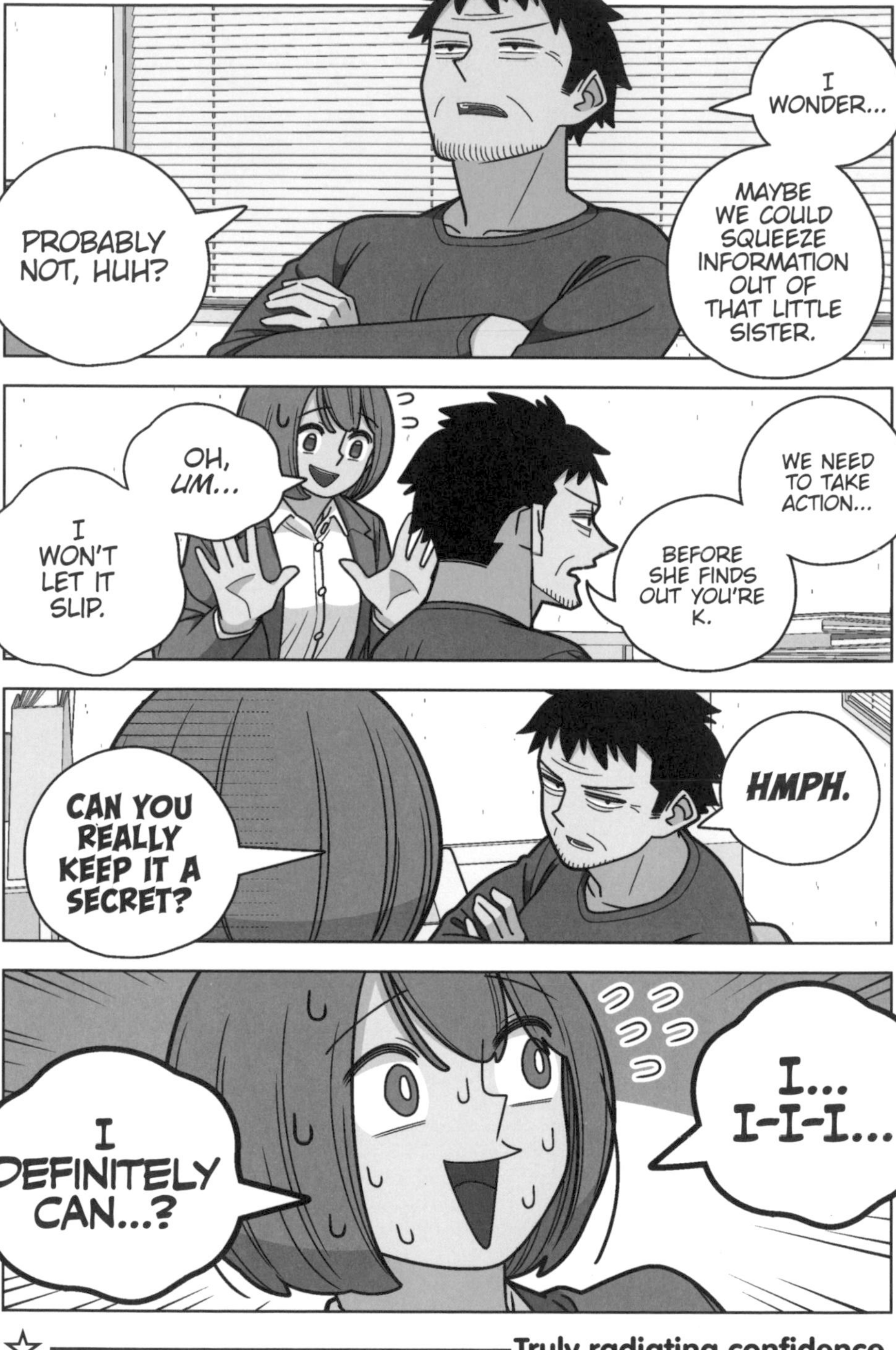
I WONDER...
MAYBE WE COULD SQUEEZE INFORMATION OUT OF THAT LITTLE SISTER.
PROBABLY NOT, HUH?
WE NEED TO TAKE ACTION...
BEFORE SHE FINDS OUT YOU'RE K.
OH, UM...
I WON'T LET IT SLIP.
HMPH.
CAN YOU REALLY KEEP IT A SECRET?
I... I-I-I...
I DEFINITELY CAN...?

☆———Truly radiating confidence.

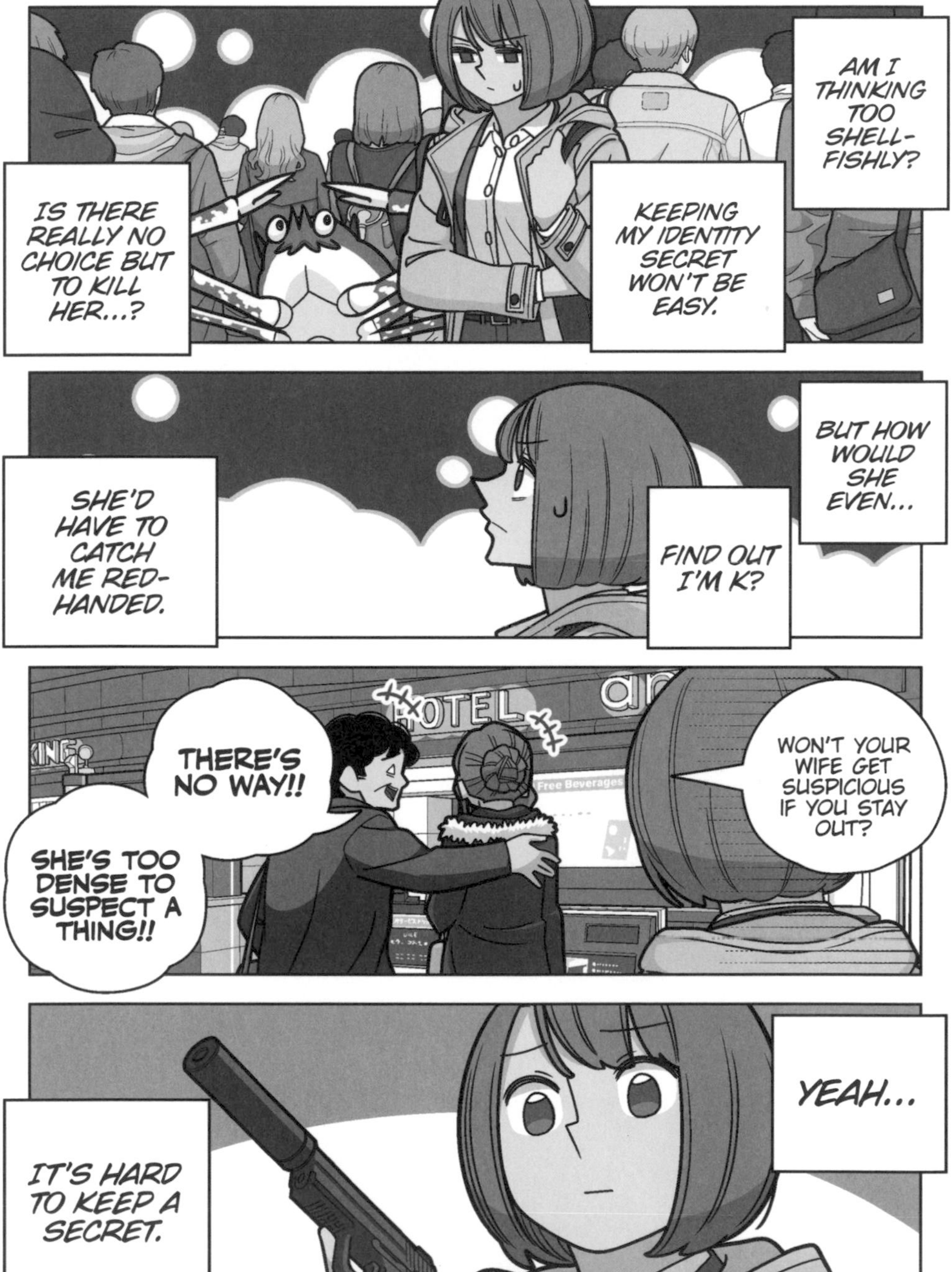
AM I THINKING TOO SHELL-FISHLY?
KEEPING MY IDENTITY SECRET WON'T BE EASY.
IS THERE REALLY NO CHOICE BUT TO KILL HER...?
BUT HOW WOULD SHE EVEN...
FIND OUT I'M K?
SHE'D HAVE TO CATCH ME RED-HANDED.
HOTEL
Free Beverages
WON'T YOUR WIFE GET SUSPICIOUS IF YOU STAY OUT?
THERE'S NO WAY!!
SHE'S TOO DENSE TO SUSPECT A THING!!
YEAH...
IT'S HARD TO KEEP A SECRET.

Can never be too careful. ☆

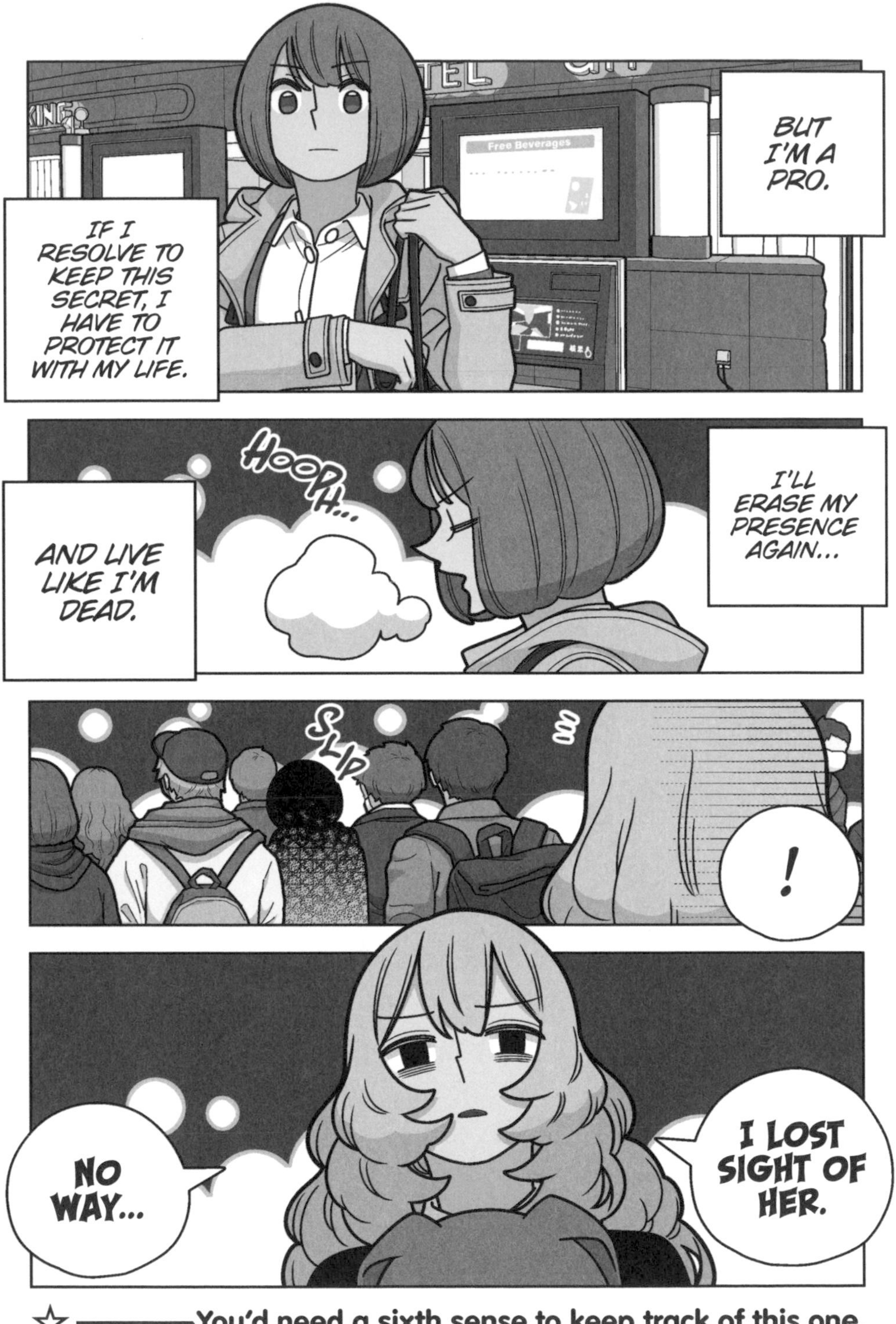
BUT I'M A PRO.
IF I RESOLVE TO KEEP THIS SECRET, I HAVE TO PROTECT IT WITH MY LIFE.
Free Beverages
I'LL ERASE MY PRESENCE AGAIN...
HOOPH...
AND LIVE LIKE I'M DEAD.
!
SLIP
I LOST SIGHT OF HER.
NO WAY...

☆———You'd need a sixth sense to keep track of this one.

071

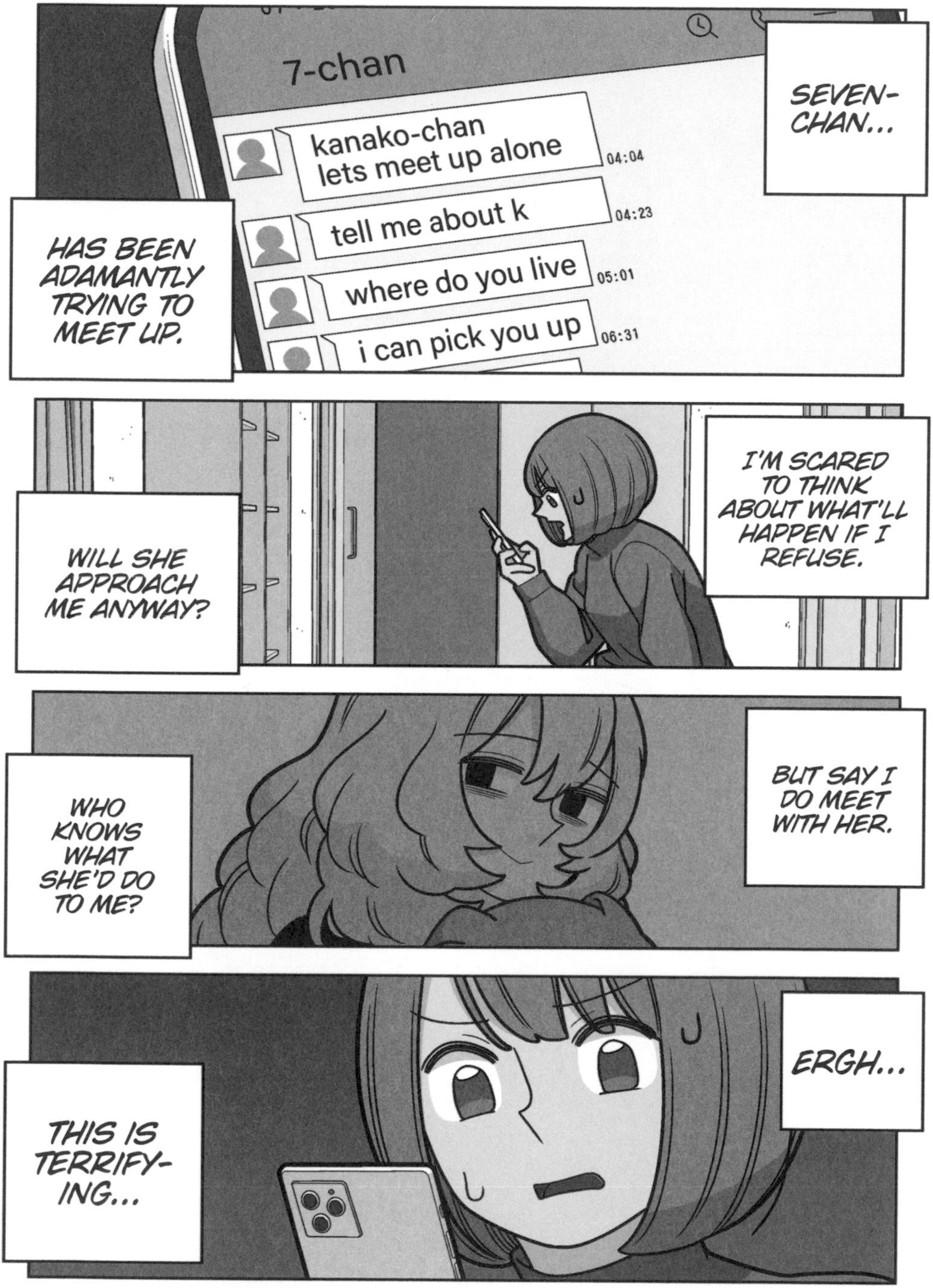
SEVEN-CHAN...
7-chan
kanako-chan lets meet up alone
04:04
tell me about k
04:23
where do you live
05:01
i can pick you up
06:31
HAS BEEN ADAMANTLY TRYING TO MEET UP.
I'M SCARED TO THINK ABOUT WHAT'LL HAPPEN IF I REFUSE.
WILL SHE APPROACH ME ANYWAY?
BUT SAY I DO MEET WITH HER.
WHO KNOWS WHAT SHE'D DO TO ME?
ERGH...
THIS IS TERRIFYING...

Be afraid, be very afraid. ☆

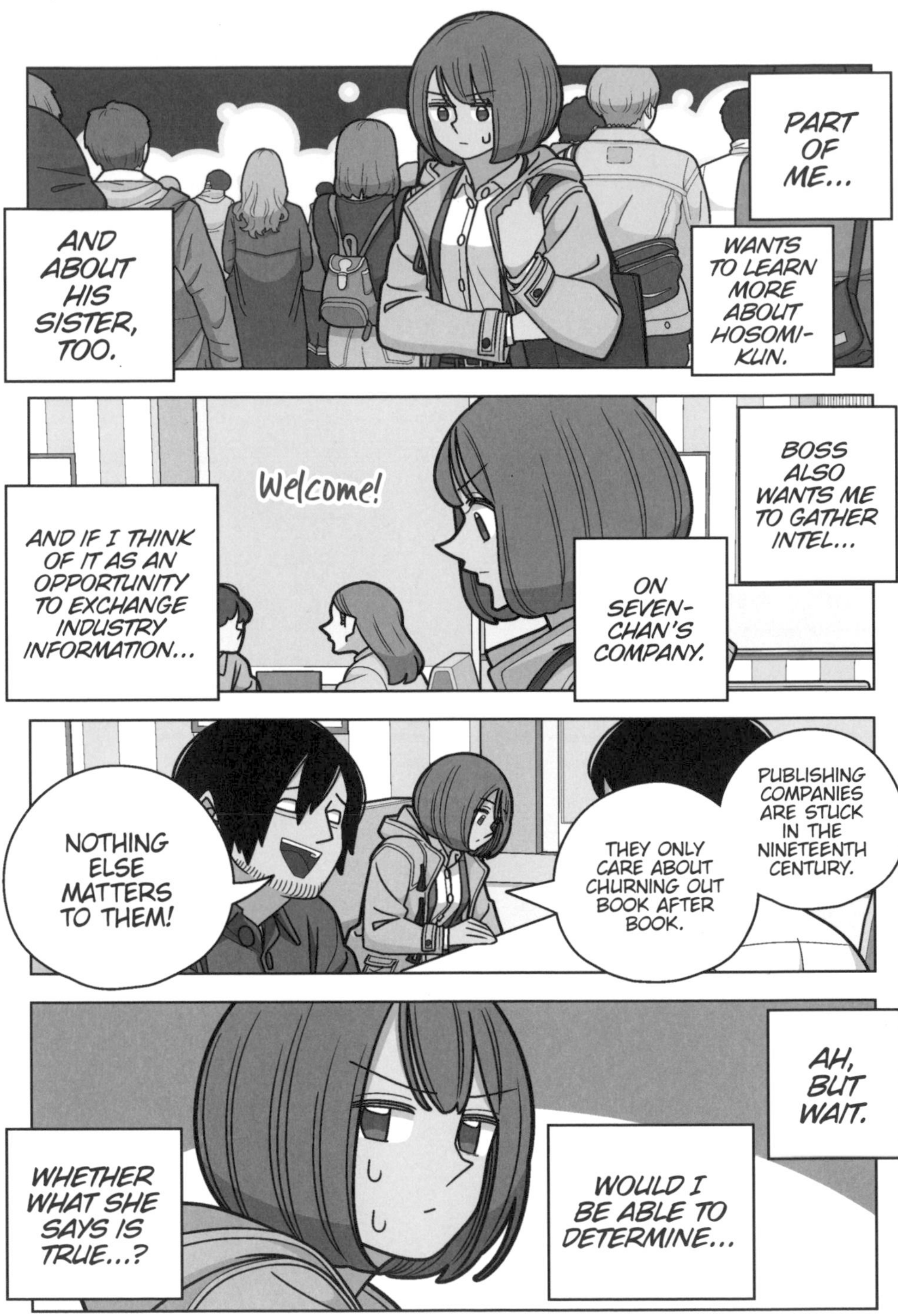
PART OF ME...
WANTS TO LEARN MORE ABOUT HOSOMI-KUN.
AND ABOUT HIS SISTER, TOO.
BOSS ALSO WANTS ME TO GATHER INTEL...
ON SEVEN-CHAN'S COMPANY.
Welcome!
AND IF I THINK OF IT AS AN OPPORTUNITY TO EXCHANGE INDUSTRY INFORMATION...
PUBLISHING COMPANIES ARE STUCK IN THE NINETEENTH CENTURY.
THEY ONLY CARE ABOUT CHURNING OUT BOOK AFTER BOOK.
NOTHING ELSE MATTERS TO THEM!
AH, BUT WAIT.
WOULD I BE ABLE TO DETERMINE...
WHETHER WHAT SHE SAYS IS TRUE...?

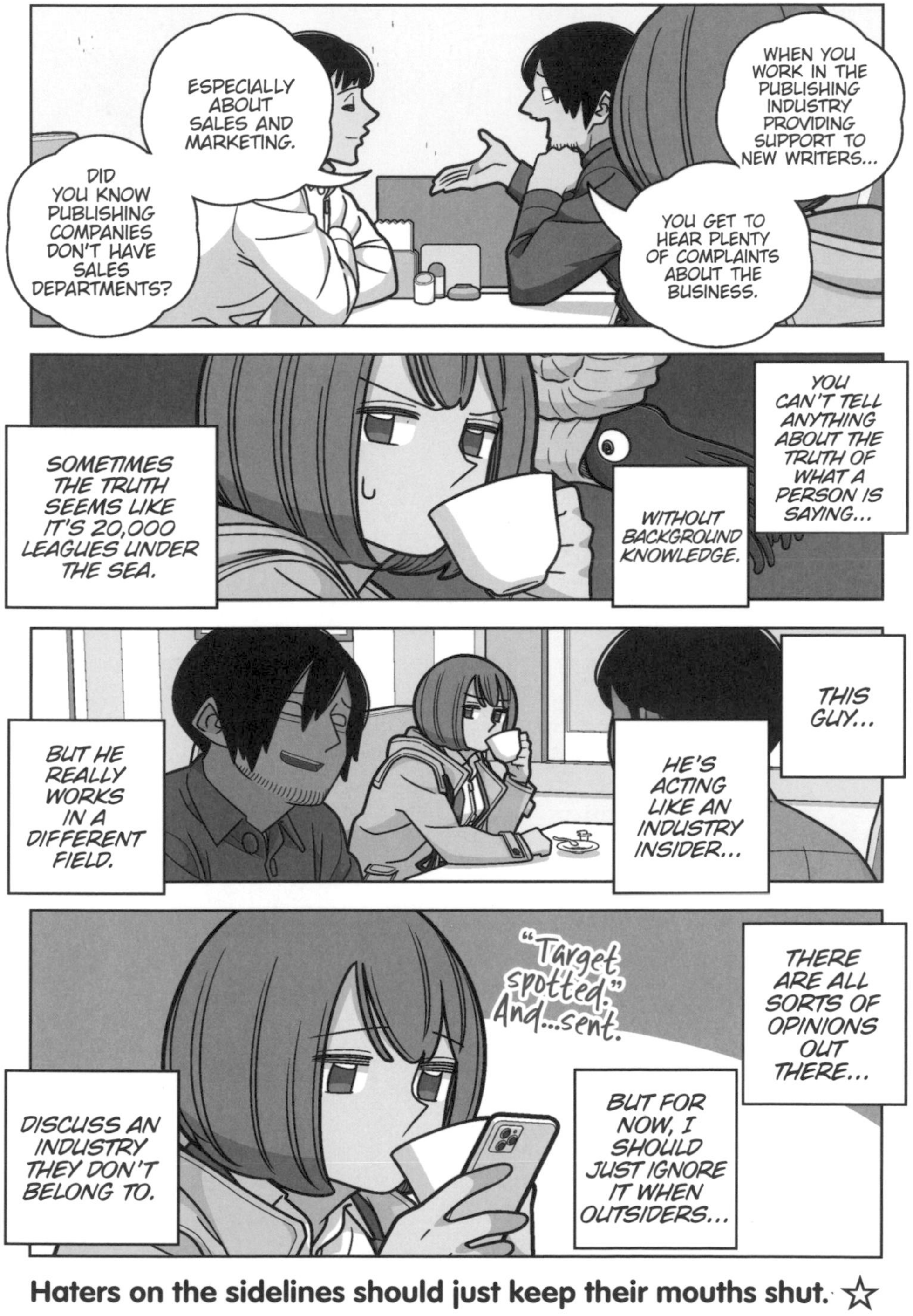
WHEN YOU WORK IN THE PUBLISHING INDUSTRY PROVIDING SUPPORT TO NEW WRITERS...
YOU GET TO HEAR PLENTY OF COMPLAINTS ABOUT THE BUSINESS.
ESPECIALLY ABOUT SALES AND MARKETING.
DID YOU KNOW PUBLISHING COMPANIES DON'T HAVE SALES DEPARTMENTS?
YOU CAN'T TELL ANYTHING ABOUT THE TRUTH OF WHAT A PERSON IS SAYING...
WITHOUT BACKGROUND KNOWLEDGE.
SOMETIMES THE TRUTH SEEMS LIKE IT'S 20,000 LEAGUES UNDER THE SEA.
THIS GUY...
HE'S ACTING LIKE AN INDUSTRY INSIDER...
BUT HE REALLY WORKS IN A DIFFERENT FIELD.
THERE ARE ALL SORTS OF OPINIONS OUT THERE...
"Target spotted." And...sent.
BUT FOR NOW, I SHOULD JUST IGNORE IT WHEN OUTSIDERS...
DISCUSS AN INDUSTRY THEY DON'T BELONG TO.

Haters on the sidelines should just keep their mouths shut. ☆

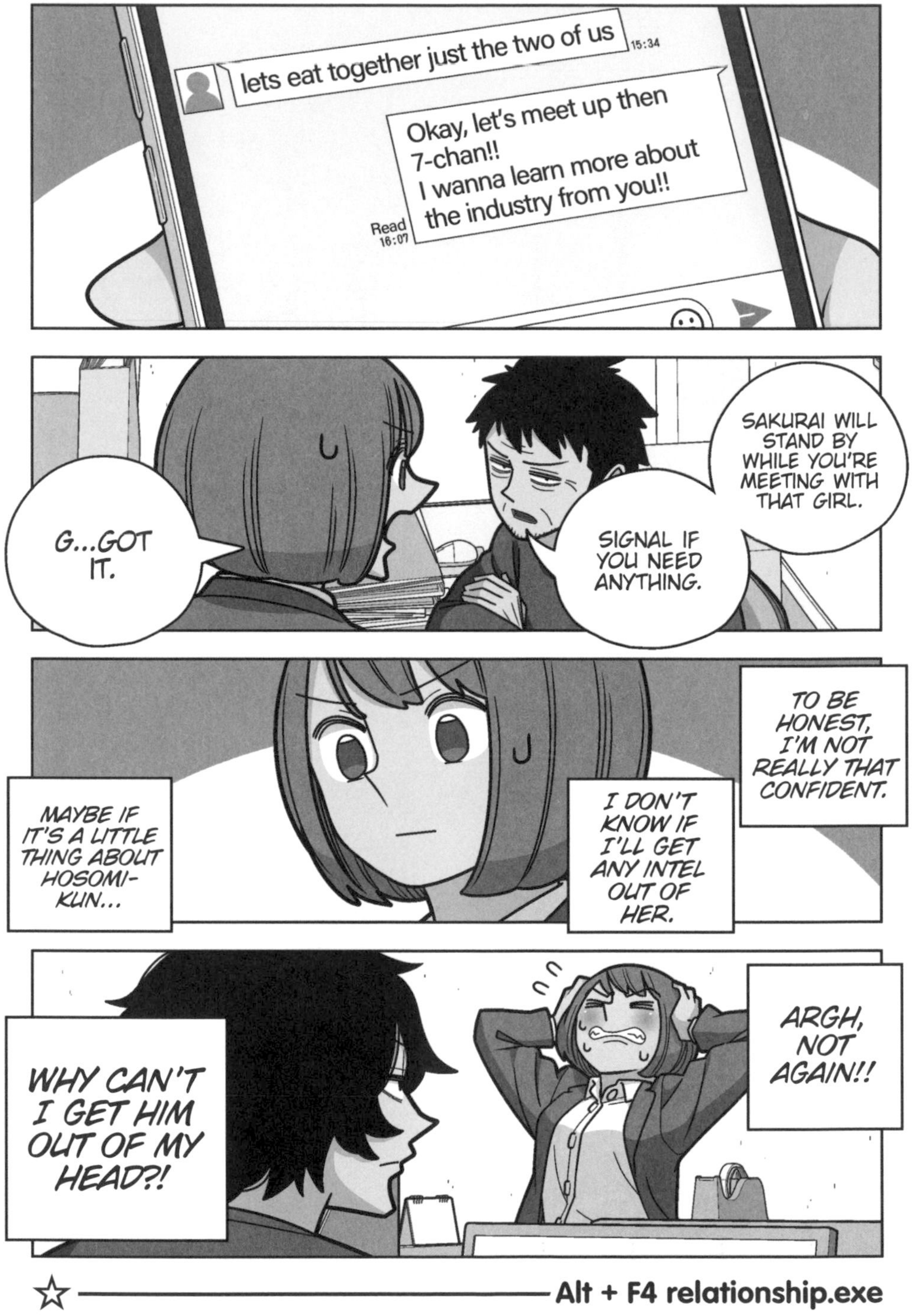

lets eat together just the two of us
15:34
Okay, let's meet up then 7-chan!! I wanna learn more about the industry from you!!
Read 16:07
SAKURAI WILL STAND BY WHILE YOU'RE MEETING WITH THAT GIRL.
SIGNAL IF YOU NEED ANYTHING.
G...GOT IT.
TO BE HONEST, I'M NOT REALLY THAT CONFIDENT.
I DON'T KNOW IF I'LL GET ANY INTEL OUT OF HER.
MAYBE IF IT'S A LITTLE THING ABOUT HOSOMI-KUN...
ARGH, NOT AGAIN!!
WHY CAN'T I GET HIM OUT OF MY HEAD?!

072

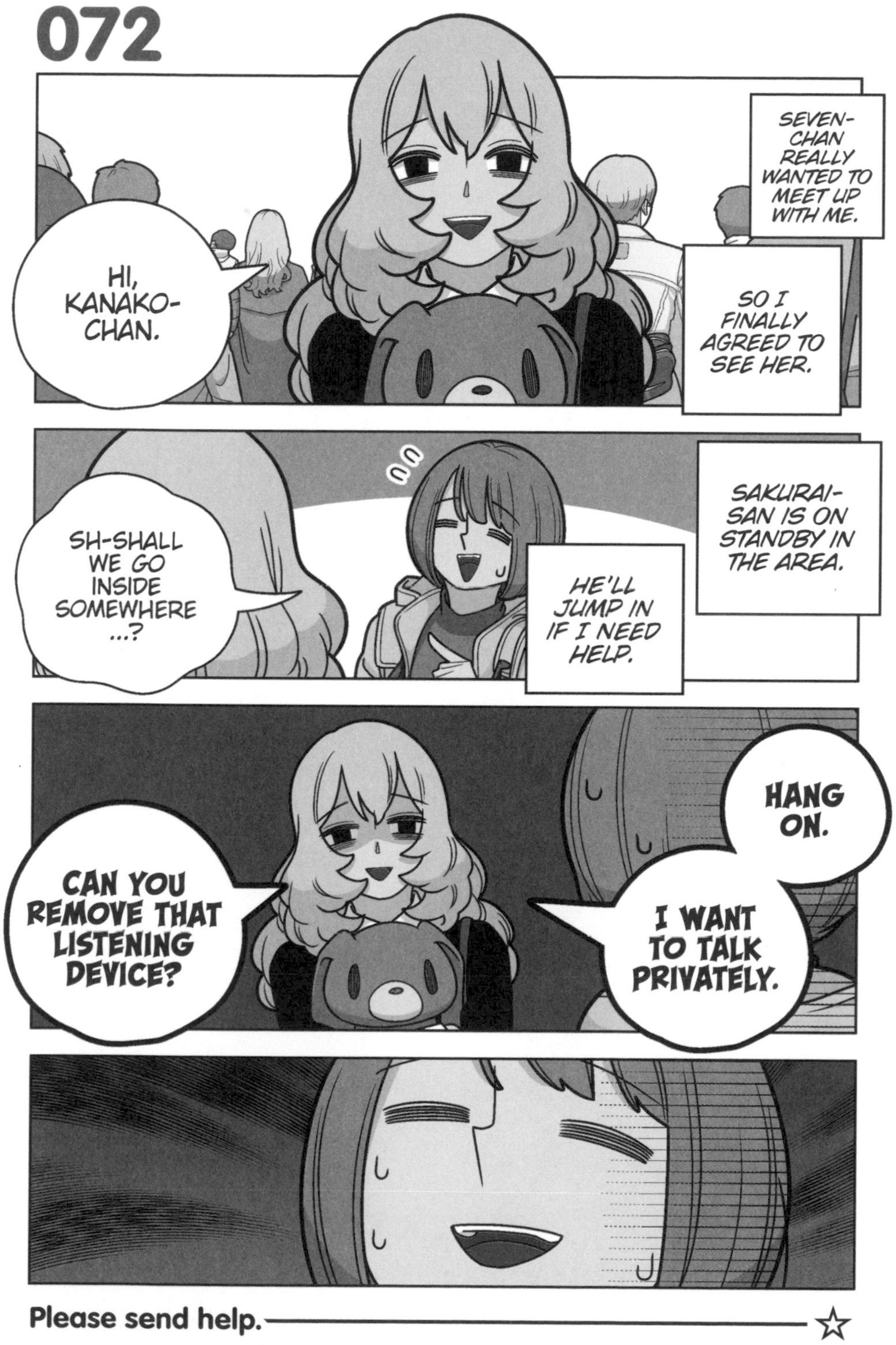
SEVEN-CHAN REALLY WANTED TO MEET UP WITH ME.
SO I FINALLY AGREED TO SEE HER.
HI, KANAKO-CHAN.
SAKURAI-SAN IS ON STANDBY IN THE AREA.
HE'LL JUMP IN IF I NEED HELP.
SH-SHALL WE GO INSIDE SOMEWHERE ...?
HANG ON.
I WANT TO TALK PRIVATELY.
CAN YOU REMOVE THAT LISTENING DEVICE?

Please send help. ☆

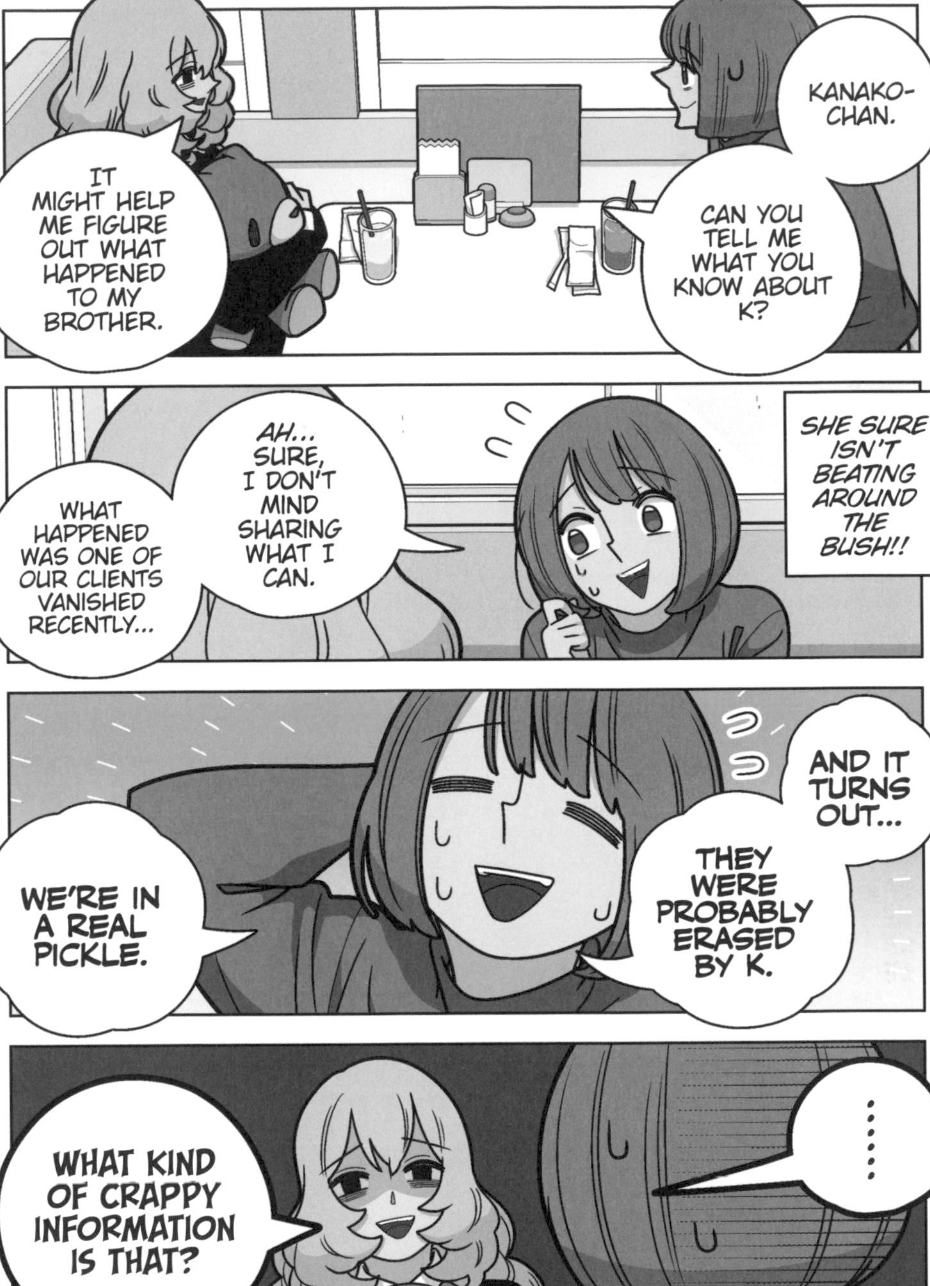
KANAKO-CHAN.
CAN YOU TELL ME WHAT YOU KNOW ABOUT K?
IT MIGHT HELP ME FIGURE OUT WHAT HAPPENED TO MY BROTHER.
SHE SURE ISN'T BEATING AROUND THE BUSH!!
AH... SURE, I DON'T MIND SHARING WHAT I CAN.
WHAT HAPPENED WAS ONE OF OUR CLIENTS VANISHED RECENTLY...
AND IT TURNS OUT...
THEY WERE PROBABLY ERASED BY K.
WE'RE IN A REAL PICKLE.
......
WHAT KIND OF CRAPPY INFORMATION IS THAT?

☆ I'm in a real pickle.

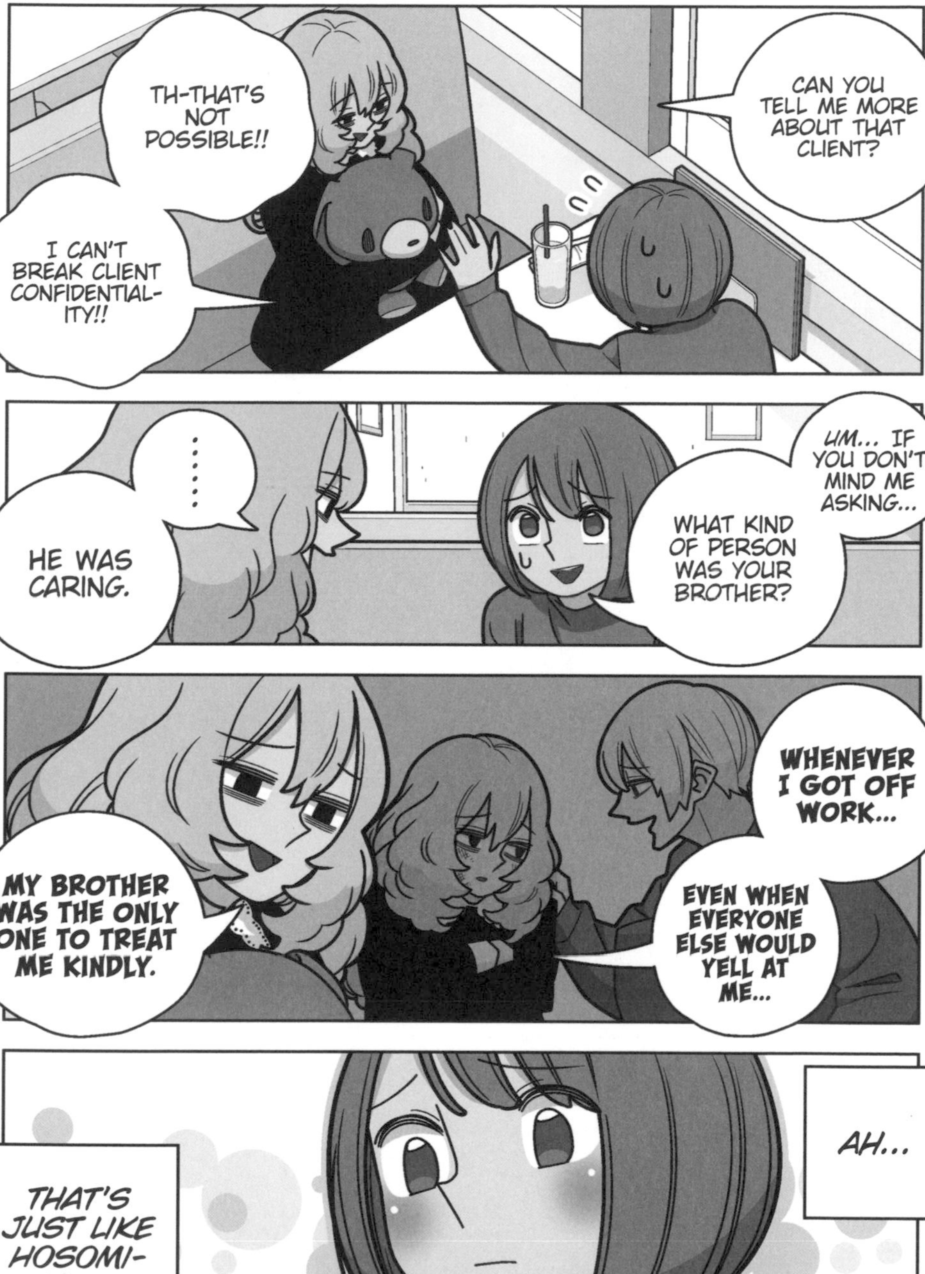
CAN YOU TELL ME MORE ABOUT THAT CLIENT?
TH-THAT'S NOT POSSIBLE!!
I CAN'T BREAK CLIENT CONFIDENTIAL-ITY!!
UM... IF YOU DON'T MIND ME ASKING...
WHAT KIND OF PERSON WAS YOUR BROTHER?
......
HE WAS CARING.
WHENEVER I GOT OFF WORK...
EVEN WHEN EVERYONE ELSE WOULD YELL AT ME...
MY BROTHER WAS THE ONLY ONE TO TREAT ME KINDLY.
AH...
THAT'S JUST LIKE HOSOMI-KUN.

I'm still the one who killed him, though.——— ☆

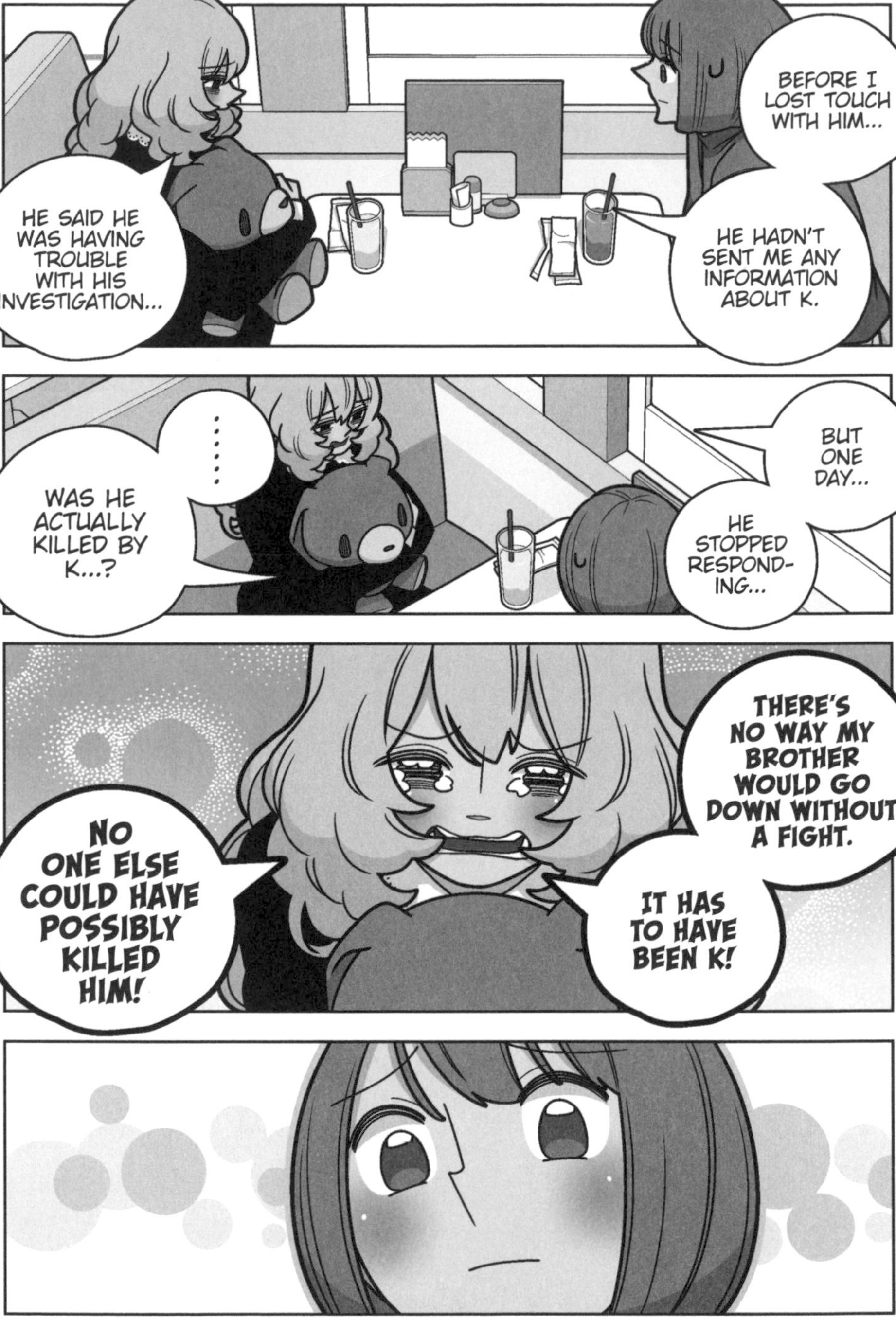
BEFORE I LOST TOUCH WITH HIM...
HE HADN'T SENT ME ANY INFORMATION ABOUT K.
HE SAID HE WAS HAVING TROUBLE WITH HIS INVESTIGATION...
BUT ONE DAY...
HE STOPPED RESPOND-ING...
......
WAS HE ACTUALLY KILLED BY K...?
THERE'S NO WAY MY BROTHER WOULD GO DOWN WITHOUT A FIGHT.
IT HAS TO HAVE BEEN K!
NO ONE ELSE COULD HAVE POSSIBLY KILLED HIM!

☆ —— He was a tough one.

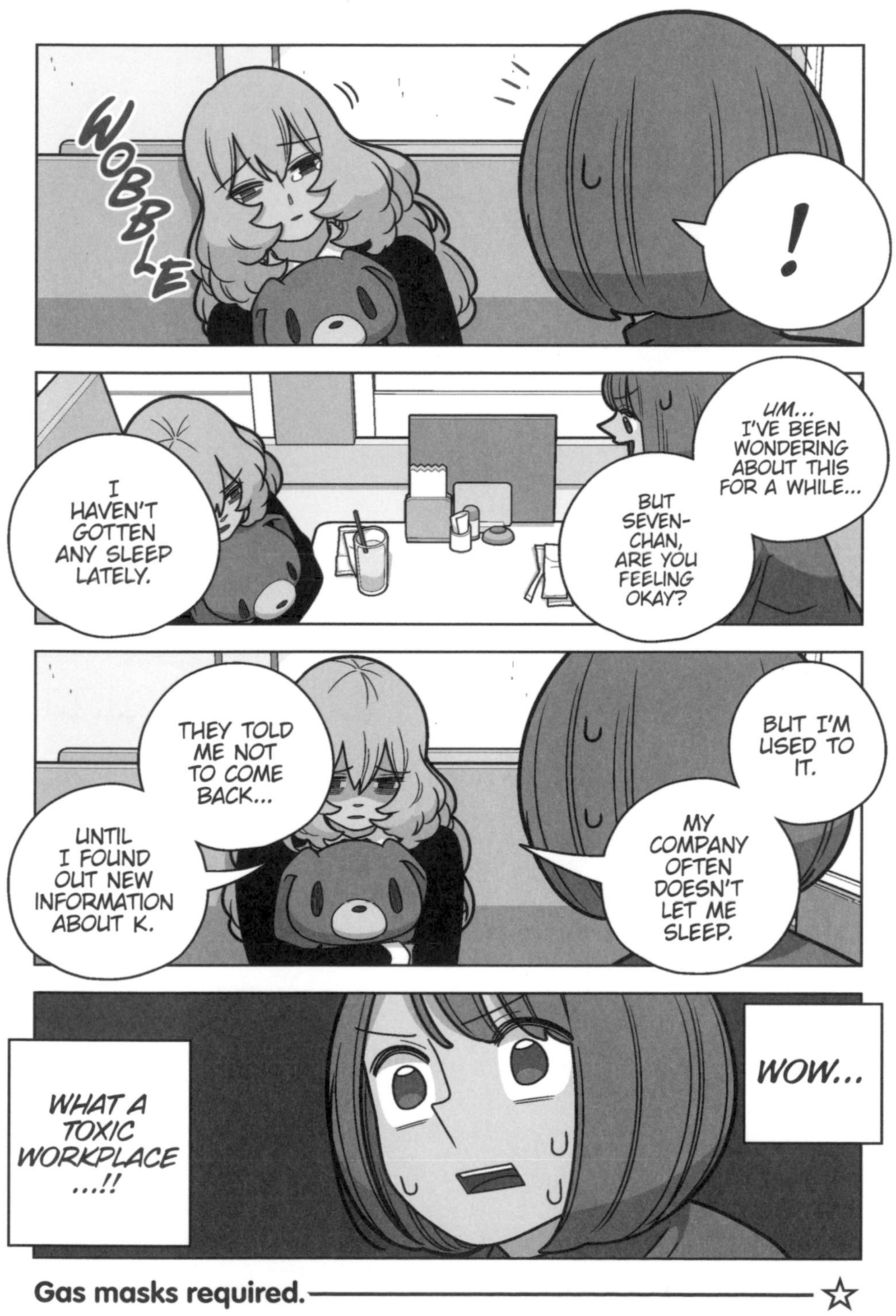
!
WOBBLE
UM... I'VE BEEN WONDERING ABOUT THIS FOR A WHILE...
BUT SEVEN-CHAN, ARE YOU FEELING OKAY?
I HAVEN'T GOTTEN ANY SLEEP LATELY.
MY COMPANY OFTEN DOESN'T LET ME SLEEP.
BUT I'M USED TO IT.
THEY TOLD ME NOT TO COME BACK...
UNTIL I FOUND OUT NEW INFORMATION ABOUT K.
WOW...
WHAT A TOXIC WORKPLACE ...!!

Gas masks required. ☆

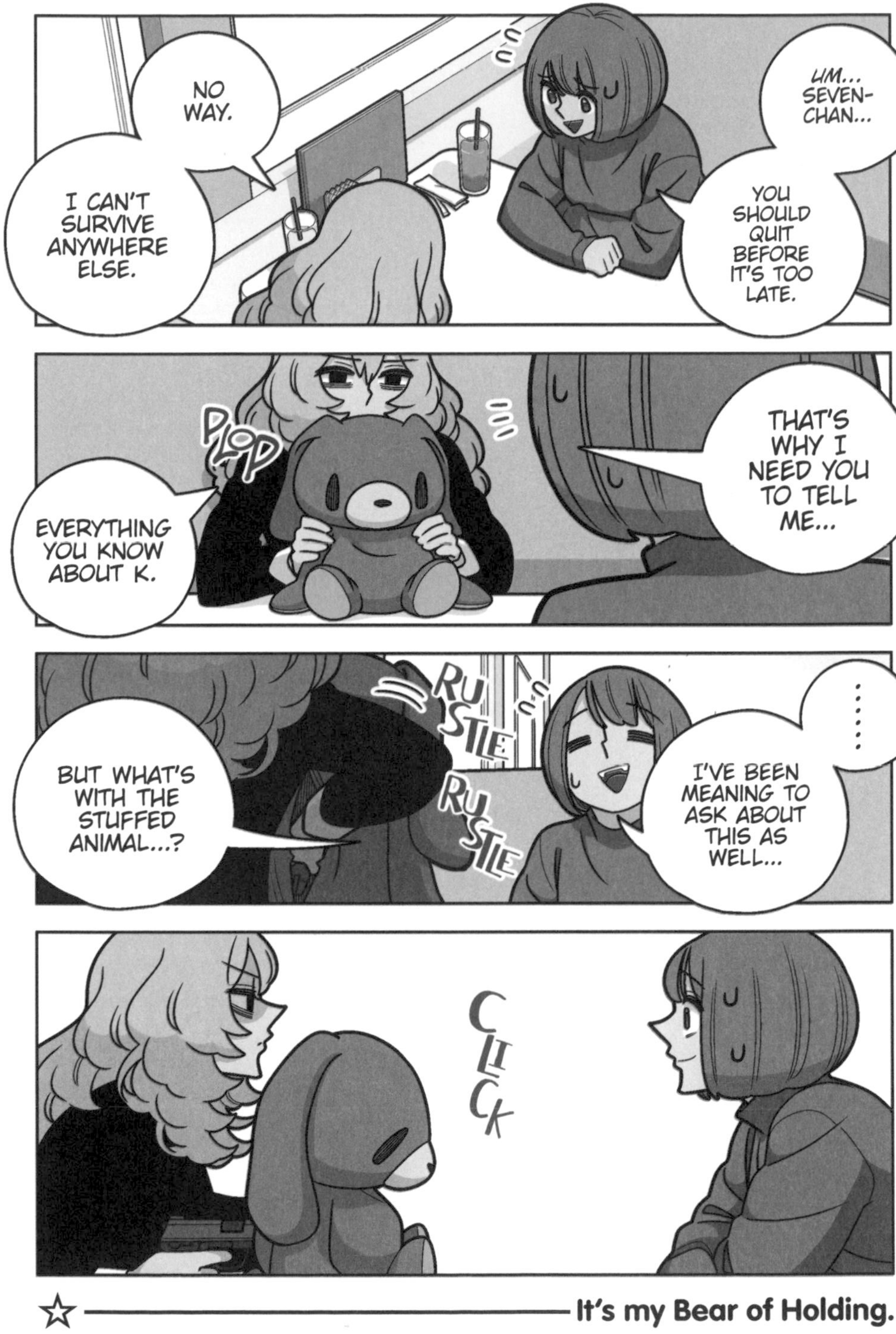
UM... SEVEN-CHAN...
YOU SHOULD QUIT BEFORE IT'S TOO LATE.
NO WAY.
I CAN'T SURVIVE ANYWHERE ELSE.
THAT'S WHY I NEED YOU TO TELL ME...
PLOP
EVERYTHING YOU KNOW ABOUT K.
......
I'VE BEEN MEANING TO ASK ABOUT THIS AS WELL...
RUSTLE
RUSTLE
BUT WHAT'S WITH THE STUFFED ANIMAL...?
CLICK

☆ —— **It's my Bear of Holding.**

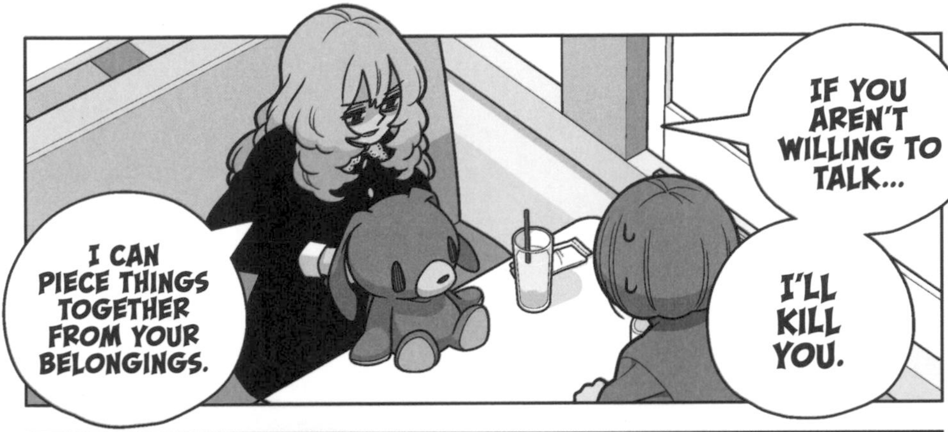
IF YOU AREN'T WILLING TO TALK...
I'LL KILL YOU.
I CAN PIECE THINGS TOGETHER FROM YOUR BELONGINGS.

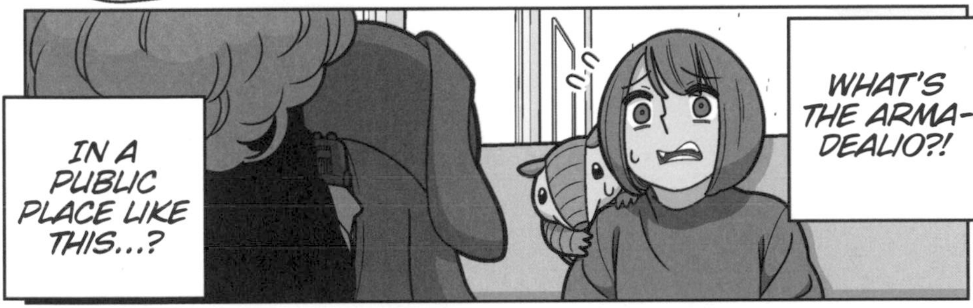
WHAT'S THE ARMA-DEALIO?!
IN A PUBLIC PLACE LIKE THIS...?

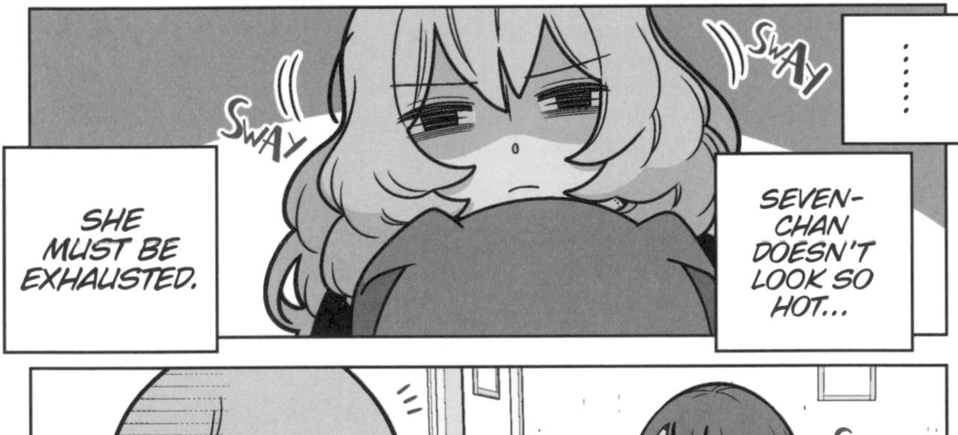
......
SWAY
SWAY
SEVEN-CHAN DOESN'T LOOK SO HOT...
SHE MUST BE EXHAUSTED.

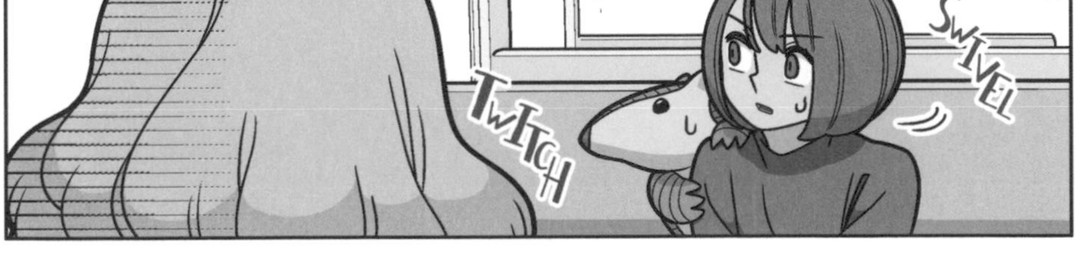
SWIVEL
TWITCH

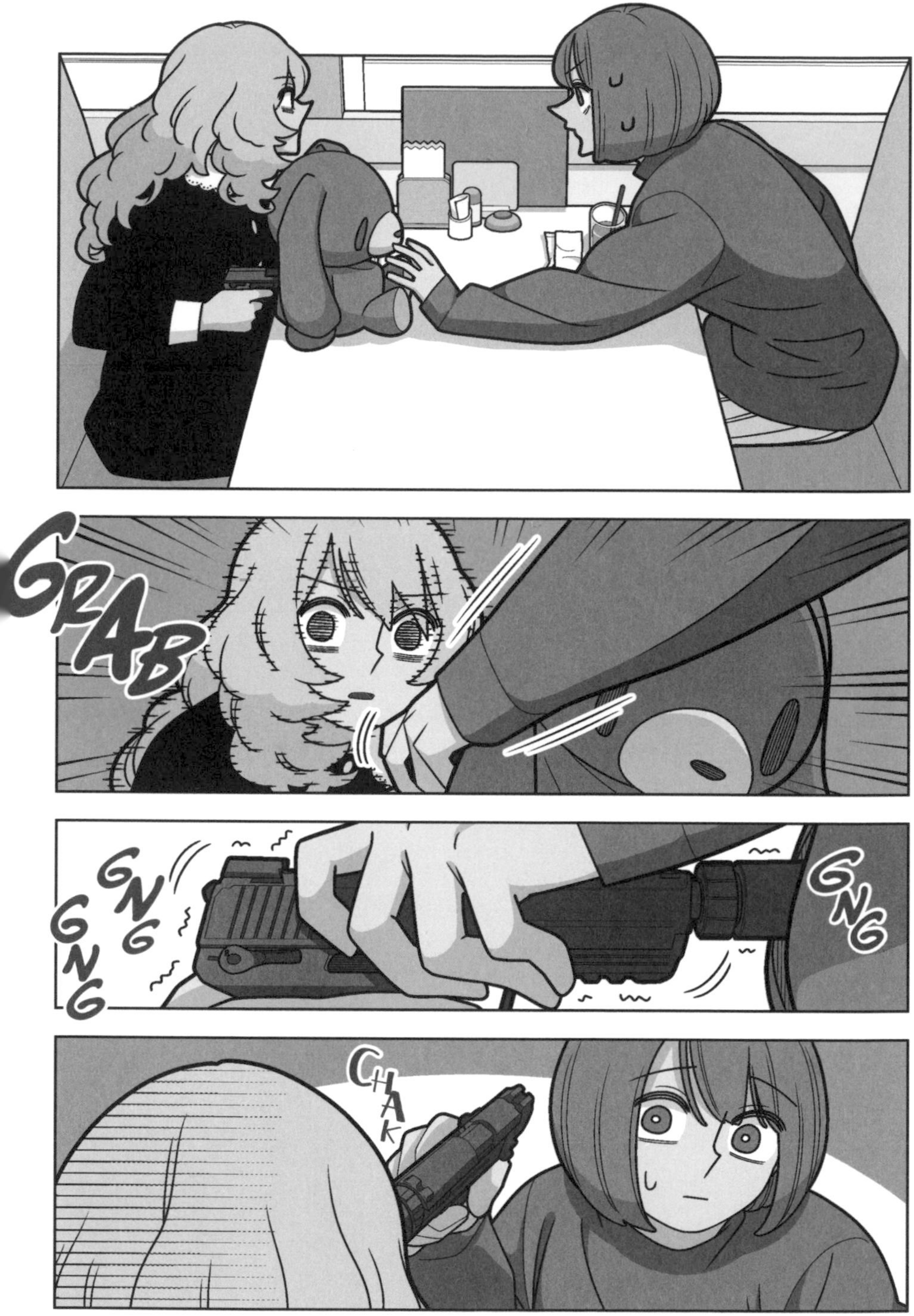
GRAB
GNG
GNG
GNG
CHAK

☆ ——— True colors: Shown.

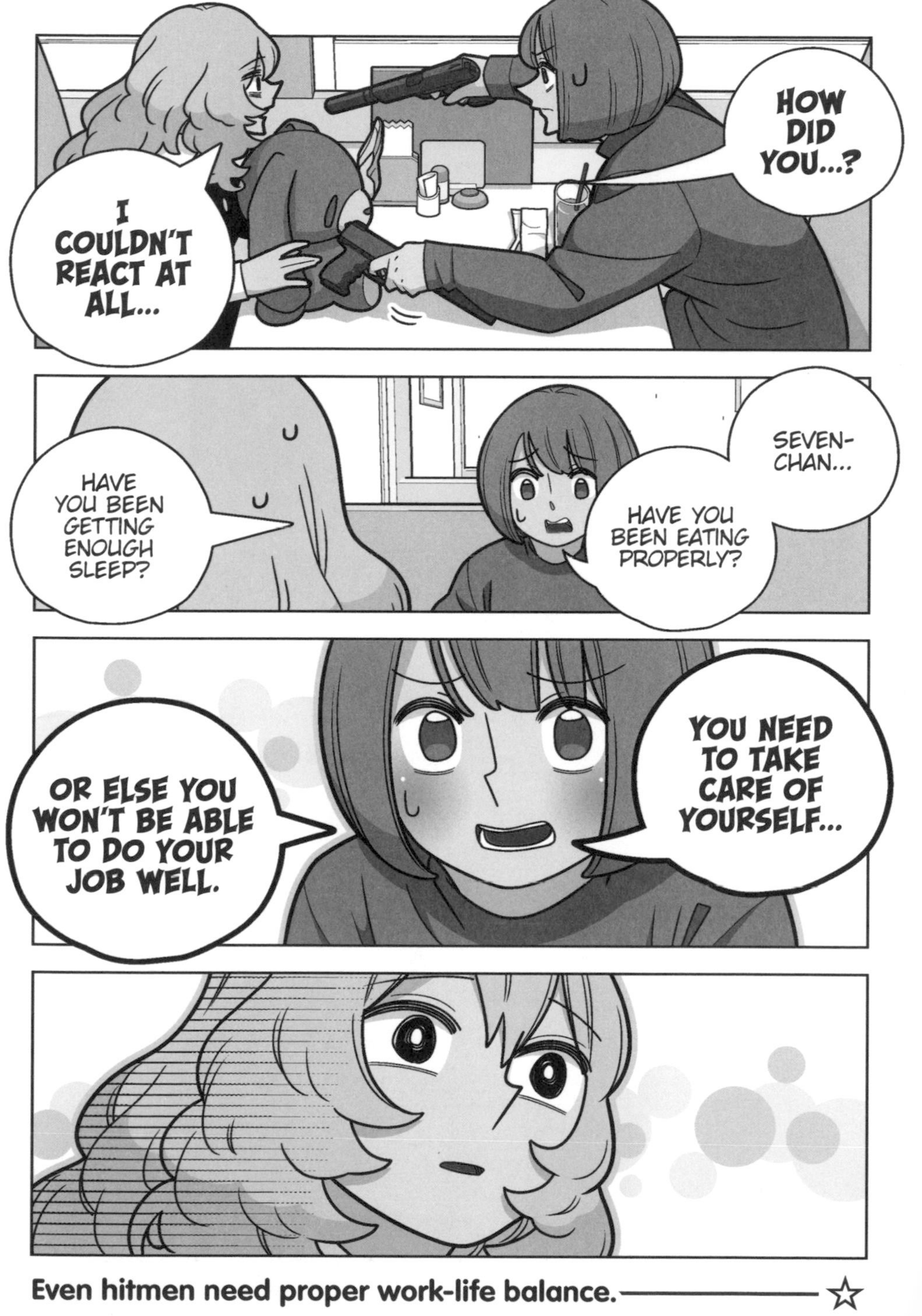
HOW DID YOU...?
I COULDN'T REACT AT ALL...
SEVEN-CHAN...
HAVE YOU BEEN EATING PROPERLY?
HAVE YOU BEEN GETTING ENOUGH SLEEP?
YOU NEED TO TAKE CARE OF YOURSELF...
OR ELSE YOU WON'T BE ABLE TO DO YOUR JOB WELL.

Even hitmen need proper work-life balance. ☆

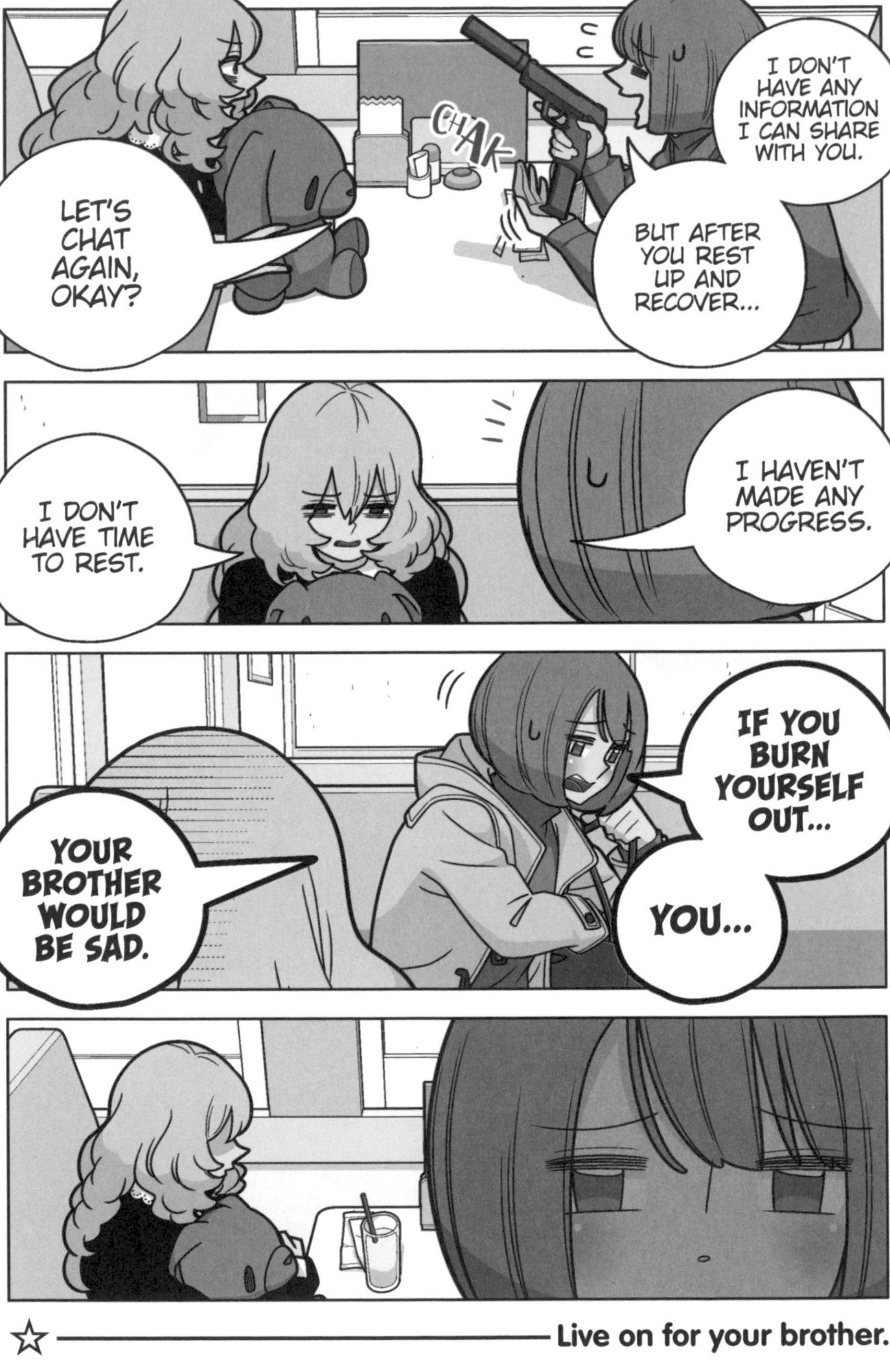
I DON'T HAVE ANY INFORMATION I CAN SHARE WITH YOU.
BUT AFTER YOU REST UP AND RECOVER...
CHAK
LET'S CHAT AGAIN, OKAY?
I HAVEN'T MADE ANY PROGRESS.
I DON'T HAVE TIME TO REST.
IF YOU BURN YOURSELF OUT...
YOU...
YOUR BROTHER WOULD BE SAD.

☆ —— Live on for your brother.

Happy Kanako's
Killer Life

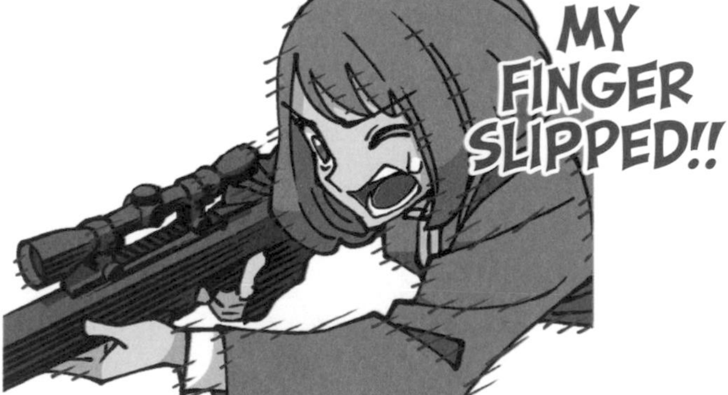
MY FINGER SLIPPED!!

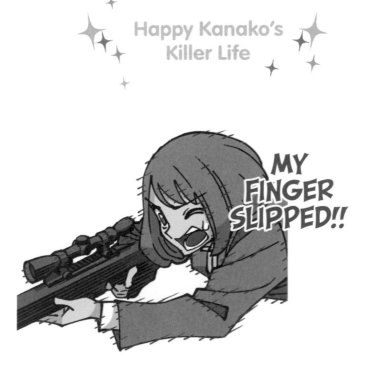

Happy Kanako's
Killer Life

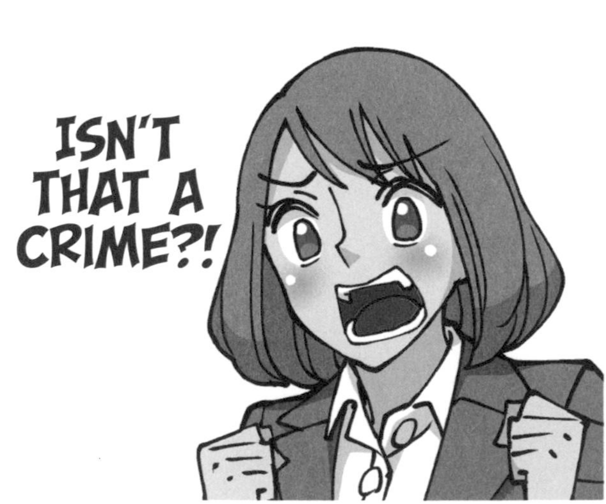
ISN'T THAT A CRIME?!

Bonus

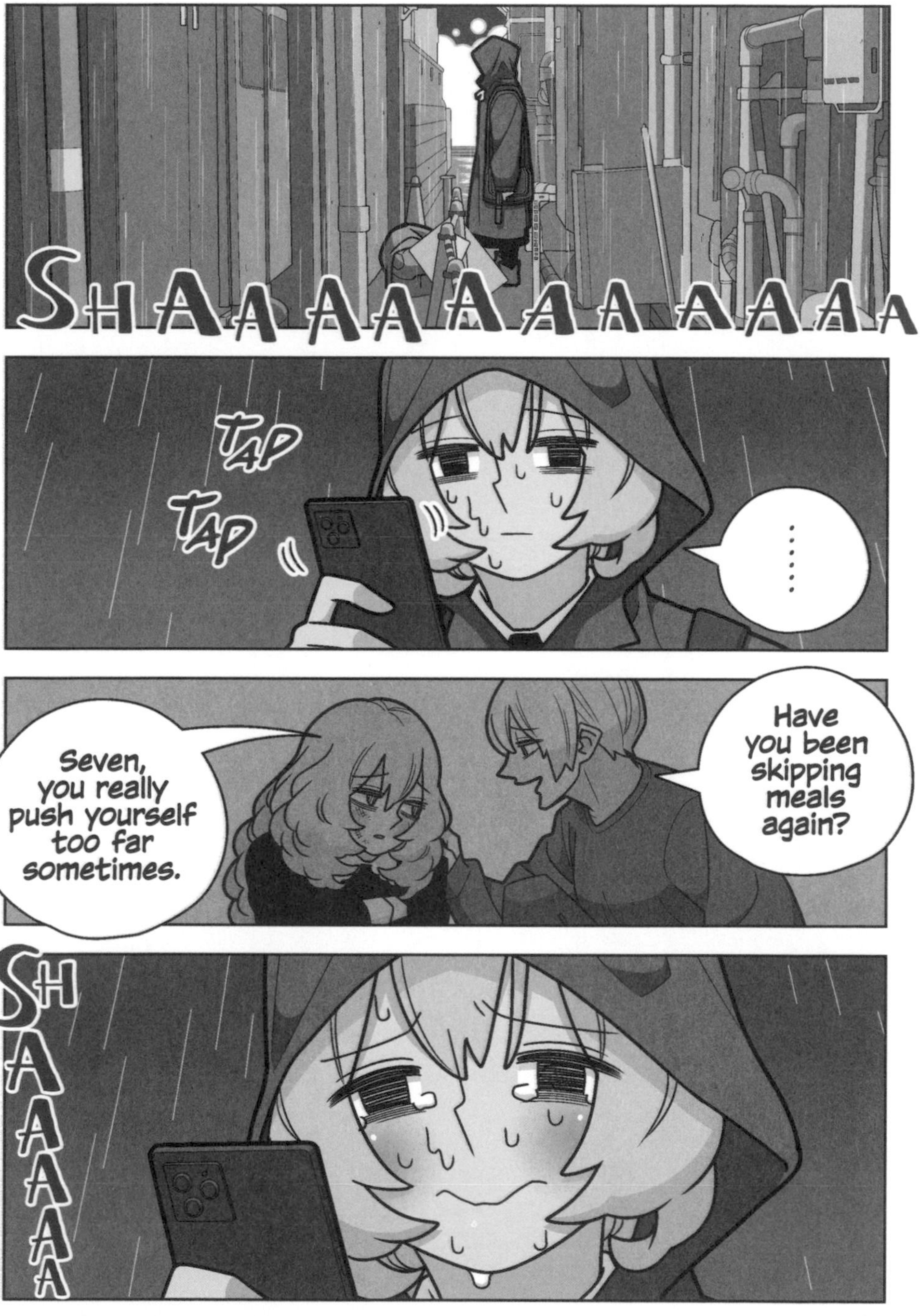
SHAAAAAAAAAAAA
TAP TAP
......
Have you been skipping meals again?
Seven, you really push yourself too far sometimes.
SHAAAAAAA

Another day of overtime. ☆

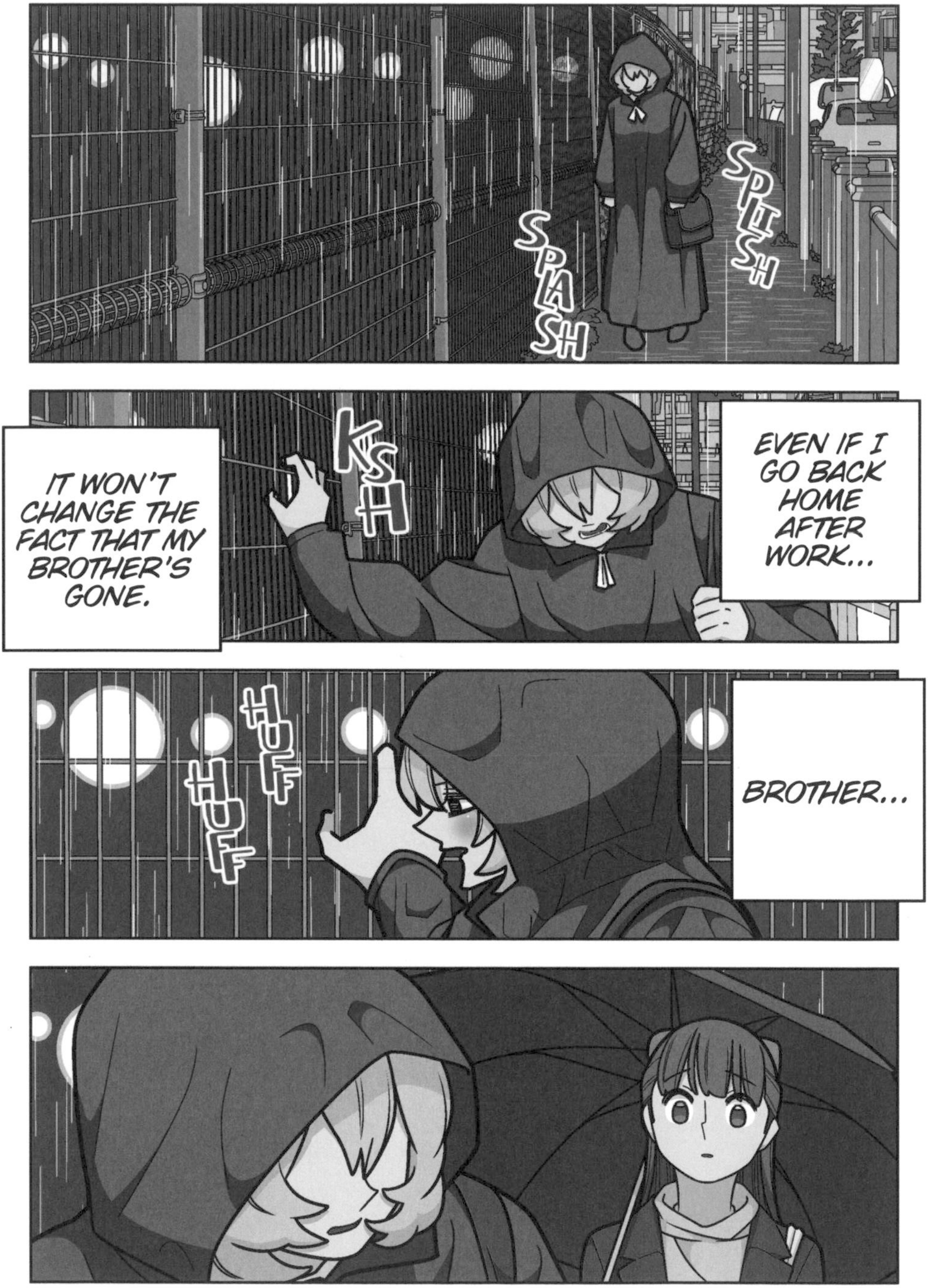
SPLISH
SPLASH
EVEN IF I GO BACK HOME AFTER WORK...
KSH
IT WON'T CHANGE THE FACT THAT MY BROTHER'S GONE.
BROTHER...
HUFF
HUFF

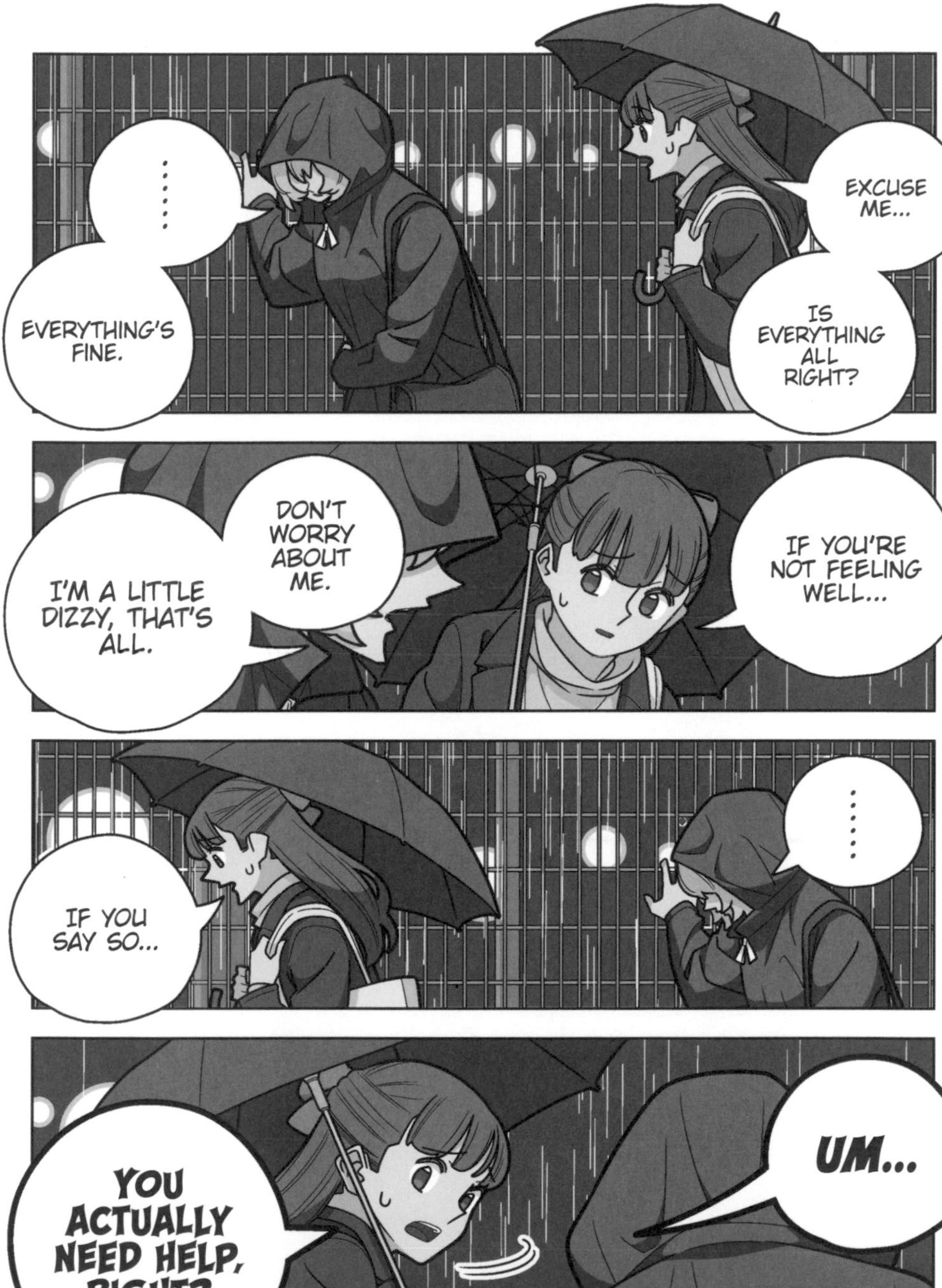
EXCUSE ME...
IS EVERYTHING ALL RIGHT?
......
EVERYTHING'S FINE.
IF YOU'RE NOT FEELING WELL...
DON'T WORRY ABOUT ME.
I'M A LITTLE DIZZY, THAT'S ALL.
......
IF YOU SAY SO...
UM...
YOU ACTUALLY NEED HELP, RIGHT?

Can't overlook someone in trouble. ☆

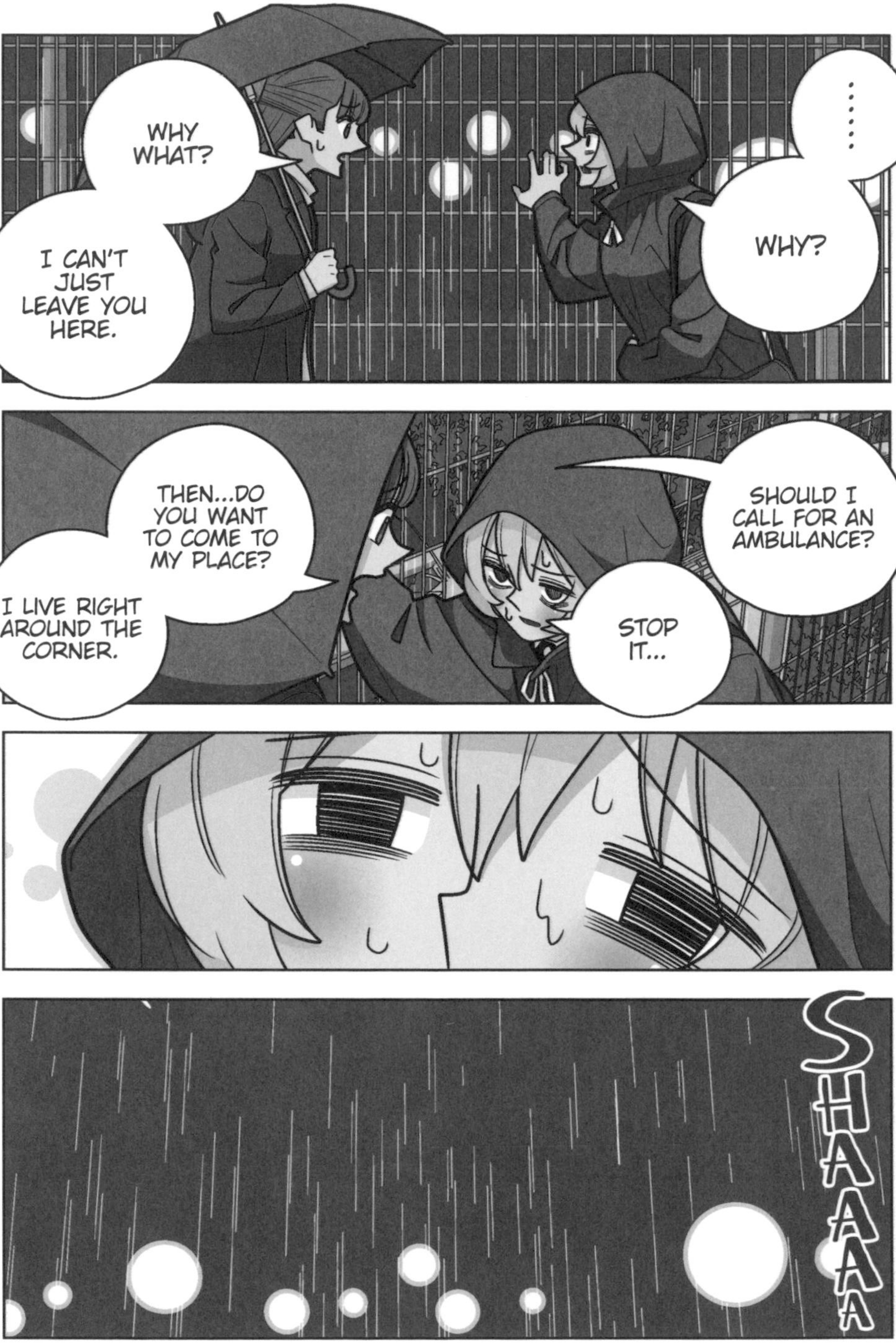
......
WHY?
WHY WHAT?
I CAN'T JUST LEAVE YOU HERE.
SHOULD I CALL FOR AN AMBULANCE?
STOP IT...
THEN...DO YOU WANT TO COME TO MY PLACE?
I LIVE RIGHT AROUND THE CORNER.
SHAAAAA

☆ **A sister.**

Happy Kanako's
Killer Life

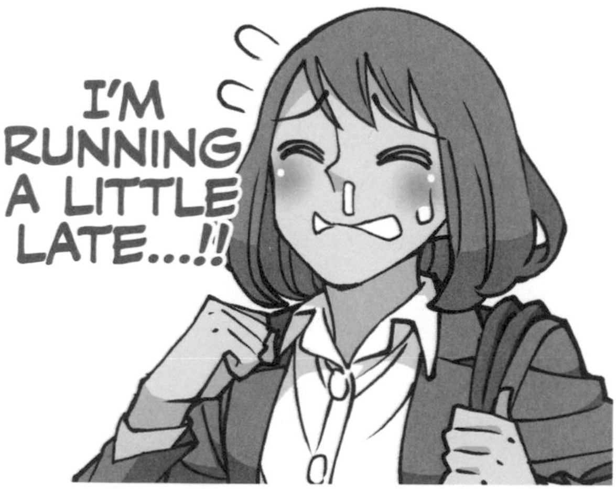
I'M RUNNING A LITTLE LATE...!!

Happy Kanako's
Killer Life

073

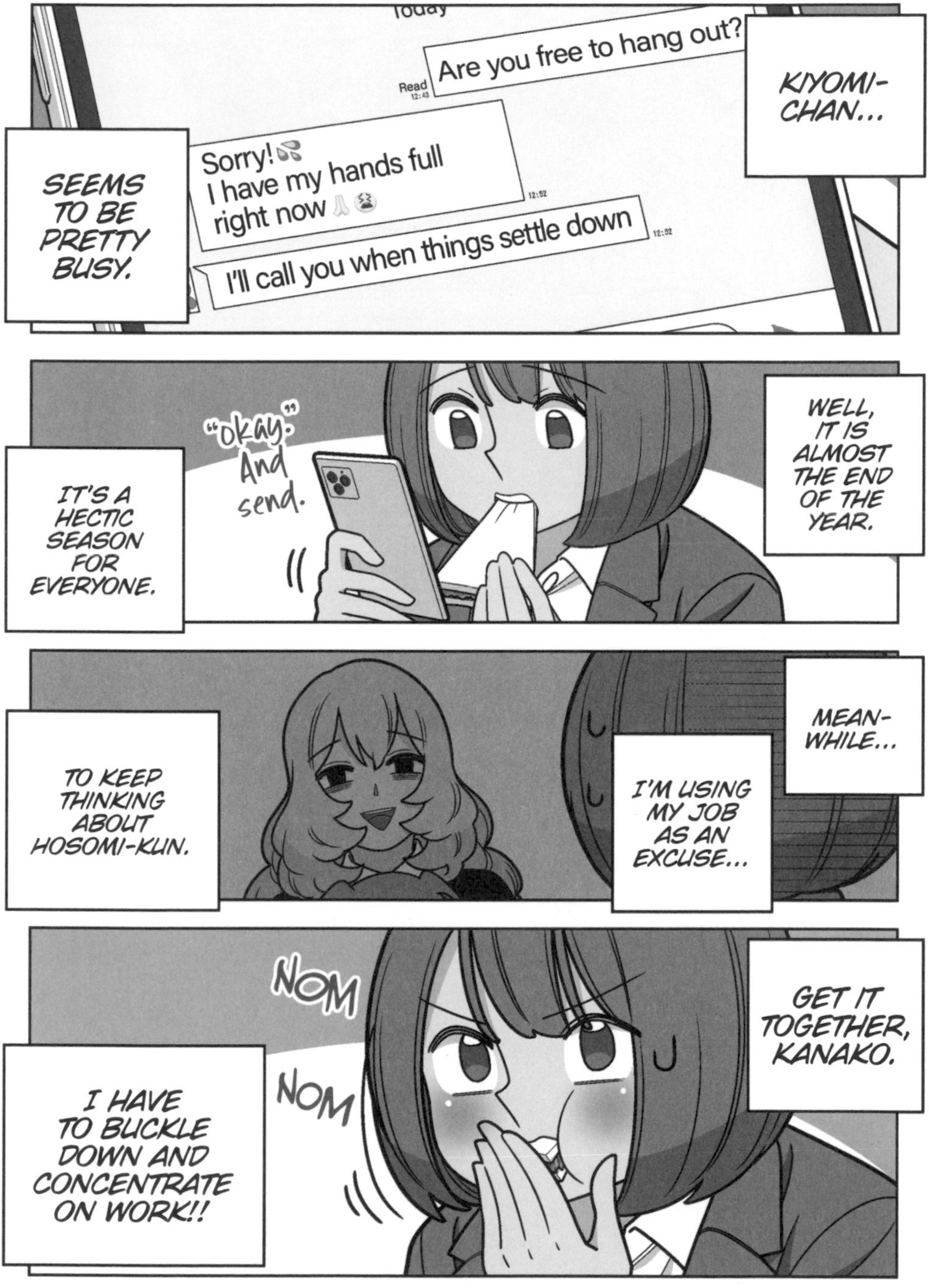
KIYOMI-CHAN...
Today
Are you free to hang out?
Read 12:43
Sorry! I have my hands full right now
12:52
I'll call you when things settle down
12:52
SEEMS TO BE PRETTY BUSY.
WELL, IT IS ALMOST THE END OF THE YEAR.
"okay." And send.
IT'S A HECTIC SEASON FOR EVERYONE.
MEAN-WHILE...
I'M USING MY JOB AS AN EXCUSE...
TO KEEP THINKING ABOUT HOSOMI-KUN.
GET IT TOGETHER, KANAKO.
NOM
NOM
I HAVE TO BUCKLE DOWN AND CONCENTRATE ON WORK!!

Total Concentration. ☆

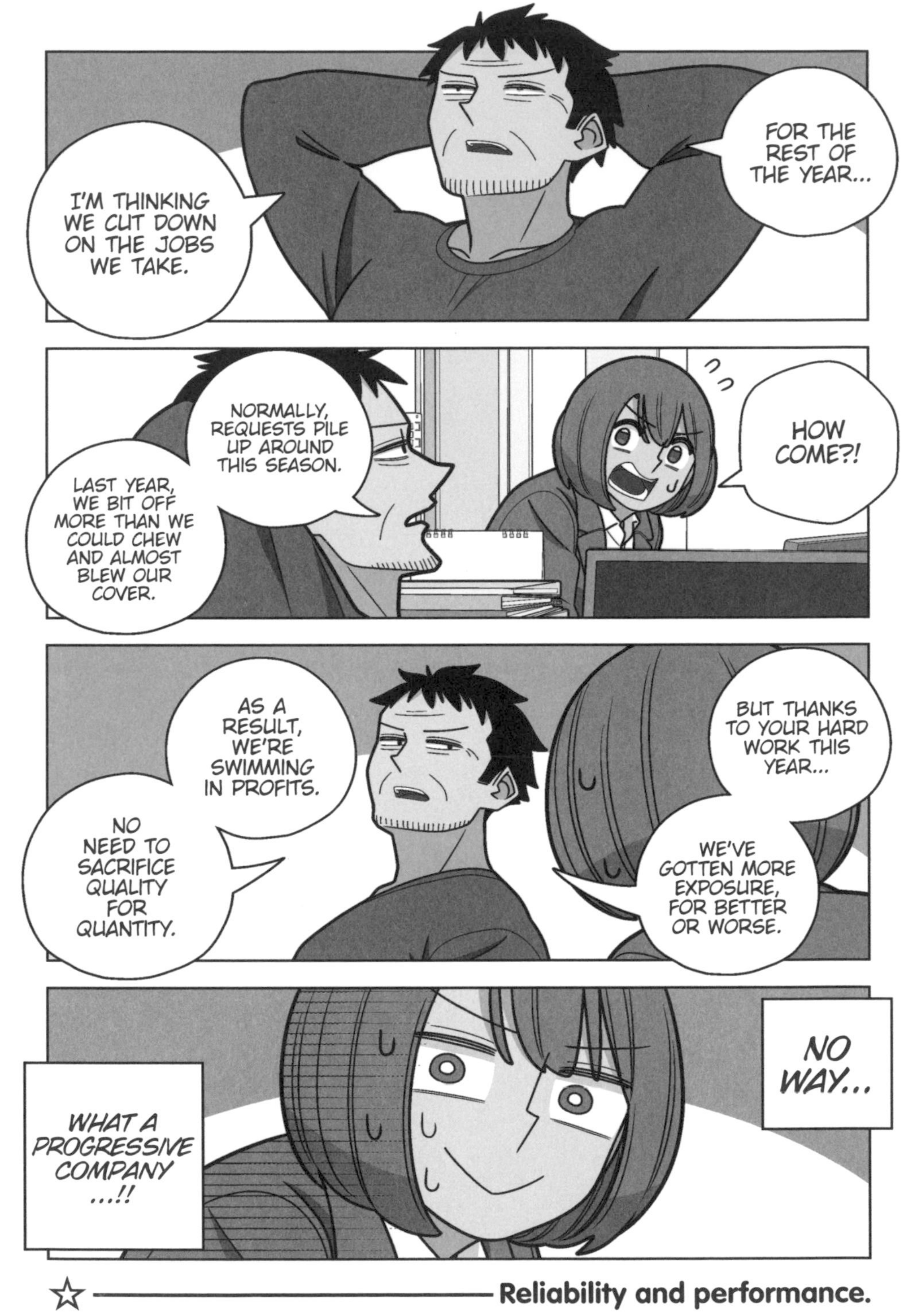
FOR THE REST OF THE YEAR...
I'M THINKING WE CUT DOWN ON THE JOBS WE TAKE.
HOW COME?!
NORMALLY, REQUESTS PILE UP AROUND THIS SEASON.
LAST YEAR, WE BIT OFF MORE THAN WE COULD CHEW AND ALMOST BLEW OUR COVER.
BUT THANKS TO YOUR HARD WORK THIS YEAR...
WE'VE GOTTEN MORE EXPOSURE, FOR BETTER OR WORSE.
AS A RESULT, WE'RE SWIMMING IN PROFITS.
NO NEED TO SACRIFICE QUALITY FOR QUANTITY.
NO WAY...
WHAT A PROGRESSIVE COMPANY ...!!

☆ **Reliability and performance.**

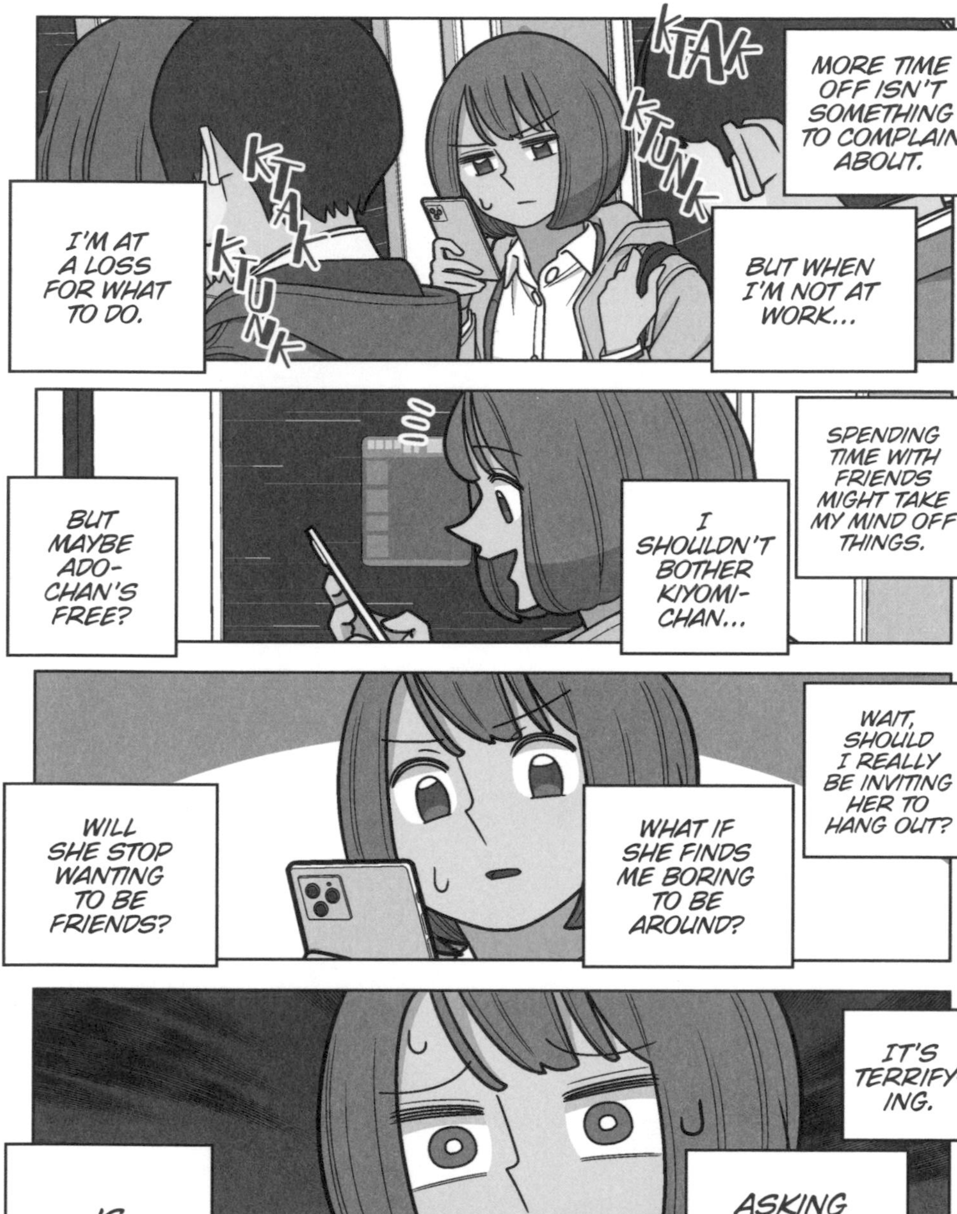
KTAK
MORE TIME OFF ISN'T SOMETHING TO COMPLAIN ABOUT.
KTUNK
BUT WHEN I'M NOT AT WORK...
KTAK
KTUNK
I'M AT A LOSS FOR WHAT TO DO.
SPENDING TIME WITH FRIENDS MIGHT TAKE MY MIND OFF THINGS.
I SHOULDN'T BOTHER KIYOMI-CHAN...
BUT MAYBE ADO-CHAN'S FREE?
WAIT, SHOULD I REALLY BE INVITING HER TO HANG OUT?
WHAT IF SHE FINDS ME BORING TO BE AROUND?
WILL SHE STOP WANTING TO BE FRIENDS?
IT'S TERRIFY-ING.
ASKING OTHERS TO HANG OUT...
IS TERRIFY-ING!!

Always waiting for an invitation. ☆

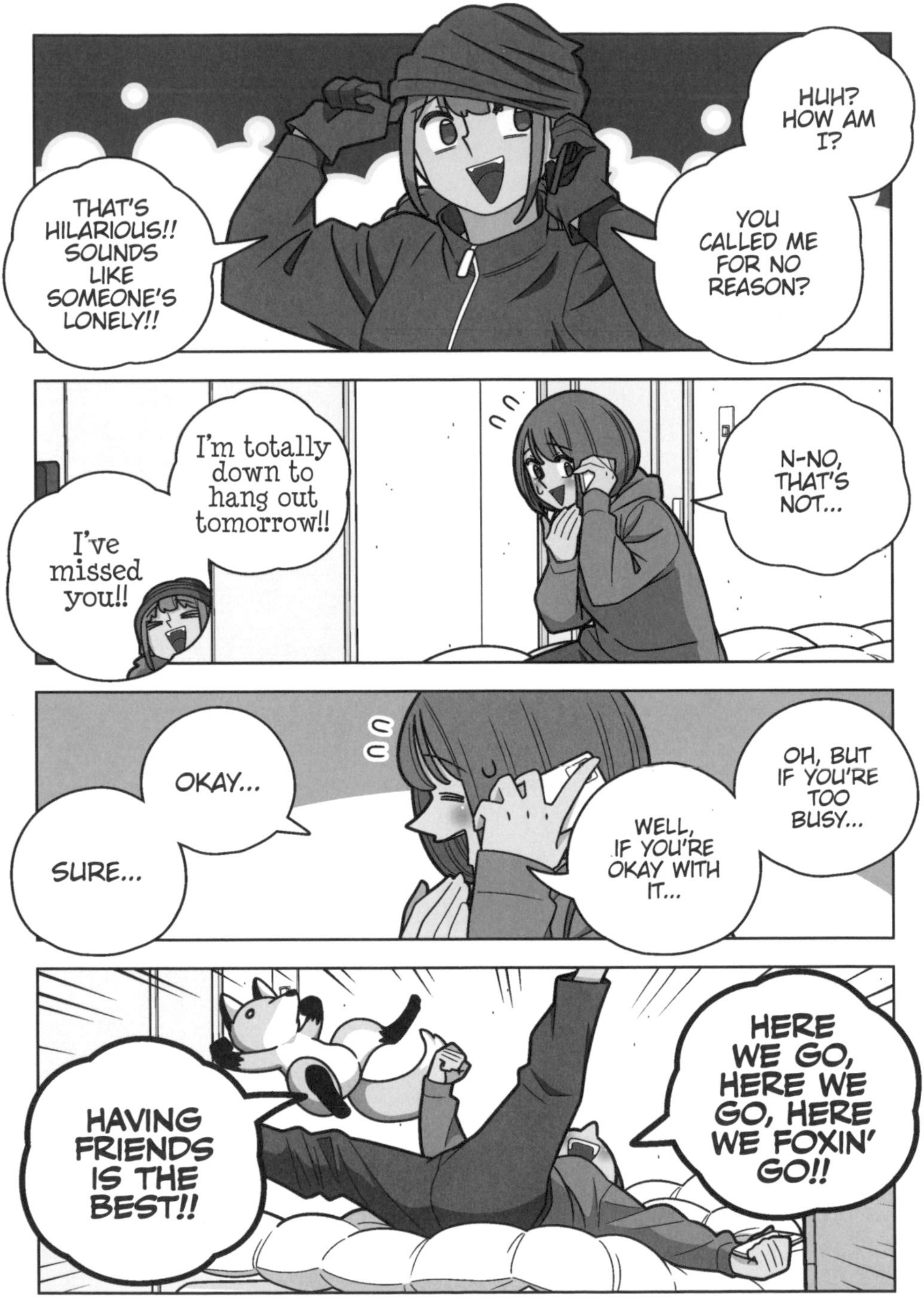
HUH? HOW AM I?
YOU CALLED ME FOR NO REASON?
THAT'S HILARIOUS!! SOUNDS LIKE SOMEONE'S LONELY!!
N-NO, THAT'S NOT...
I'm totally down to hang out tomorrow!!
I've missed you!!
OH, BUT IF YOU'RE TOO BUSY...
WELL, IF YOU'RE OKAY WITH IT...
OKAY...
SURE...
HERE WE GO, HERE WE GO, HERE WE FOXIN' GO!!
HAVING FRIENDS IS THE BEST!!

☆ —— **Pretty much all my friends are bad people.**

074

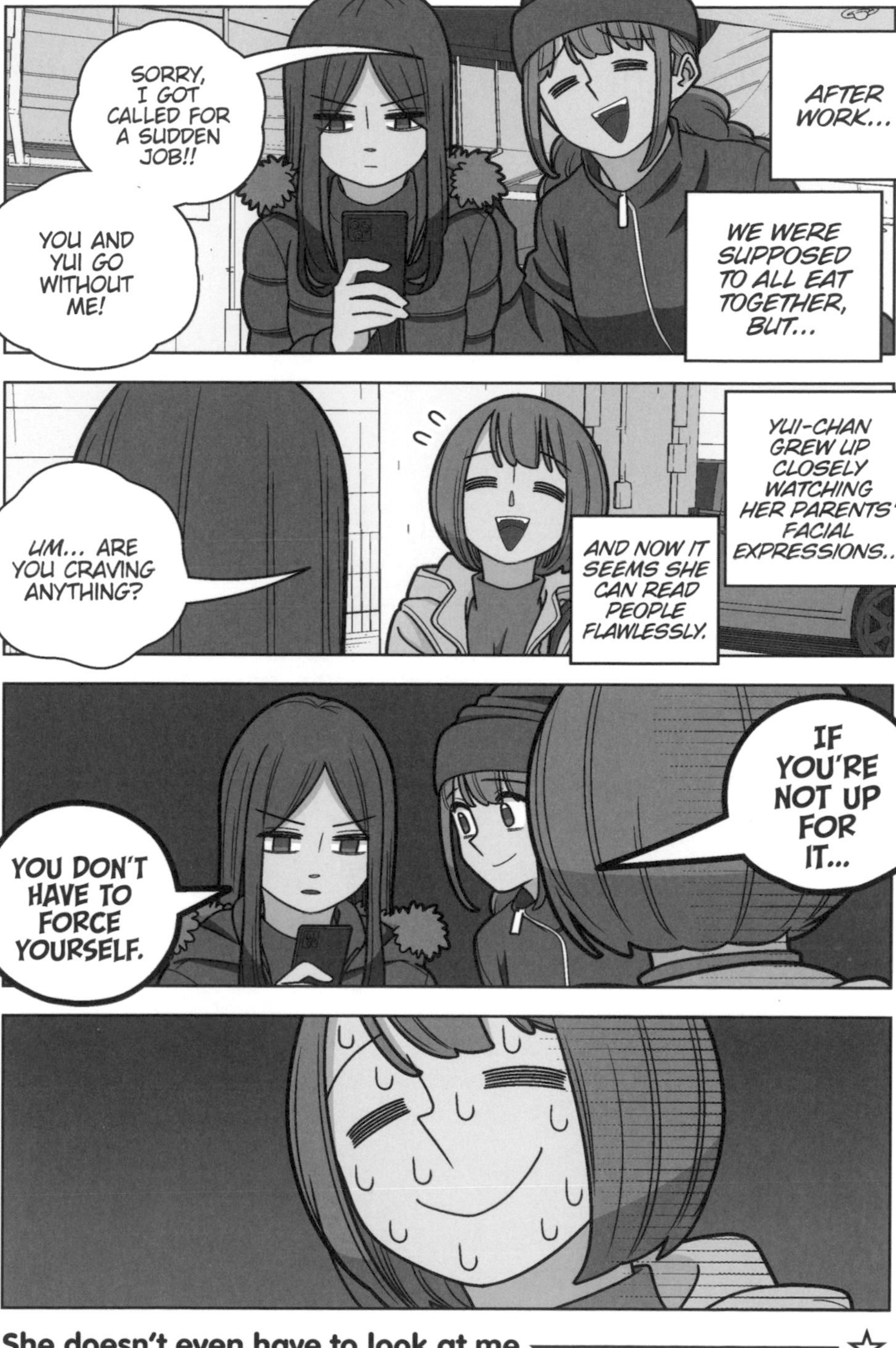
AFTER WORK...
WE WERE SUPPOSED TO ALL EAT TOGETHER, BUT...
SORRY, I GOT CALLED FOR A SUDDEN JOB!!
YOU AND YUI GO WITHOUT ME!
YUI-CHAN GREW UP CLOSELY WATCHING HER PARENTS' FACIAL EXPRESSIONS...
AND NOW IT SEEMS SHE CAN READ PEOPLE FLAWLESSLY.
UM... ARE YOU CRAVING ANYTHING?
IF YOU'RE NOT UP FOR IT...
YOU DON'T HAVE TO FORCE YOURSELF.

She doesn't even have to look at me. ☆

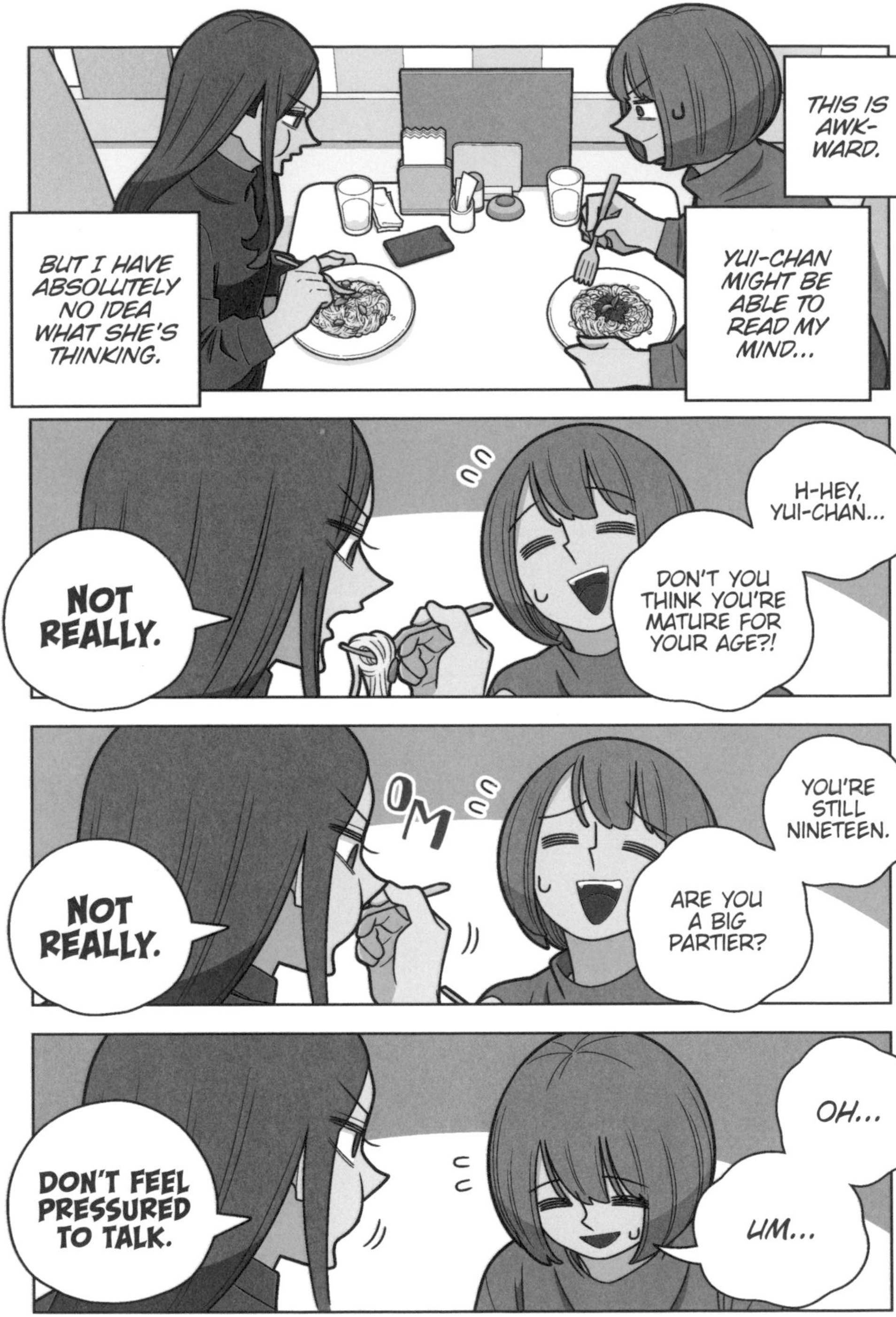
THIS IS AWK-WARD.
YUI-CHAN MIGHT BE ABLE TO READ MY MIND...
BUT I HAVE ABSOLUTELY NO IDEA WHAT SHE'S THINKING.
H-HEY, YUI-CHAN...
DON'T YOU THINK YOU'RE MATURE FOR YOUR AGE?!
NOT REALLY.
YOU'RE STILL NINETEEN.
ARE YOU A BIG PARTIER?
OM
NOT REALLY.
OH...
UM...
DON'T FEEL PRESSURED TO TALK.

☆ Silence makes me anxious.

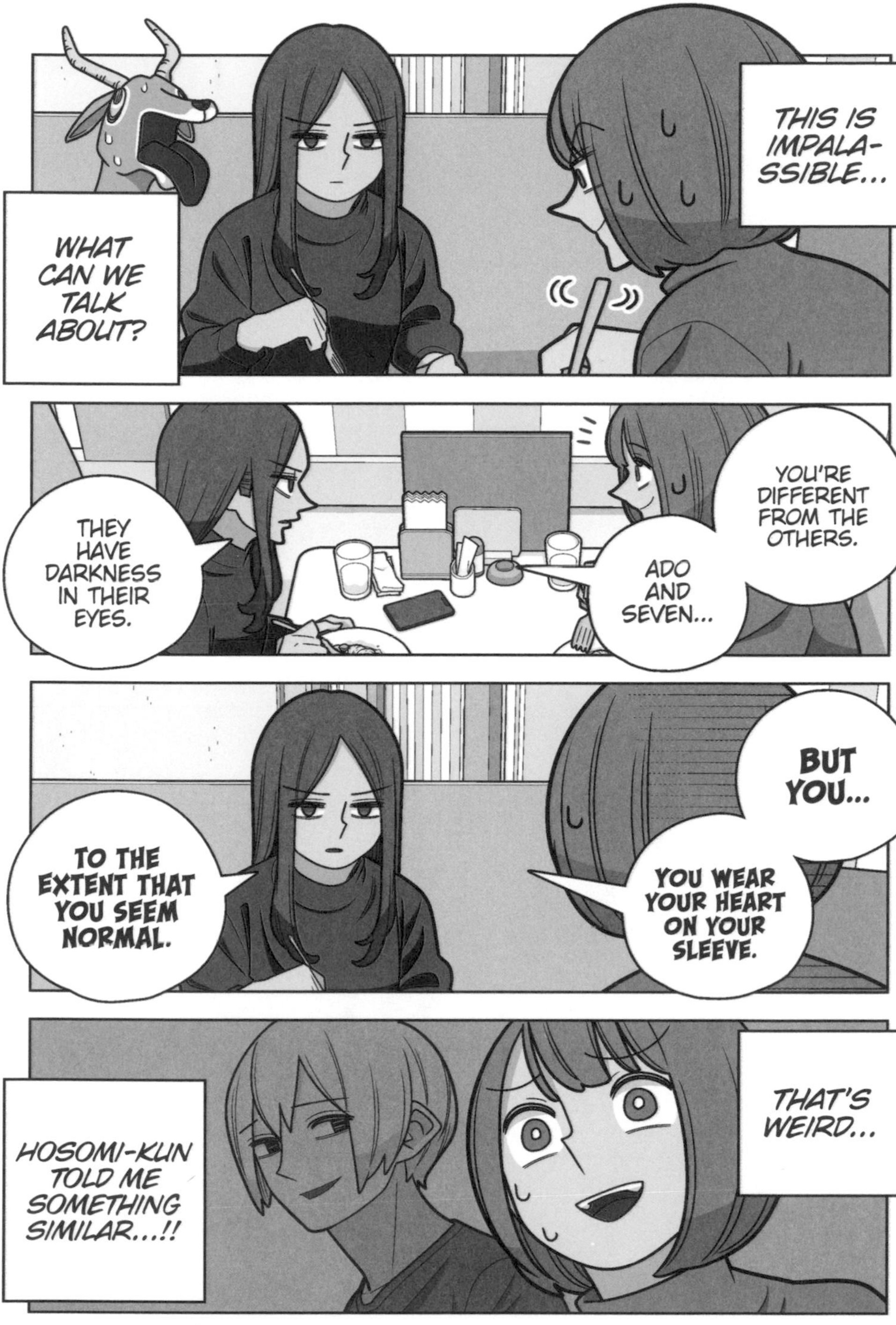
THIS IS IMPALA-SSIBLE...
WHAT CAN WE TALK ABOUT?
YOU'RE DIFFERENT FROM THE OTHERS.
ADO AND SEVEN...
THEY HAVE DARKNESS IN THEIR EYES.
BUT YOU...
YOU WEAR YOUR HEART ON YOUR SLEEVE.
TO THE EXTENT THAT YOU SEEM NORMAL.
THAT'S WEIRD...
HOSOMI-KUN TOLD ME SOMETHING SIMILAR...!!

He's always on my mind.——— ☆

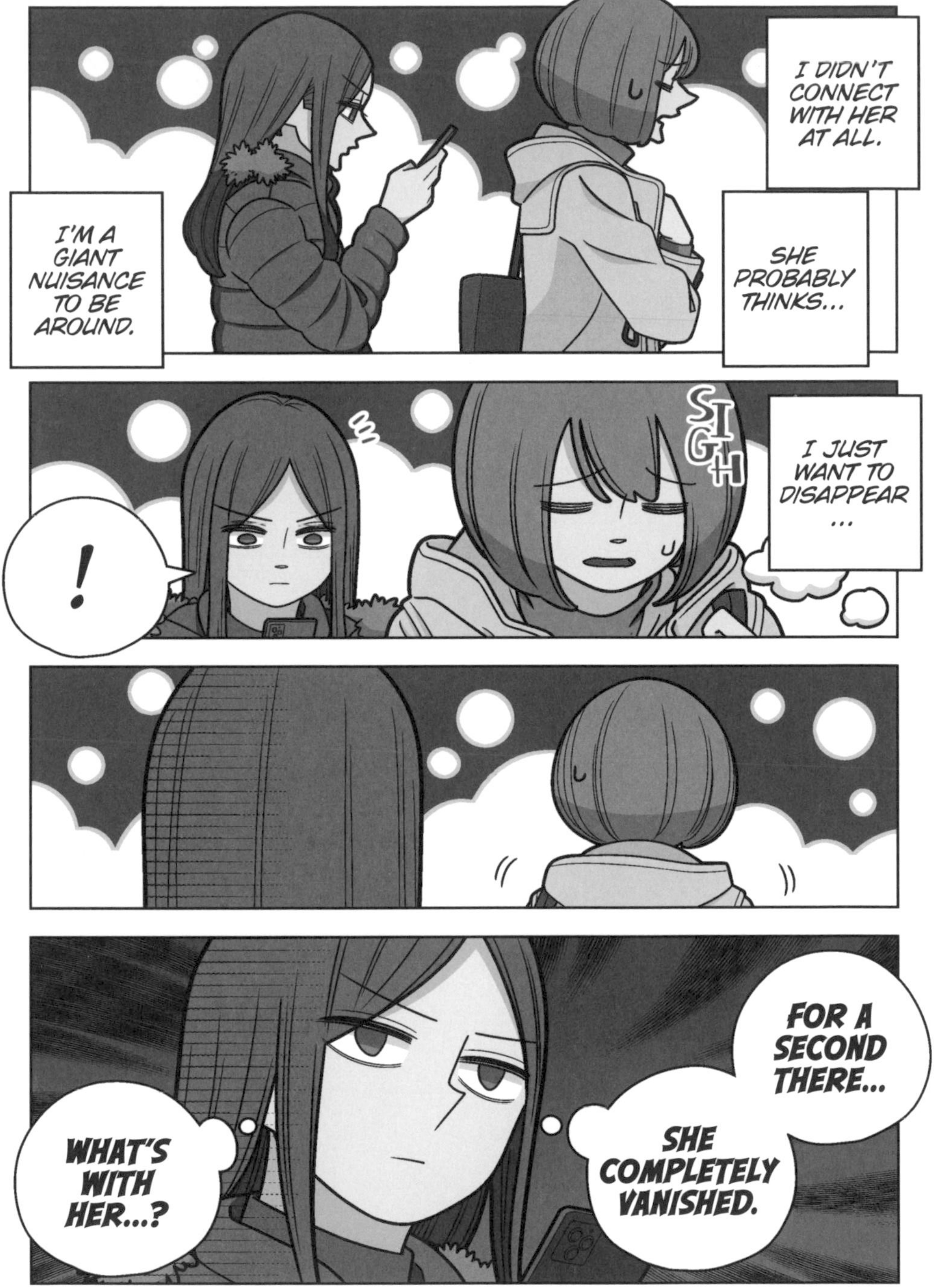
I DIDN'T CONNECT WITH HER AT ALL.
SHE PROBABLY THINKS...
I'M A GIANT NUISANCE TO BE AROUND.
I JUST WANT TO DISAPPEAR ...
SIGH
!
FOR A SECOND THERE...
SHE COMPLETELY VANISHED.
WHAT'S WITH HER...?

☆ —— It's dangerous to walk and talk.

075

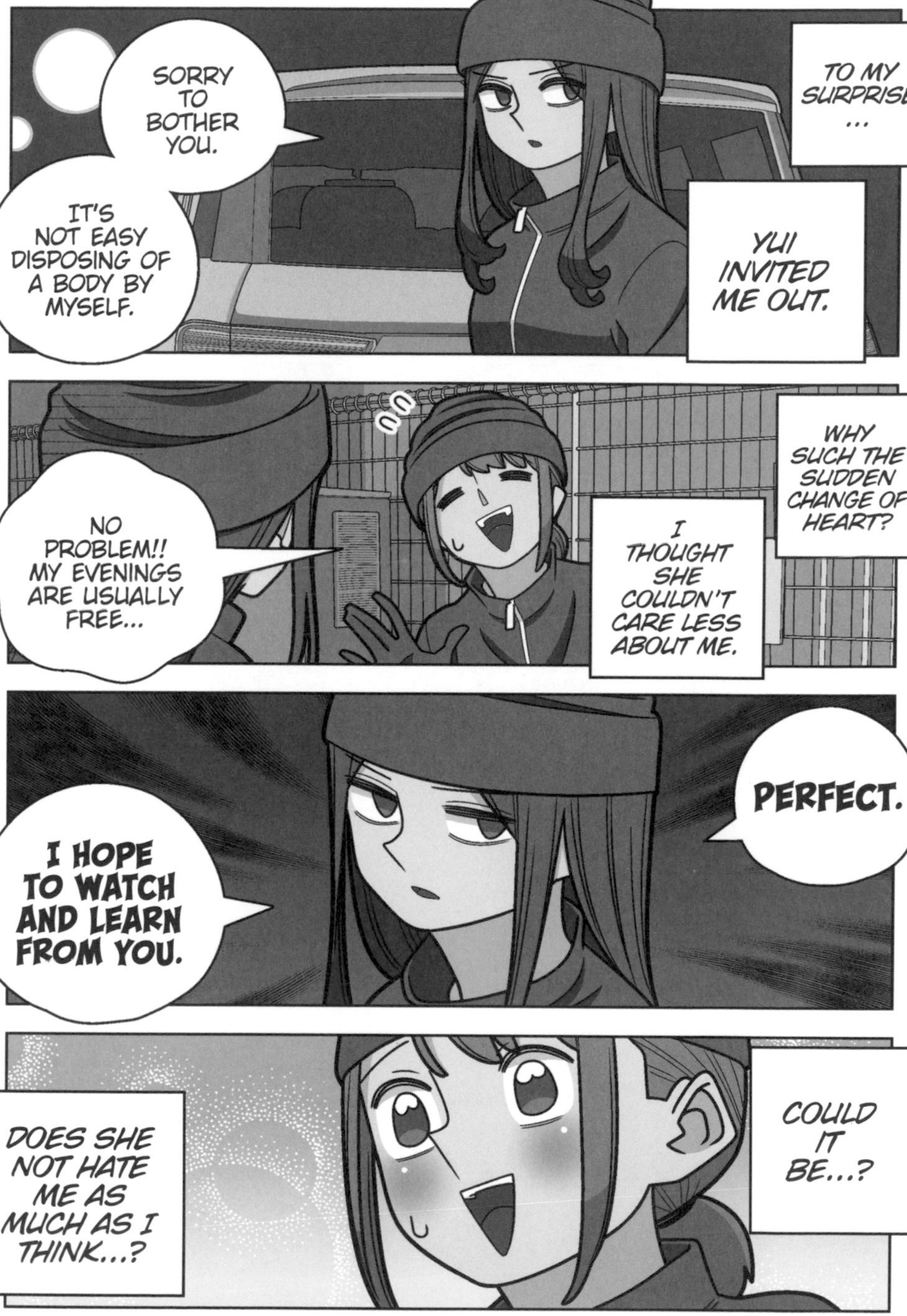
TO MY SURPRISE...
YUI INVITED ME OUT.
SORRY TO BOTHER YOU.
IT'S NOT EASY DISPOSING OF A BODY BY MYSELF.
WHY SUCH THE SUDDEN CHANGE OF HEART?
I THOUGHT SHE COULDN'T CARE LESS ABOUT ME.
NO PROBLEM!! MY EVENINGS ARE USUALLY FREE...
PERFECT.
I HOPE TO WATCH AND LEARN FROM YOU.
COULD IT BE...?
DOES SHE NOT HATE ME AS MUCH AS I THINK...?

Maybe she's just cold to everyone. ☆

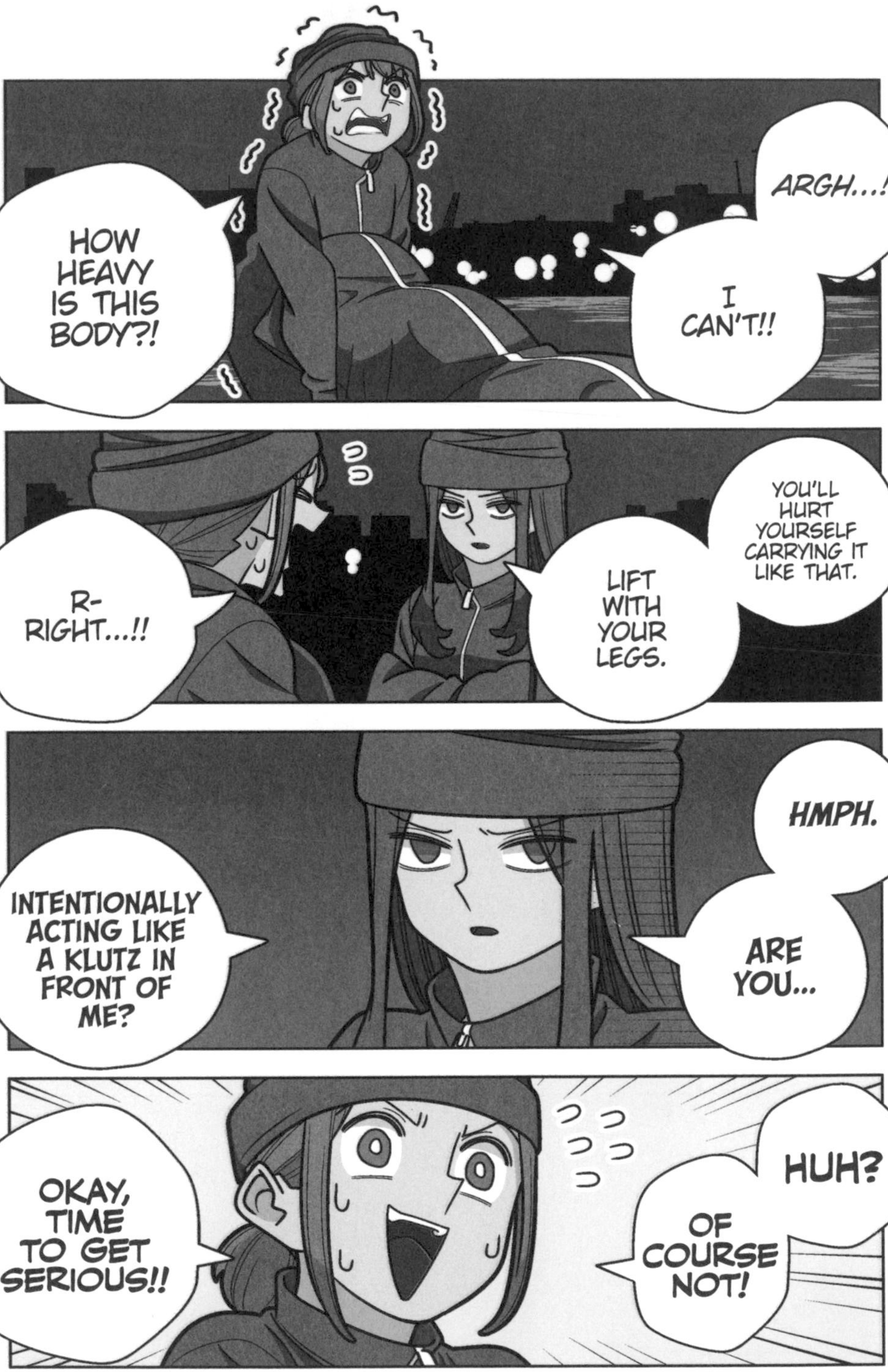
ARGH...!
I CAN'T!!
HOW HEAVY IS THIS BODY?!
YOU'LL HURT YOURSELF CARRYING IT LIKE THAT.
LIFT WITH YOUR LEGS.
R-RIGHT...!!
HMPH.
ARE YOU...
INTENTIONALLY ACTING LIKE A KLUTZ IN FRONT OF ME?
HUH?
OF COURSE NOT!
OKAY, TIME TO GET SERIOUS!!

☆ Soz.

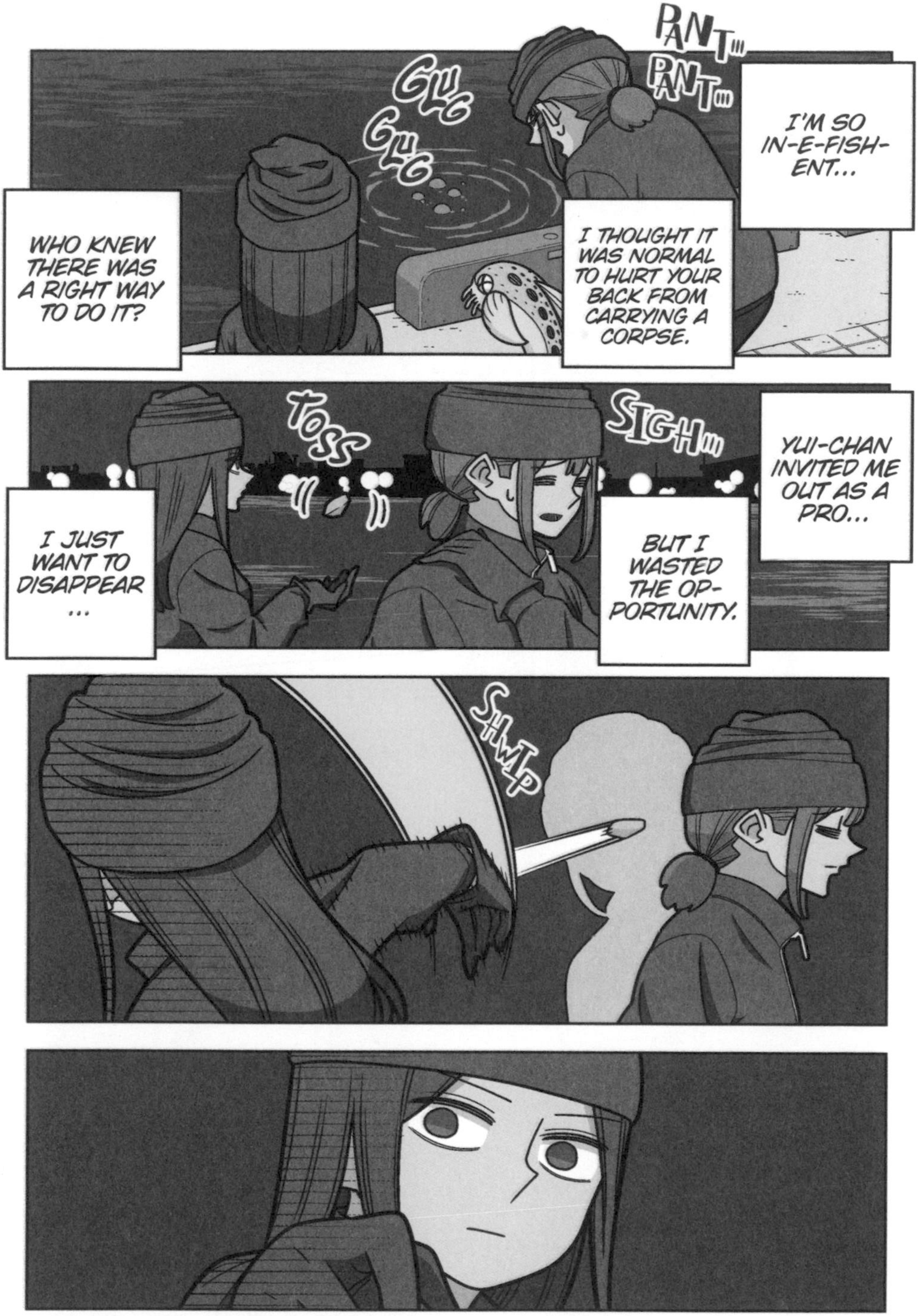
I'M SO IN-E-FISH-ENT...
PANT PANT
I THOUGHT IT WAS NORMAL TO HURT YOUR BACK FROM CARRYING A CORPSE.
GLUG GLUG
WHO KNEW THERE WAS A RIGHT WAY TO DO IT?
YUI-CHAN INVITED ME OUT AS A PRO...
BUT I WASTED THE OP-PORTUNITY.
SIGH
TOSS
I JUST WANT TO DISAPPEAR...
SHWIP

How could I misread her movements? ——— ☆

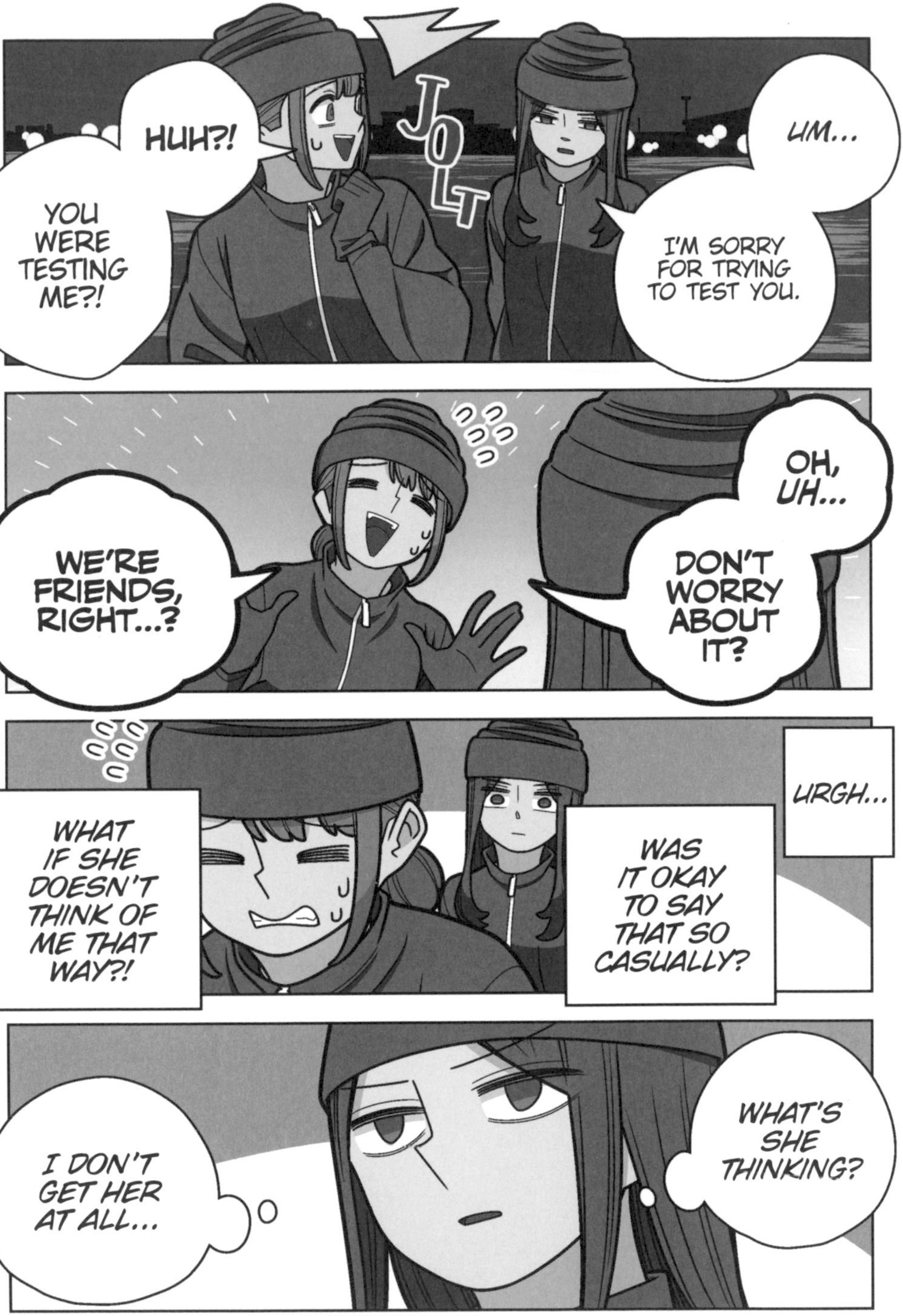
UM...
I'M SORRY FOR TRYING TO TEST YOU.
JOLT
HUH?!
YOU WERE TESTING ME?!
OH, UH...
DON'T WORRY ABOUT IT?
WE'RE FRIENDS, RIGHT...?
URGH...
WAS IT OKAY TO SAY THAT SO CASUALLY?
WHAT IF SHE DOESN'T THINK OF ME THAT WAY?!
WHAT'S SHE THINKING?
I DON'T GET HER AT ALL...

☆ —— **Either an idiot or a genius.**

076

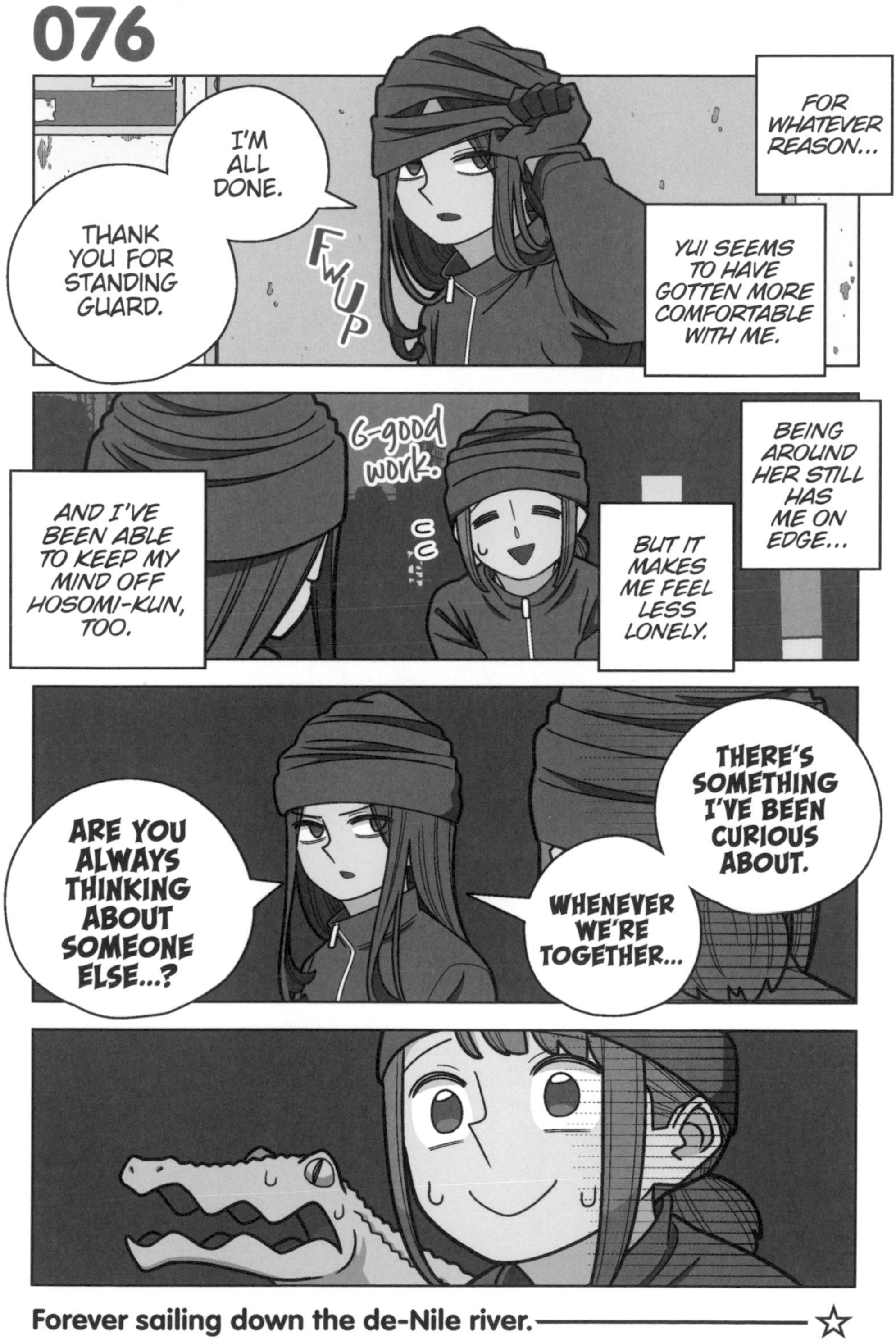
FOR WHATEVER REASON...
YUI SEEMS TO HAVE GOTTEN MORE COMFORTABLE WITH ME.
FWUP
I'M ALL DONE.
THANK YOU FOR STANDING GUARD.
BEING AROUND HER STILL HAS ME ON EDGE...
BUT IT MAKES ME FEEL LESS LONELY.
G-good work.
AND I'VE BEEN ABLE TO KEEP MY MIND OFF HOSOMI-KUN, TOO.
THERE'S SOMETHING I'VE BEEN CURIOUS ABOUT.
WHENEVER WE'RE TOGETHER...
ARE YOU ALWAYS THINKING ABOUT SOMEONE ELSE...?

Forever sailing down the de-Nile river. ☆

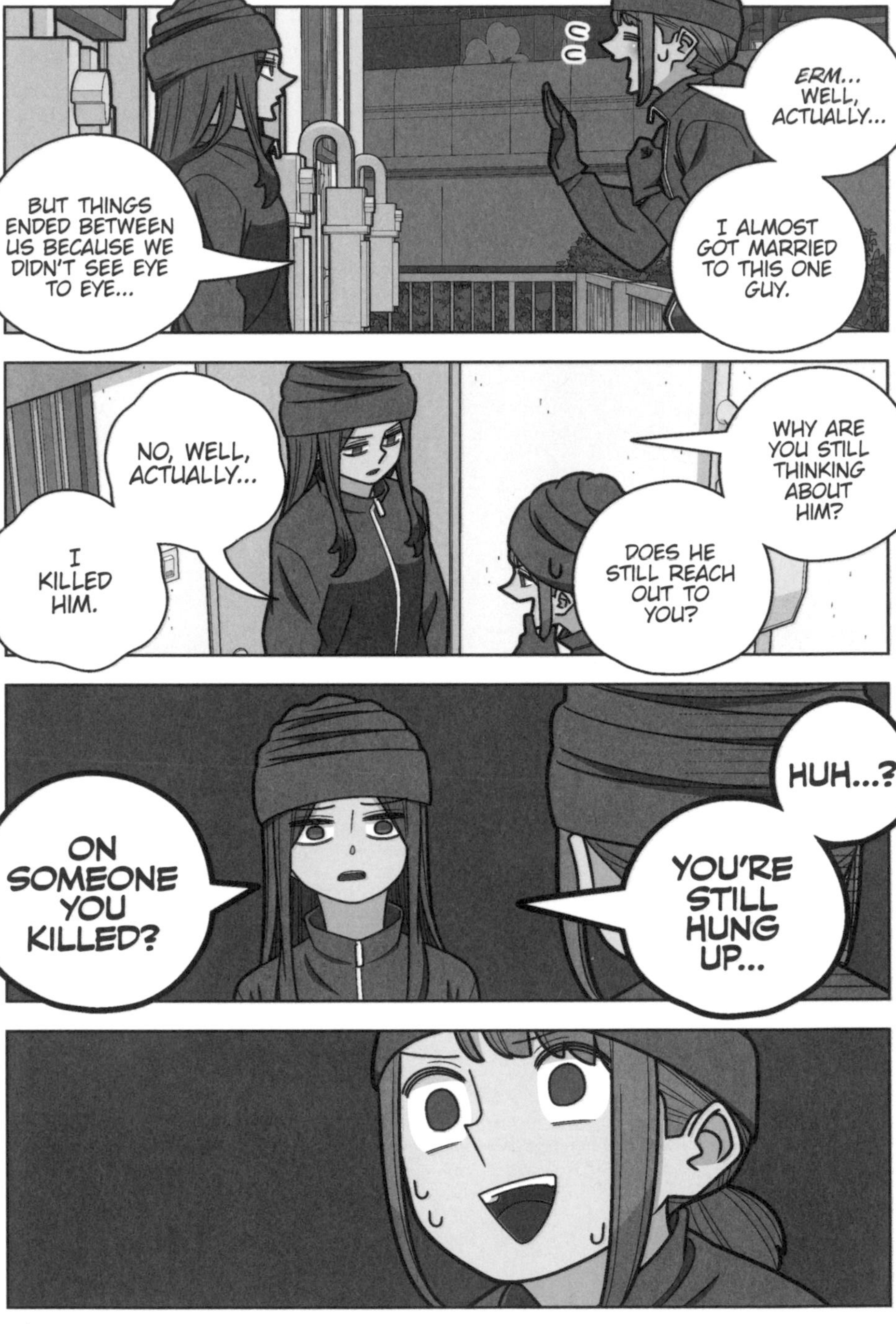
ERM... WELL, ACTUALLY...
I ALMOST GOT MARRIED TO THIS ONE GUY.
BUT THINGS ENDED BETWEEN US BECAUSE WE DIDN'T SEE EYE TO EYE...
WHY ARE YOU STILL THINKING ABOUT HIM?
DOES HE STILL REACH OUT TO YOU?
NO, WELL, ACTUALLY...
I KILLED HIM.
HUH...?
YOU'RE STILL HUNG UP...
ON SOMEONE YOU KILLED?

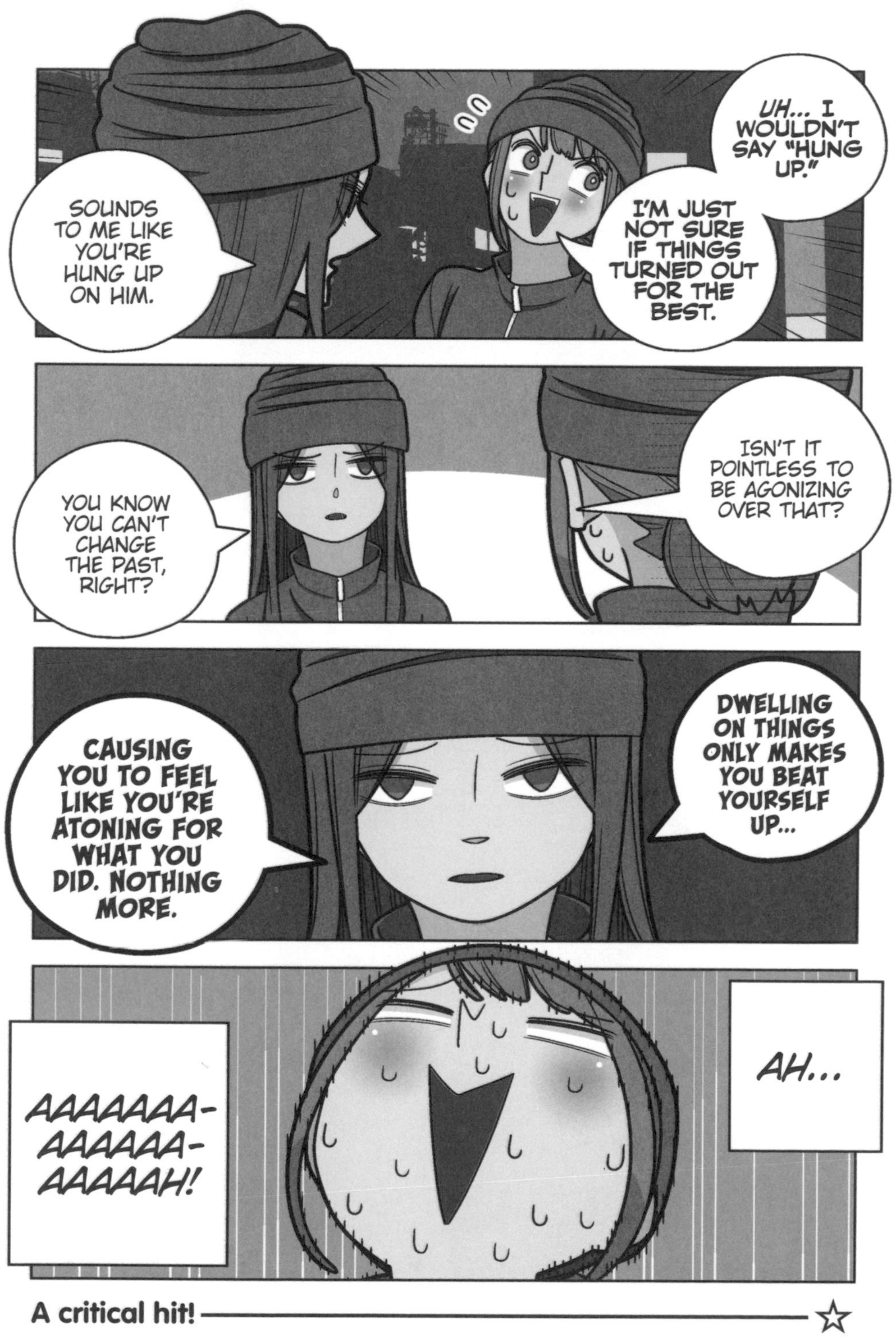
UH... I WOULDN'T SAY "HUNG UP."
I'M JUST NOT SURE IF THINGS TURNED OUT FOR THE BEST.
SOUNDS TO ME LIKE YOU'RE HUNG UP ON HIM.
ISN'T IT POINTLESS TO BE AGONIZING OVER THAT?
YOU KNOW YOU CAN'T CHANGE THE PAST, RIGHT?
DWELLING ON THINGS ONLY MAKES YOU BEAT YOURSELF UP...
CAUSING YOU TO FEEL LIKE YOU'RE ATONING FOR WHAT YOU DID. NOTHING MORE.
AH...
AAAAAAA-AAAAAA-AAAAAH!

A critical hit! ——— ☆

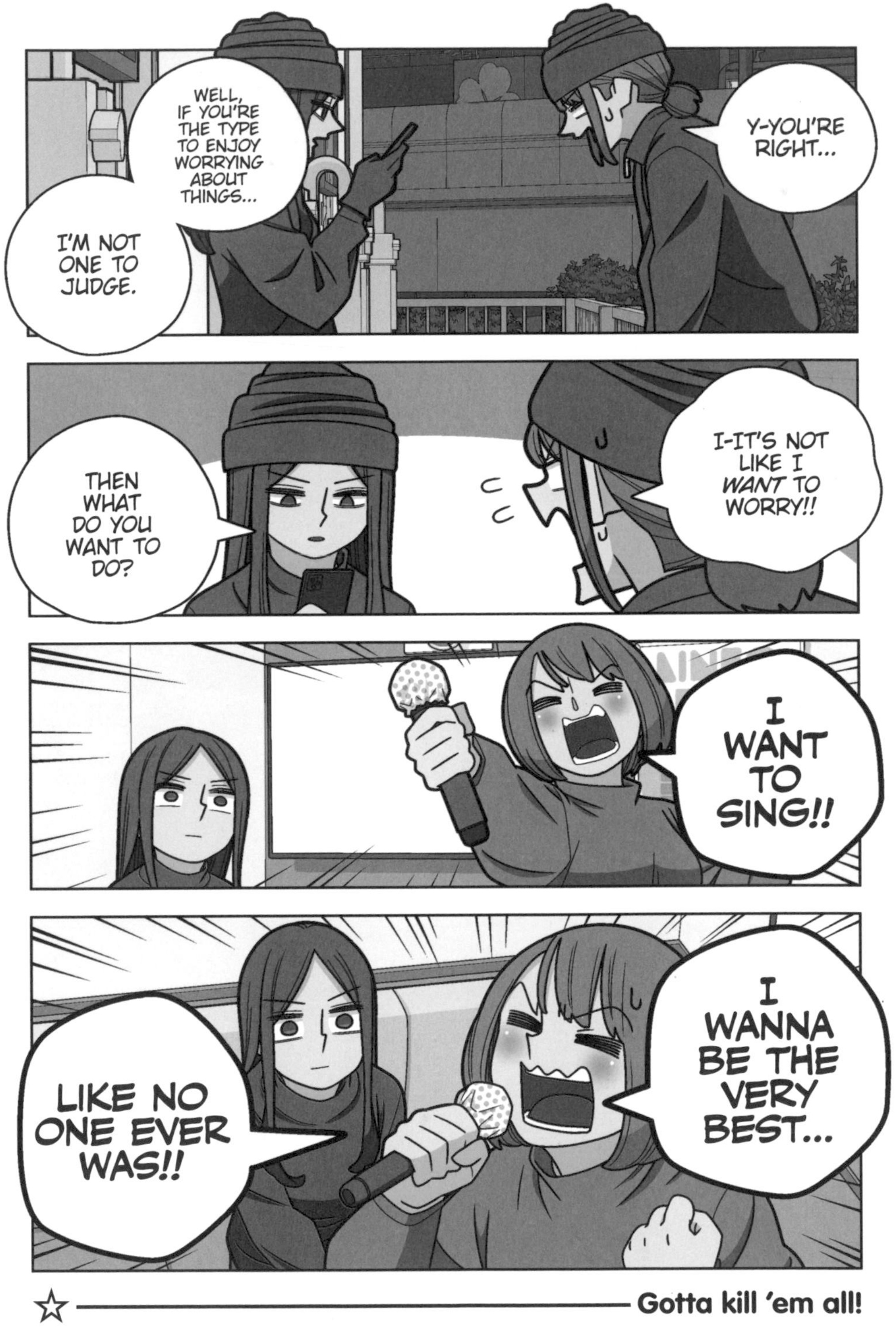
Y-YOU'RE RIGHT...
WELL, IF YOU'RE THE TYPE TO ENJOY WORRYING ABOUT THINGS...
I'M NOT ONE TO JUDGE.
I-IT'S NOT LIKE I *WANT* TO WORRY!!
THEN WHAT DO YOU WANT TO DO?
I WANT TO SING!!
I WANNA BE THE VERY BEST...
LIKE NO ONE EVER WAS!!

☆ —— **Gotta kill 'em all!**

Bonus

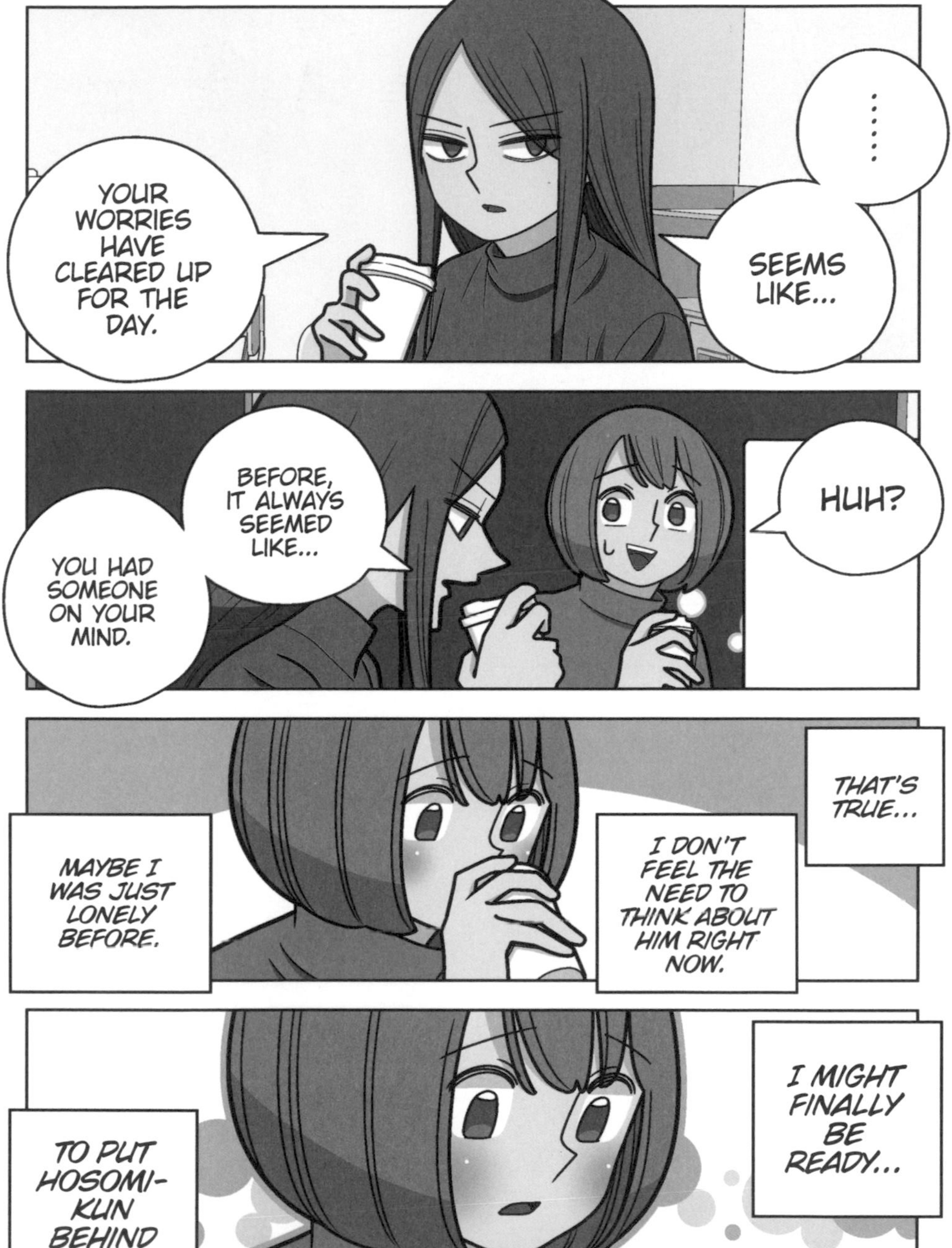
......
SEEMS LIKE...
YOUR WORRIES HAVE CLEARED UP FOR THE DAY.
HUH?
BEFORE, IT ALWAYS SEEMED LIKE...
YOU HAD SOMEONE ON YOUR MIND.
THAT'S TRUE...
I DON'T FEEL THE NEED TO THINK ABOUT HIM RIGHT NOW.
MAYBE I WAS JUST LONELY BEFORE.
I MIGHT FINALLY BE READY...
TO PUT HOSOMI-KUN BEHIND ME.

The power of song. ☆

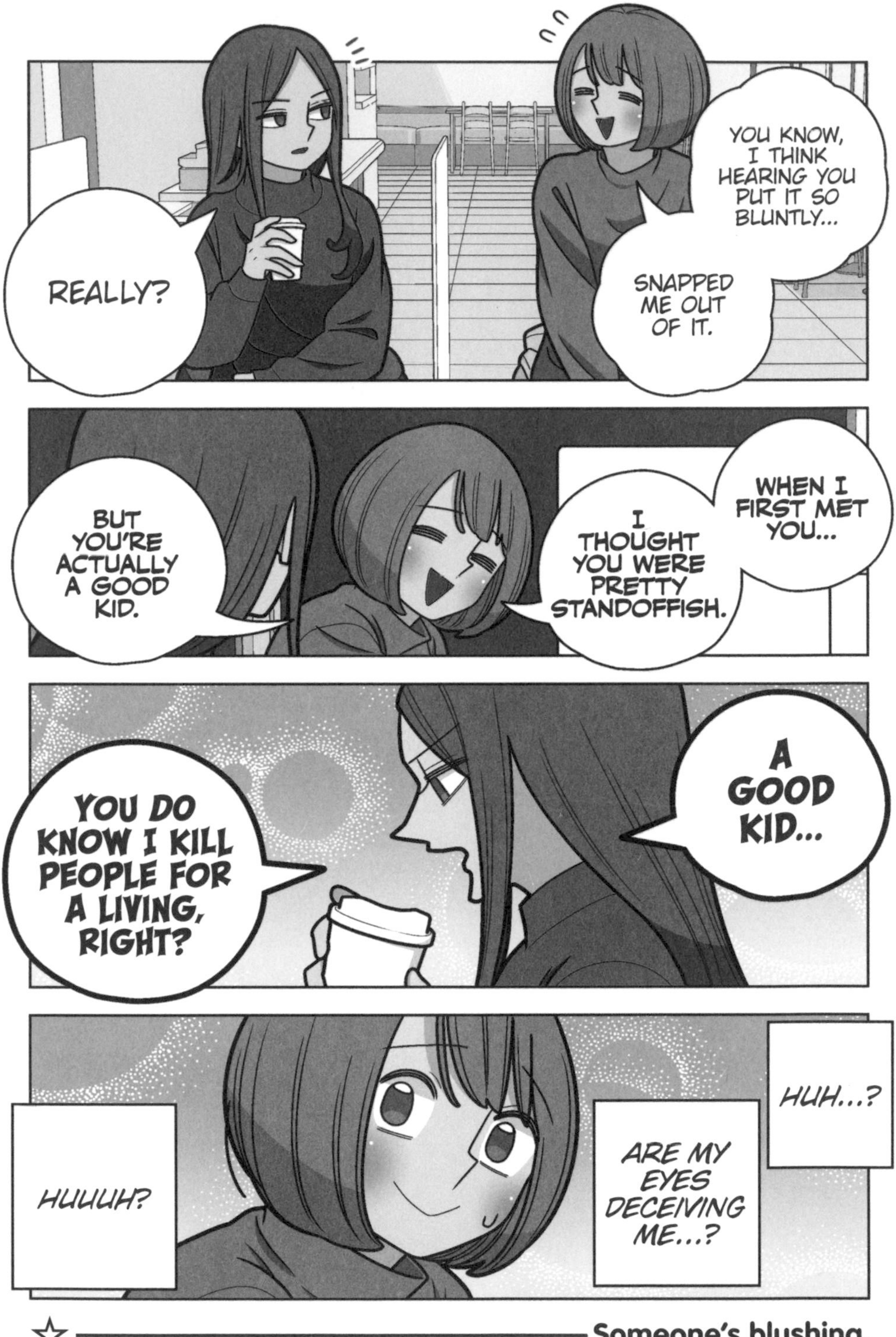
YOU KNOW, I THINK HEARING YOU PUT IT SO BLUNTLY...
SNAPPED ME OUT OF IT.
REALLY?
WHEN I FIRST MET YOU...
I THOUGHT YOU WERE PRETTY STANDOFFISH.
BUT YOU'RE ACTUALLY A GOOD KID.
A GOOD KID...
YOU DO KNOW I KILL PEOPLE FOR A LIVING, RIGHT?
HUH...?
ARE MY EYES DECEIVING ME...?
HUUUH?

☆ —— Someone's blushing.

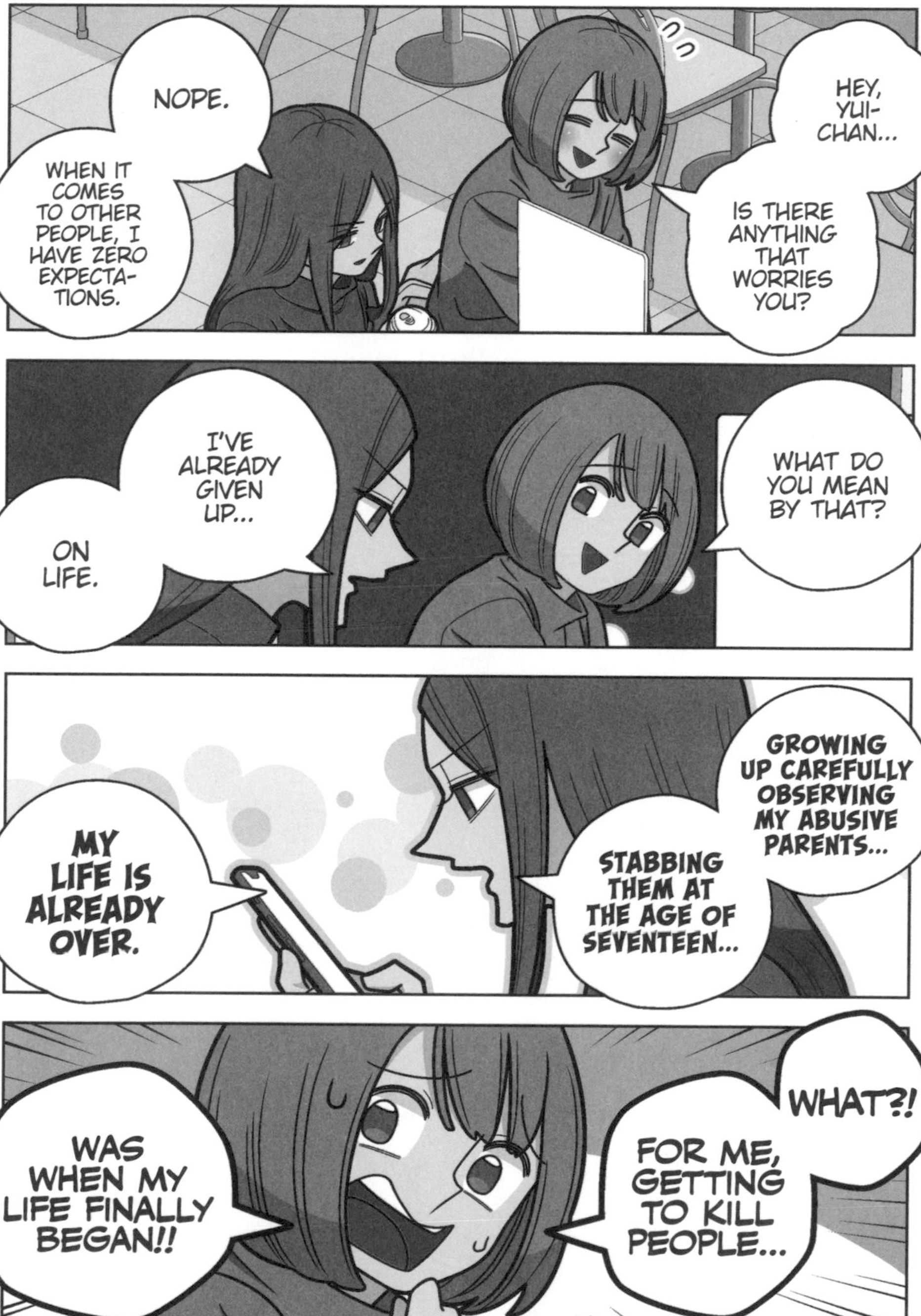
HEY, YUI-CHAN...
IS THERE ANYTHING THAT WORRIES YOU?
NOPE.
WHEN IT COMES TO OTHER PEOPLE, I HAVE ZERO EXPECTATIONS.
WHAT DO YOU MEAN BY THAT?
I'VE ALREADY GIVEN UP...
ON LIFE.
GROWING UP CAREFULLY OBSERVING MY ABUSIVE PARENTS...
STABBING THEM AT THE AGE OF SEVENTEEN...
MY LIFE IS ALREADY OVER.
WHAT?!
FOR ME, GETTING TO KILL PEOPLE...
WAS WHEN MY LIFE FINALLY BEGAN!!

Different perspectives. ☆

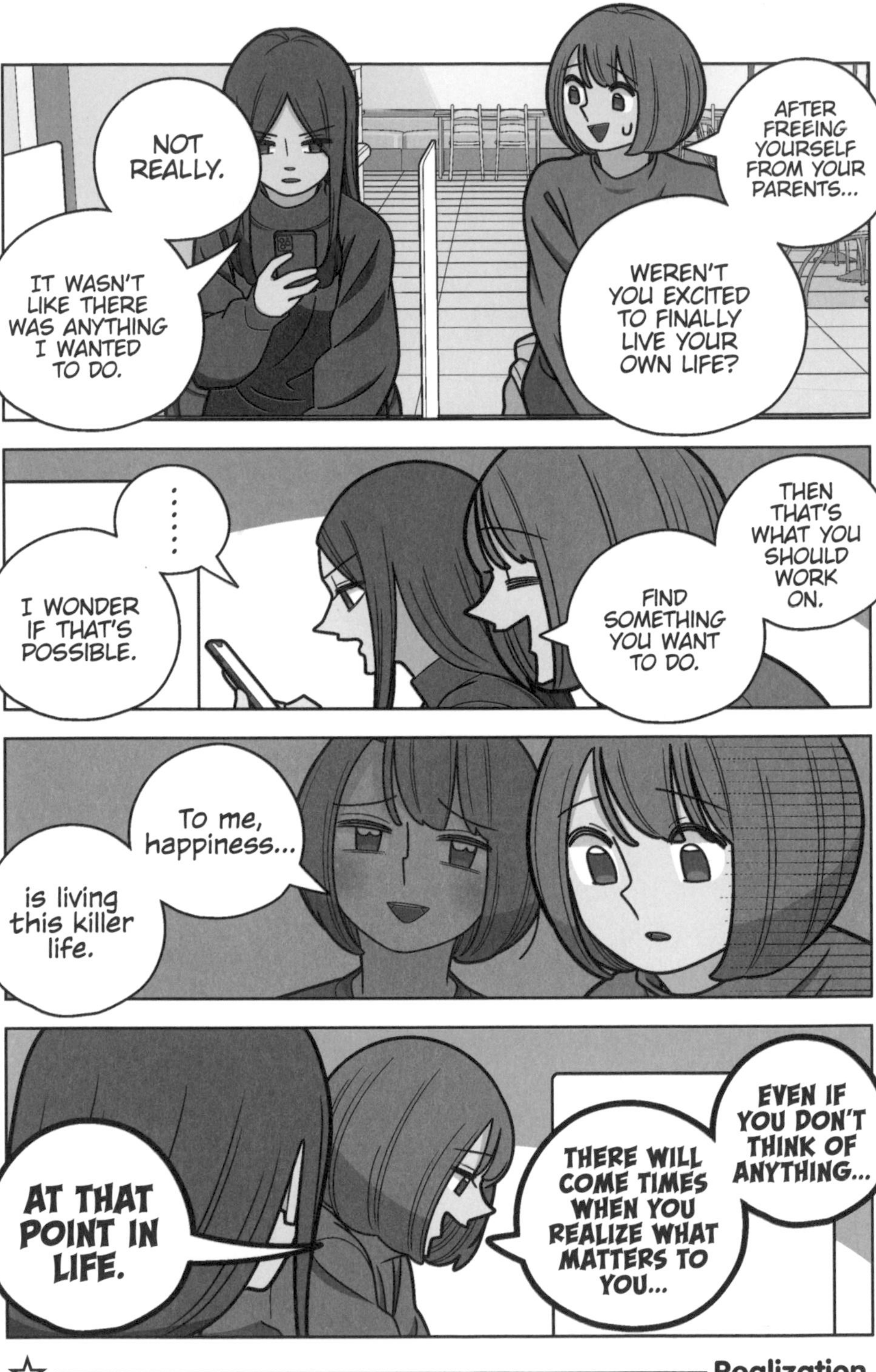
AFTER FREEING YOURSELF FROM YOUR PARENTS...
WEREN'T YOU EXCITED TO FINALLY LIVE YOUR OWN LIFE?
NOT REALLY.
IT WASN'T LIKE THERE WAS ANYTHING I WANTED TO DO.
THEN THAT'S WHAT YOU SHOULD WORK ON.
FIND SOMETHING YOU WANT TO DO.
......
I WONDER IF THAT'S POSSIBLE.
To me, happiness...
is living this killer life.
EVEN IF YOU DON'T THINK OF ANYTHING...
THERE WILL COME TIMES WHEN YOU REALIZE WHAT MATTERS TO YOU...
AT THAT POINT IN LIFE.

☆ —— Realization.

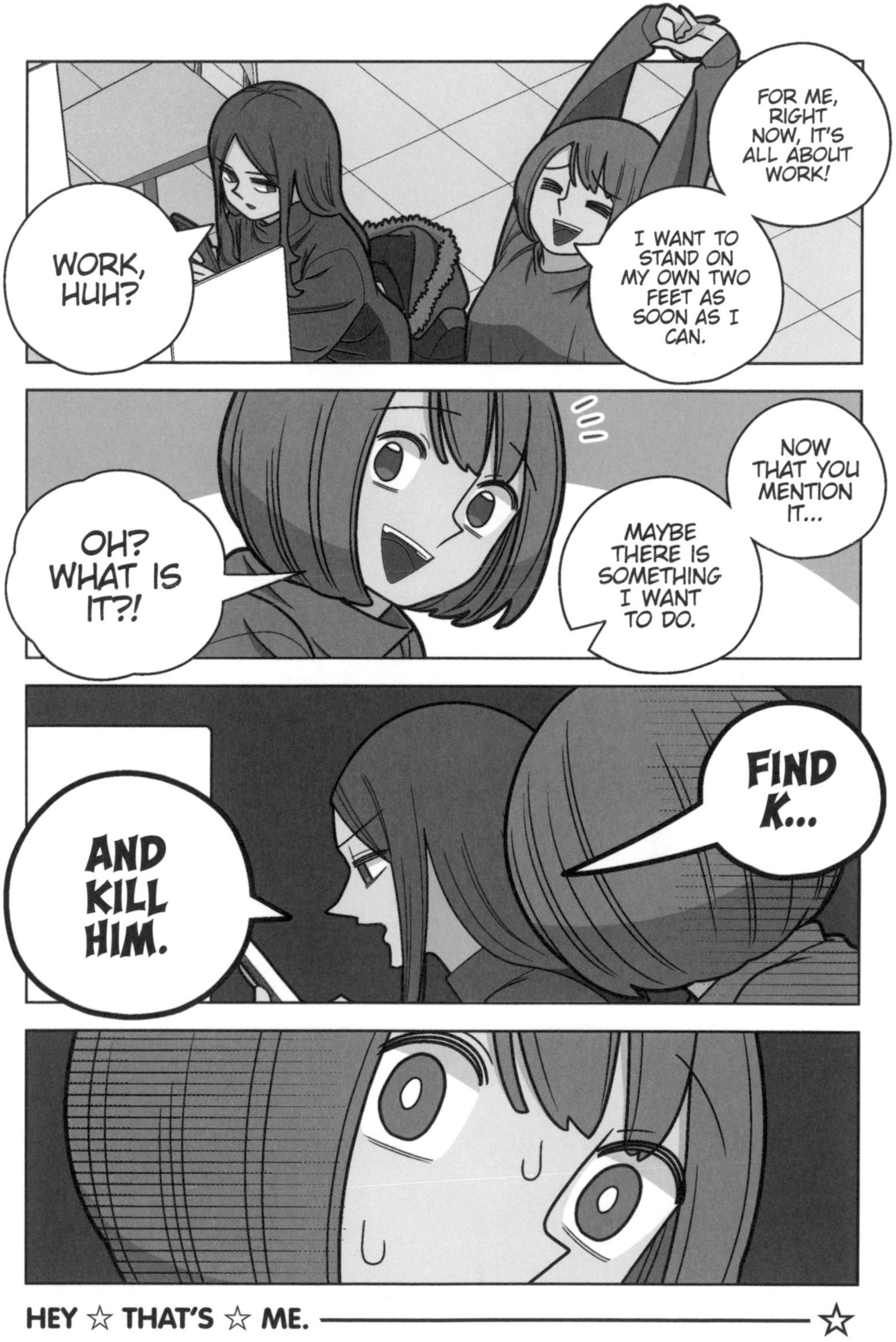
FOR ME, RIGHT NOW, IT'S ALL ABOUT WORK!
I WANT TO STAND ON MY OWN TWO FEET AS SOON AS I CAN.
WORK, HUH?
NOW THAT YOU MENTION IT...
MAYBE THERE IS SOMETHING I WANT TO DO.
OH? WHAT IS IT?!
FIND K...
AND KILL HIM.

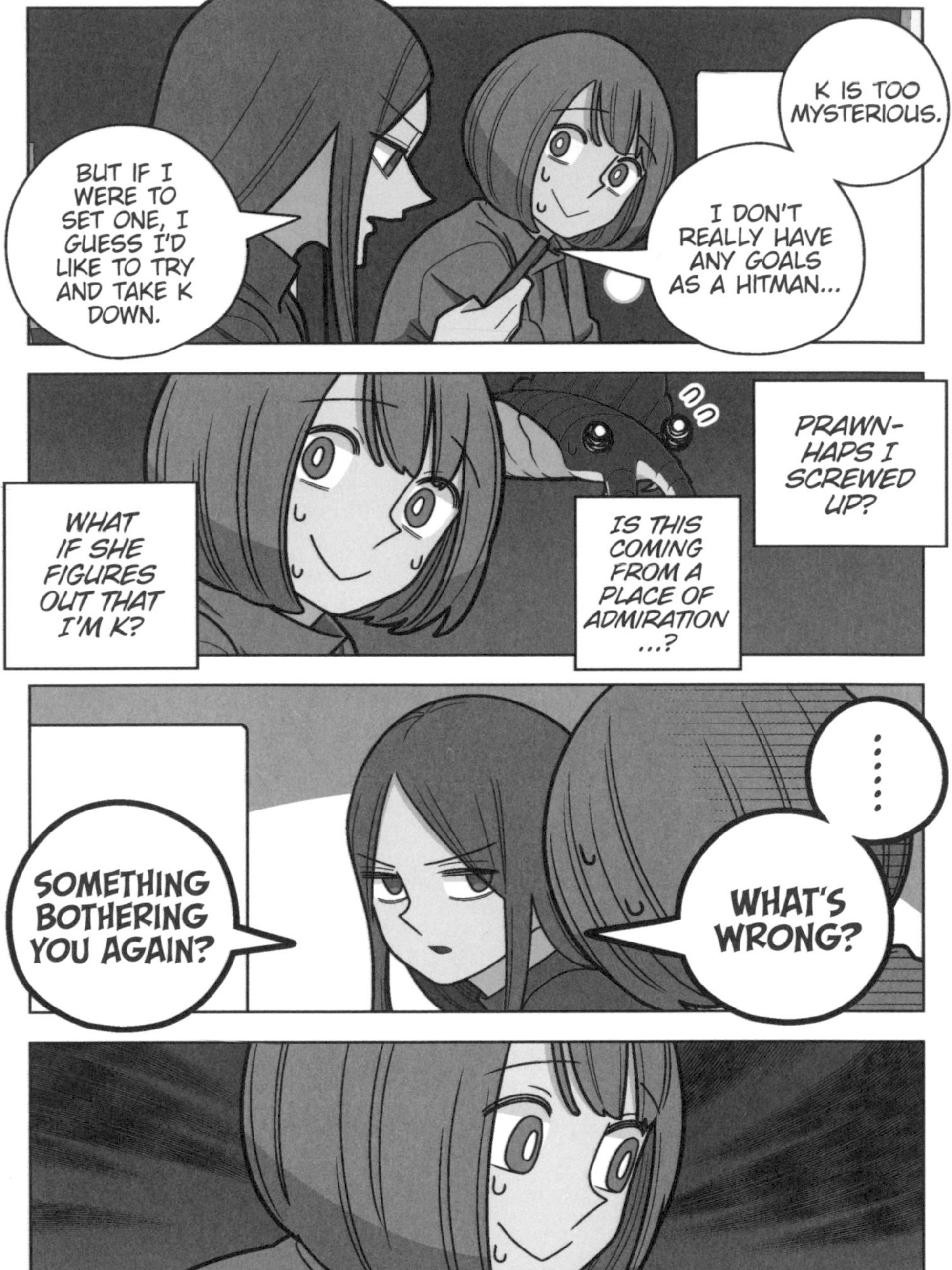
K IS TOO MYSTERIOUS.
I DON'T REALLY HAVE ANY GOALS AS A HITMAN...
BUT IF I WERE TO SET ONE, I GUESS I'D LIKE TO TRY AND TAKE K DOWN.
PRAWN-HAPS I SCREWED UP?
IS THIS COMING FROM A PLACE OF ADMIRATION ...?
WHAT IF SHE FIGURES OUT THAT I'M K?
......
WHAT'S WRONG?
SOMETHING BOTHERING YOU AGAIN?

☆ —— **Busted.**

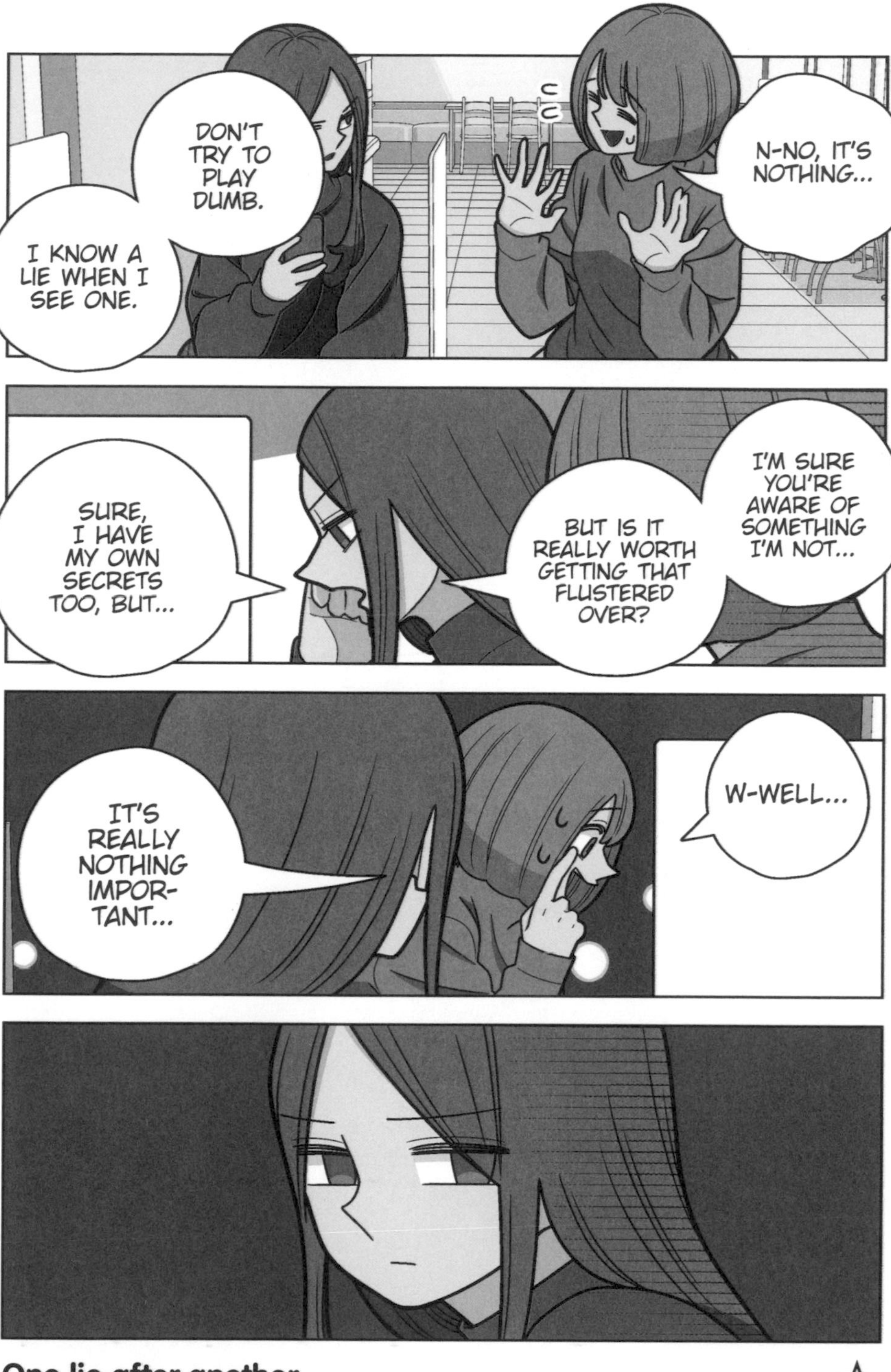
N-NO, IT'S NOTHING...
DON'T TRY TO PLAY DUMB.
I KNOW A LIE WHEN I SEE ONE.
I'M SURE YOU'RE AWARE OF SOMETHING I'M NOT...
BUT IS IT REALLY WORTH GETTING THAT FLUSTERED OVER?
SURE, I HAVE MY OWN SECRETS TOO, BUT...
W-WELL...
IT'S REALLY NOTHING IMPORTANT...

One lie after another. ☆

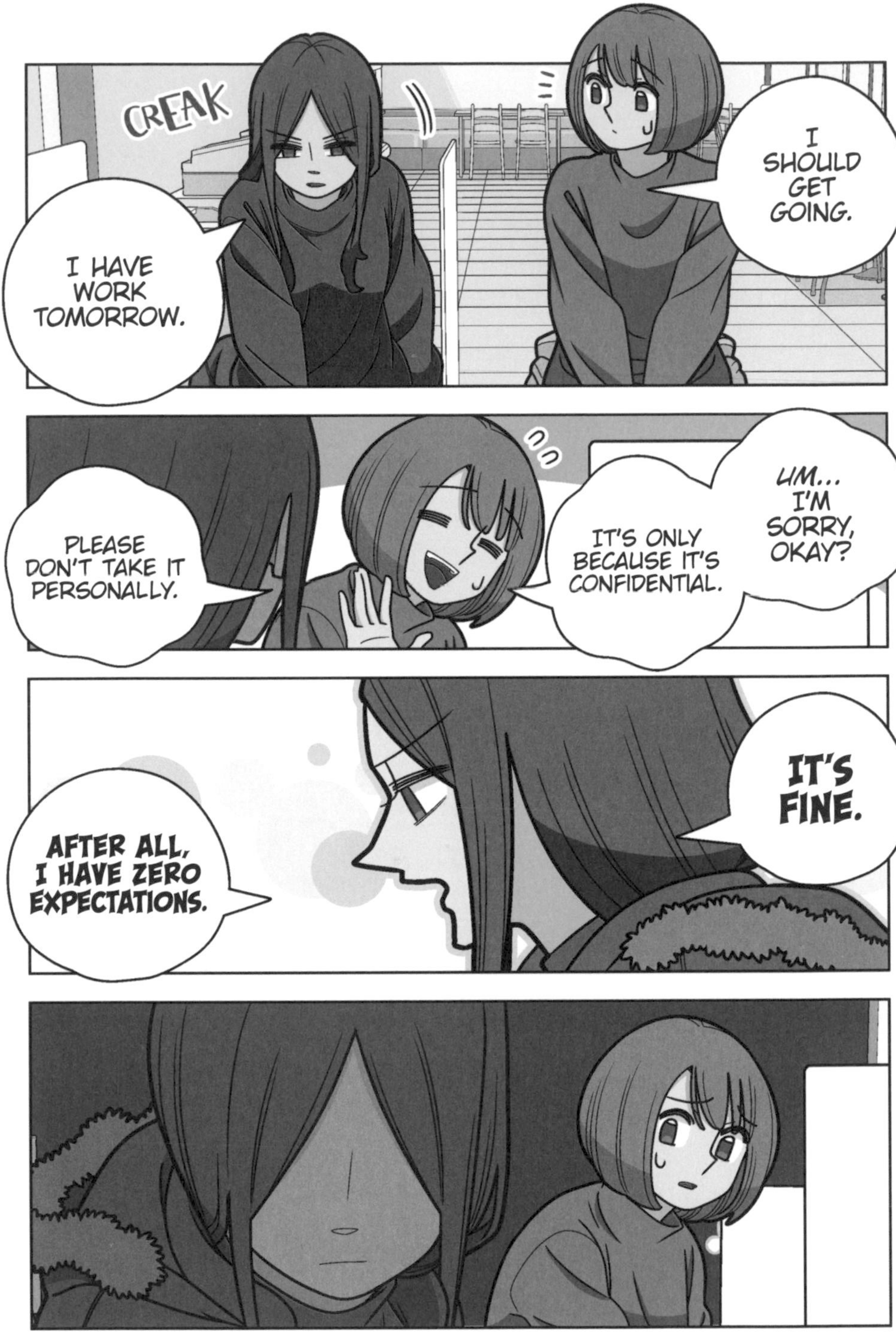
I SHOULD GET GOING.
CREAK
I HAVE WORK TOMORROW.
UM... I'M SORRY, OKAY?
IT'S ONLY BECAUSE IT'S CONFIDENTIAL.
PLEASE DON'T TAKE IT PERSONALLY.
IT'S FINE.
AFTER ALL, I HAVE ZERO EXPECTATIONS.

☆ —— I thought we were getting along.

Happy Kanako's
Killer Life

I NEED SOME TIME TO REPLY!!

Happy Kanako's
Killer Life

LURK

077

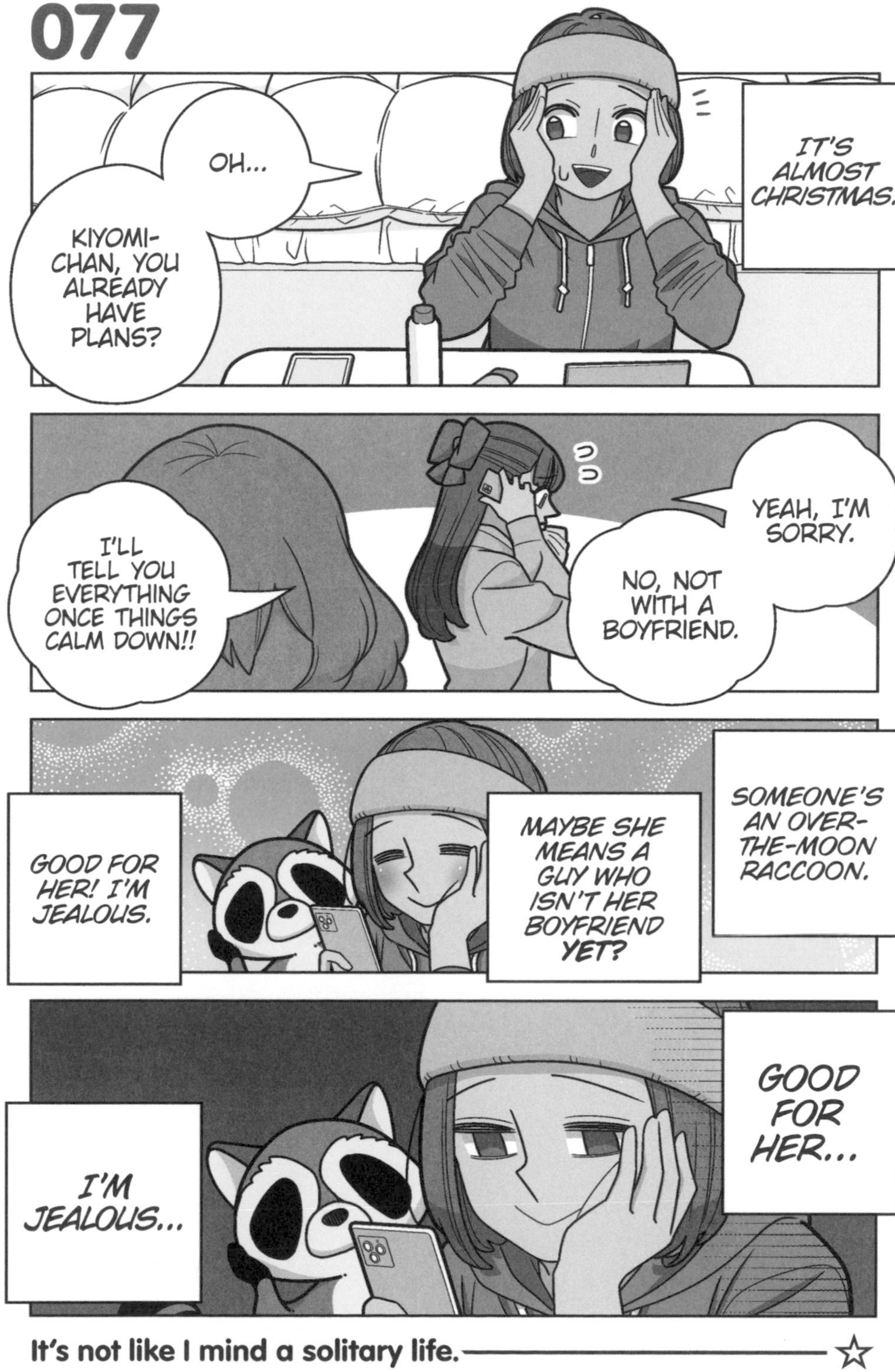
IT'S ALMOST CHRISTMAS.
OH...
KIYOMI-CHAN, YOU ALREADY HAVE PLANS?
YEAH, I'M SORRY.
NO, NOT WITH A BOYFRIEND.
I'LL TELL YOU EVERYTHING ONCE THINGS CALM DOWN!!
SOMEONE'S AN OVER-THE-MOON RACCOON.
MAYBE SHE MEANS A GUY WHO ISN'T HER BOYFRIEND YET?
GOOD FOR HER! I'M JEALOUS.
GOOD FOR HER...
I'M JEALOUS...

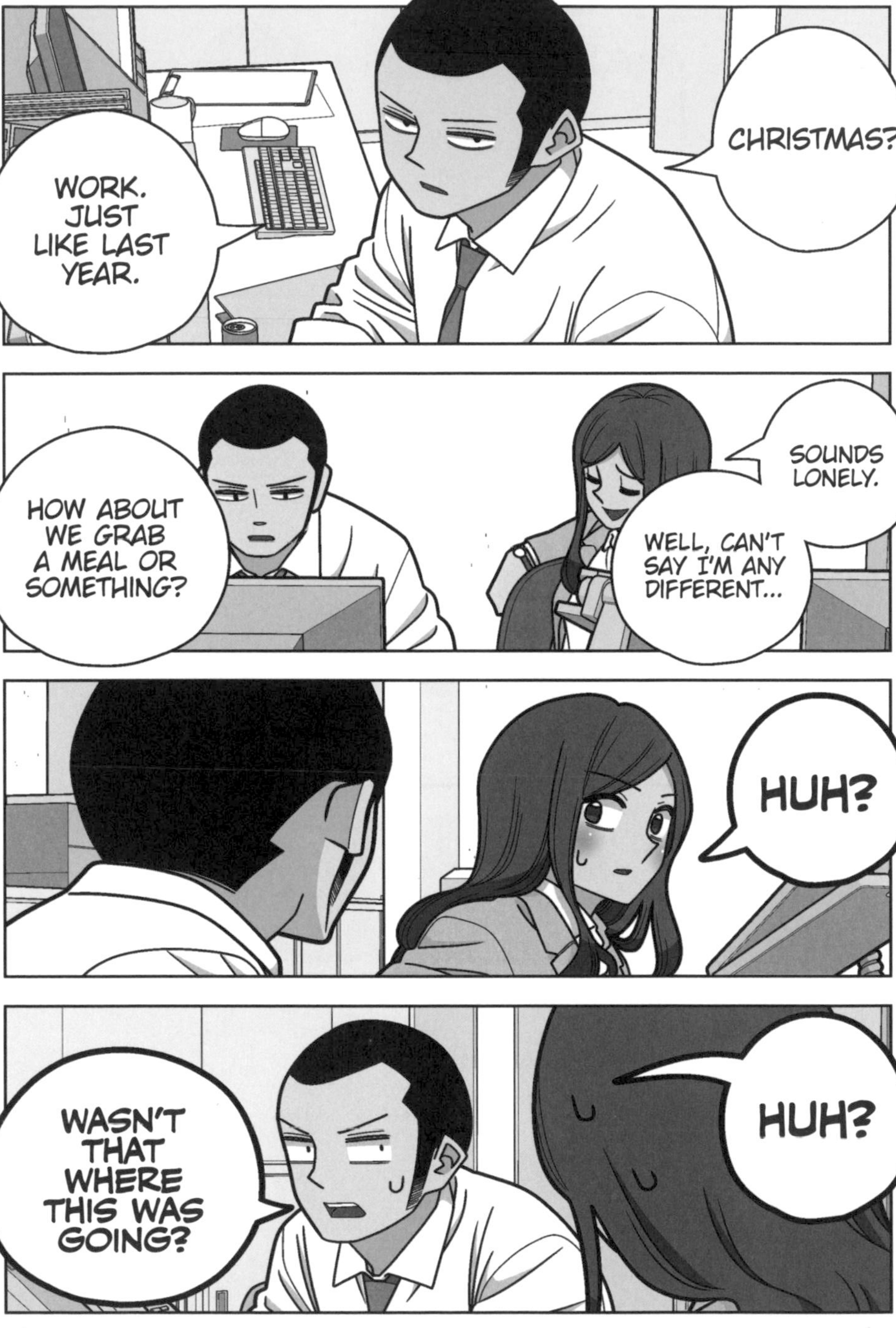
CHRISTMAS?
WORK. JUST LIKE LAST YEAR.
SOUNDS LONELY.
WELL, CAN'T SAY I'M ANY DIFFERENT...
HOW ABOUT WE GRAB A MEAL OR SOMETHING?
HUH?
HUH?
WASN'T THAT WHERE THIS WAS GOING?

☆ —— **Quick on the trigger.**

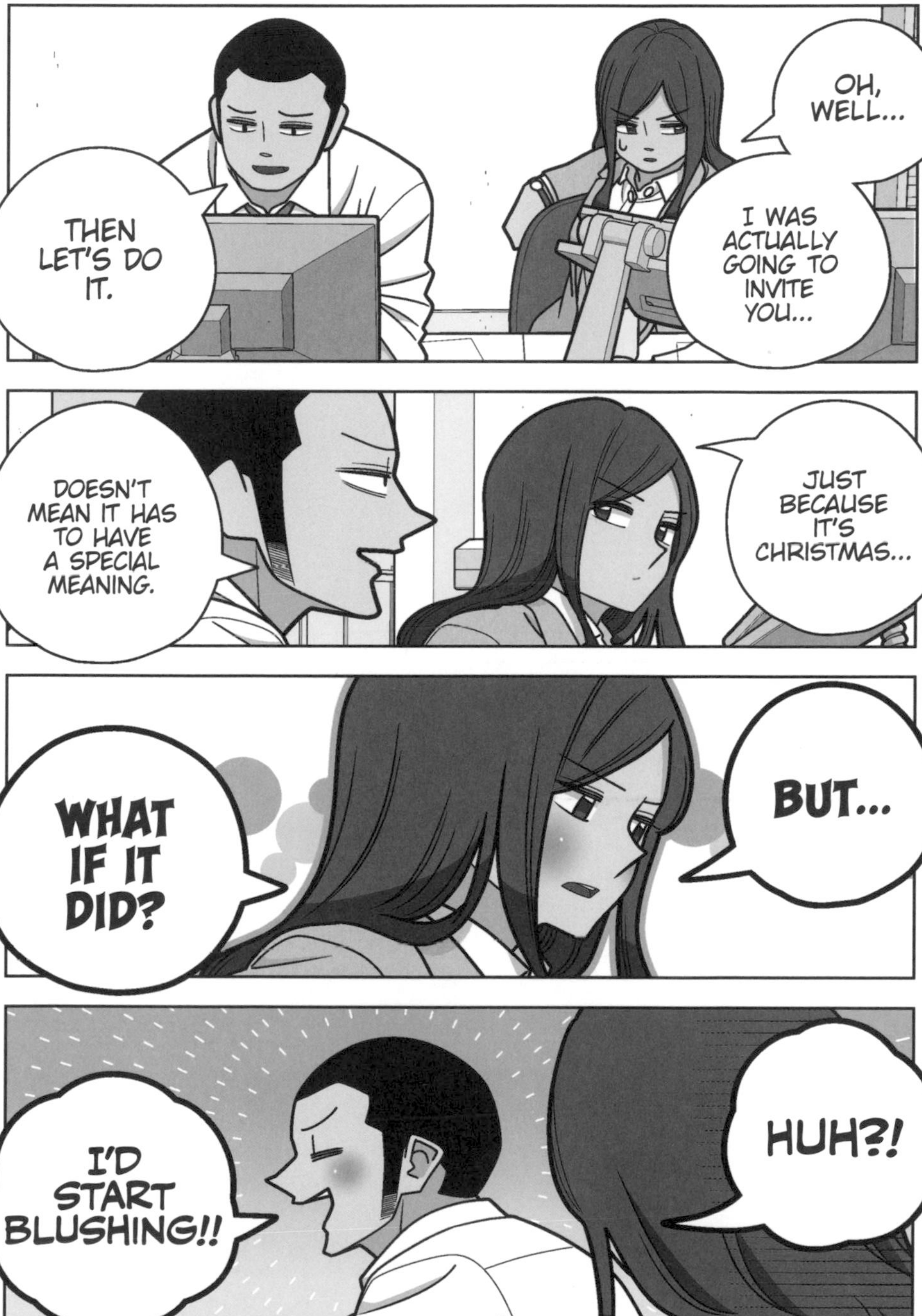
OH, WELL...
I WAS ACTUALLY GOING TO INVITE YOU...
THEN LET'S DO IT.
JUST BECAUSE IT'S CHRISTMAS...
DOESN'T MEAN IT HAS TO HAVE A SPECIAL MEANING.
BUT...
WHAT IF IT DID?
HUH?!
I'D START BLUSHING!!

How dense can he be? ——— ☆

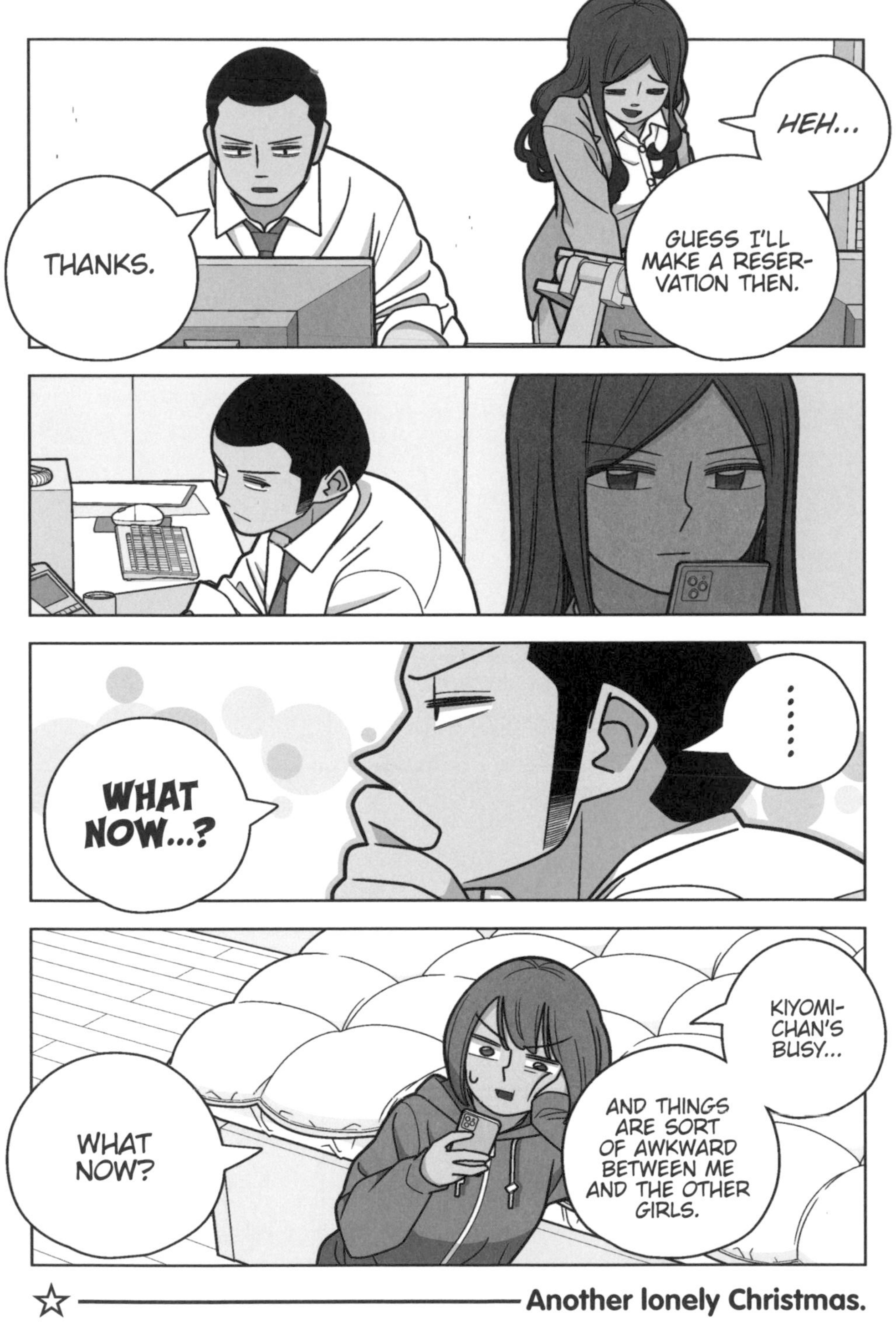
HEH...
GUESS I'LL MAKE A RESERVATION THEN.
THANKS.
......
WHAT NOW...?
KIYOMI-CHAN'S BUSY...
AND THINGS ARE SORT OF AWKWARD BETWEEN ME AND THE OTHER GIRLS.
WHAT NOW?

☆ Another lonely Christmas.

078

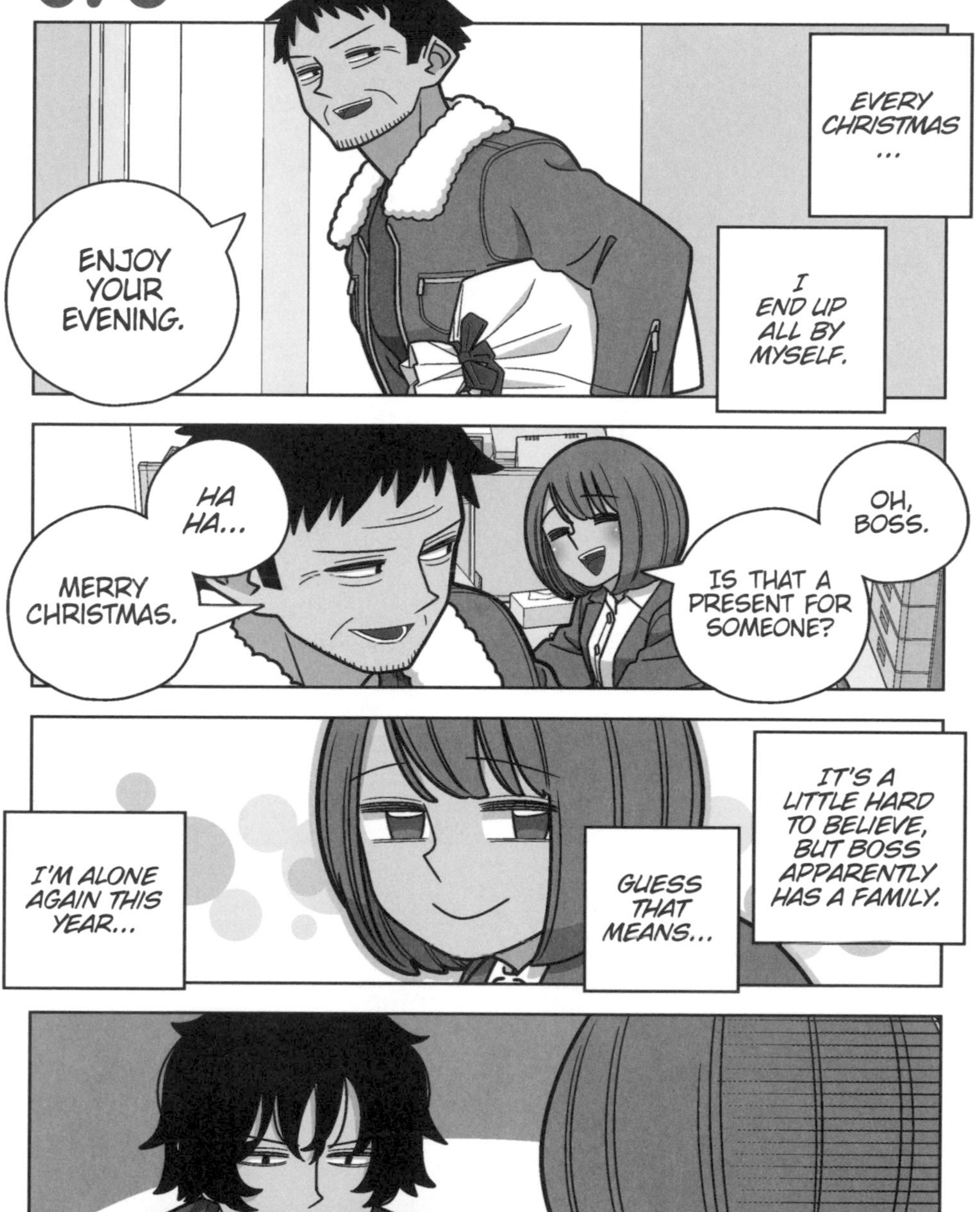
EVERY CHRISTMAS...
I END UP ALL BY MYSELF.
ENJOY YOUR EVENING.
OH, BOSS.
IS THAT A PRESENT FOR SOMEONE?
HA HA...
MERRY CHRISTMAS.
IT'S A LITTLE HARD TO BELIEVE, BUT BOSS APPARENTLY HAS A FAMILY.
GUESS THAT MEANS...
I'M ALONE AGAIN THIS YEAR...

There's someone else. ☆

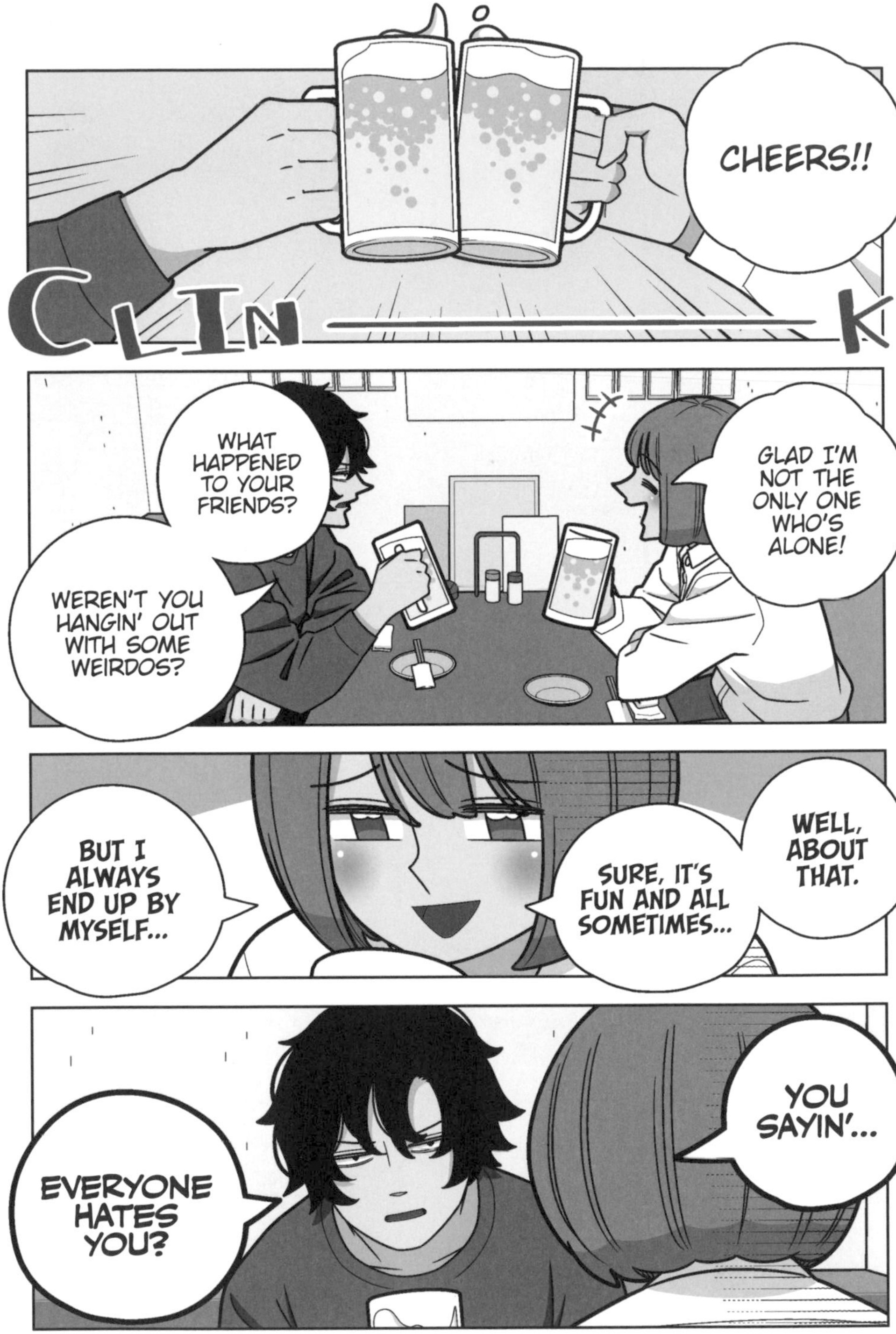
CHEERS!!
CLIN—K
GLAD I'M NOT THE ONLY ONE WHO'S ALONE!
WHAT HAPPENED TO YOUR FRIENDS?
WEREN'T YOU HANGIN' OUT WITH SOME WEIRDOS?
WELL, ABOUT THAT.
SURE, IT'S FUN AND ALL SOMETIMES...
BUT I ALWAYS END UP BY MYSELF...
YOU SAYIN'...
EVERYONE HATES YOU?

☆ — Can't deny that.

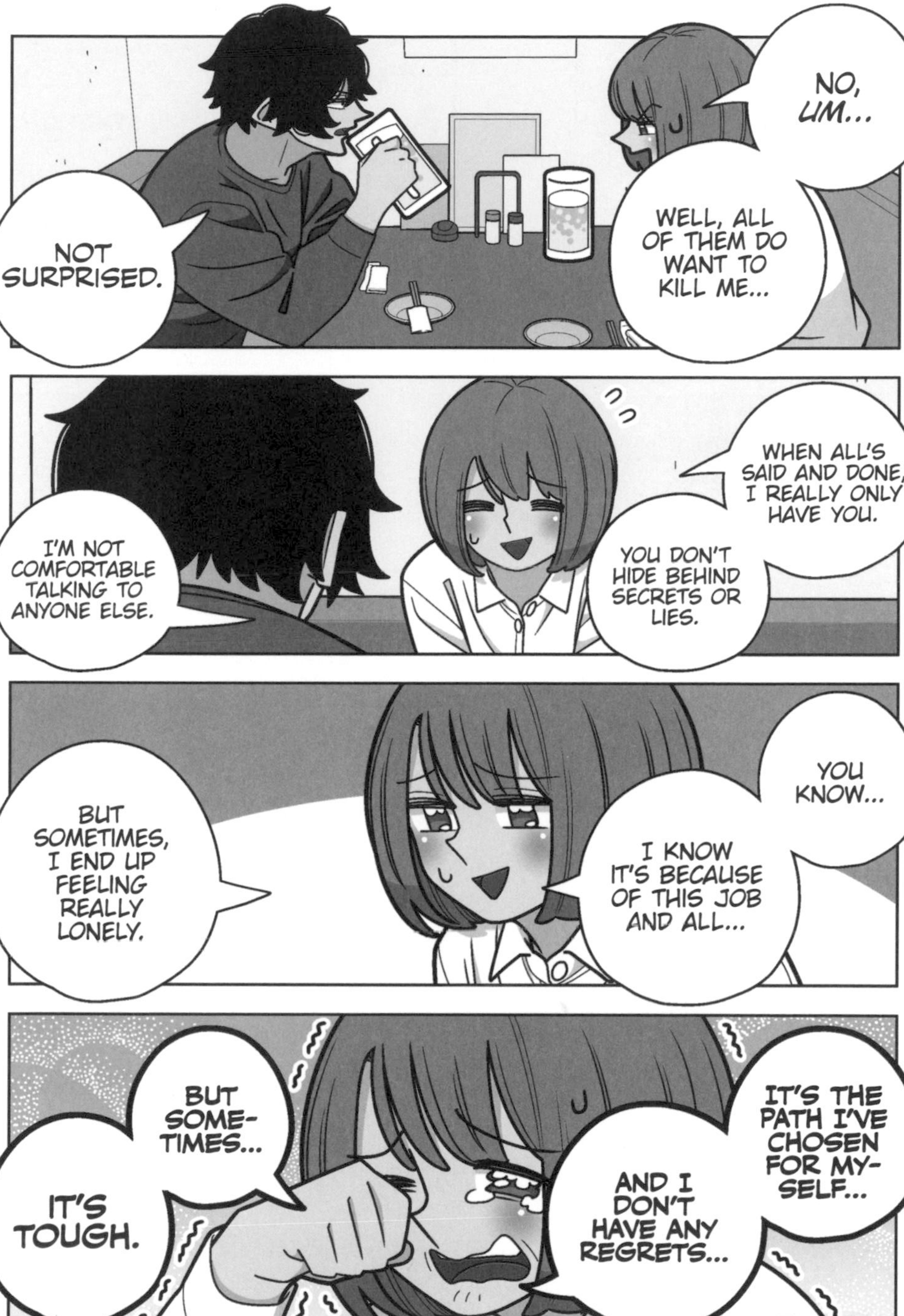
NO, UM...
WELL, ALL OF THEM DO WANT TO KILL ME...
NOT SURPRISED.
WHEN ALL'S SAID AND DONE, I REALLY ONLY HAVE YOU.
YOU DON'T HIDE BEHIND SECRETS OR LIES.
I'M NOT COMFORTABLE TALKING TO ANYONE ELSE.
YOU KNOW...
I KNOW IT'S BECAUSE OF THIS JOB AND ALL...
BUT SOMETIMES, I END UP FEELING REALLY LONELY.
IT'S THE PATH I'VE CHOSEN FOR MY-SELF...
AND I DON'T HAVE ANY REGRETS...
BUT SOME-TIMES...
IT'S TOUGH.

Not always rainbows and butterflies. ☆

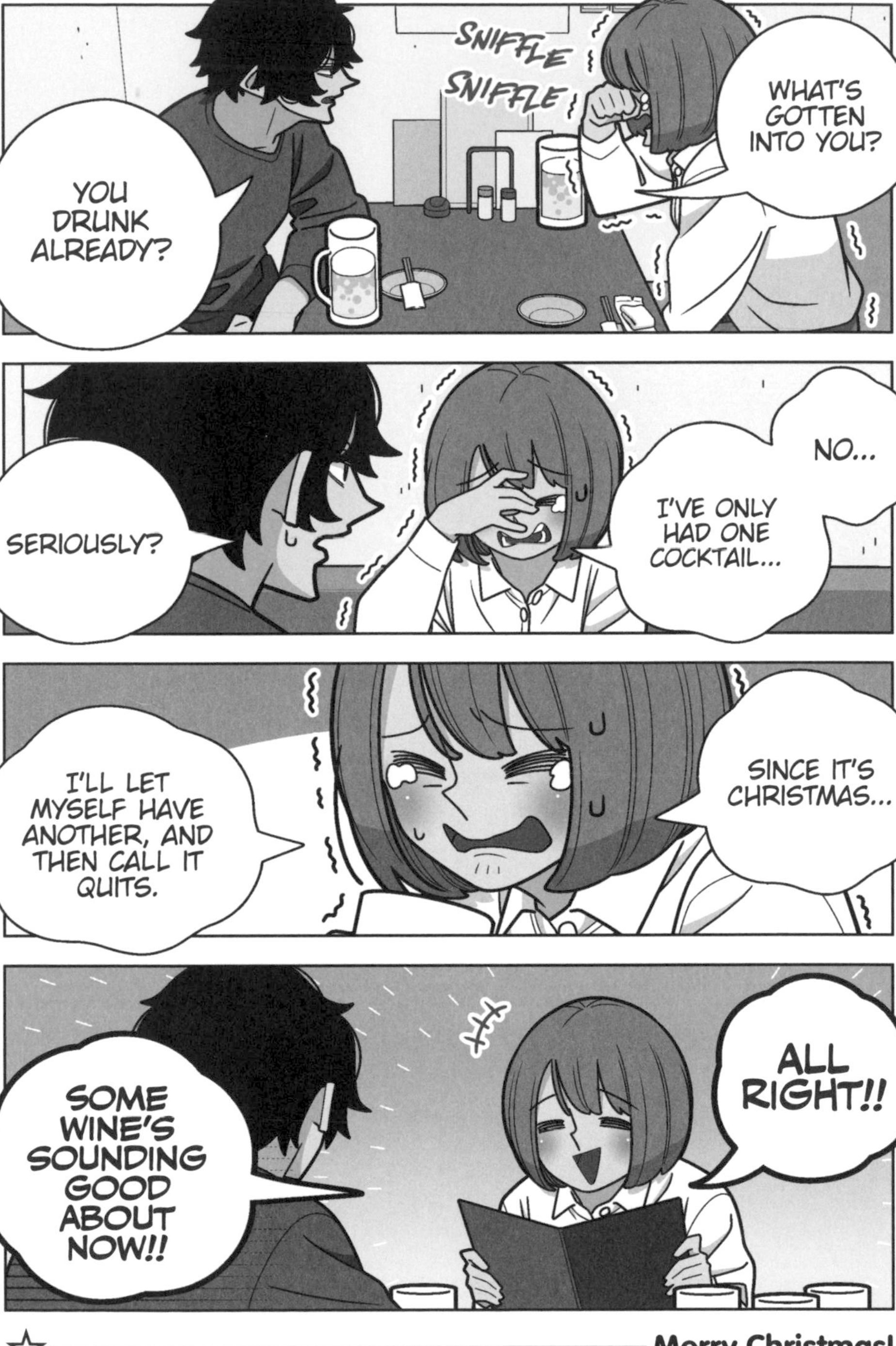
WHAT'S GOTTEN INTO YOU?
SNIFFLE
SNIFFLE
YOU DRUNK ALREADY?
NO...
I'VE ONLY HAD ONE COCKTAIL...
SERIOUSLY?
SINCE IT'S CHRISTMAS...
I'LL LET MYSELF HAVE ANOTHER, AND THEN CALL IT QUITS.
ALL RIGHT!!
SOME WINE'S SOUNDING GOOD ABOUT NOW!!

☆ Merry Christmas!

079

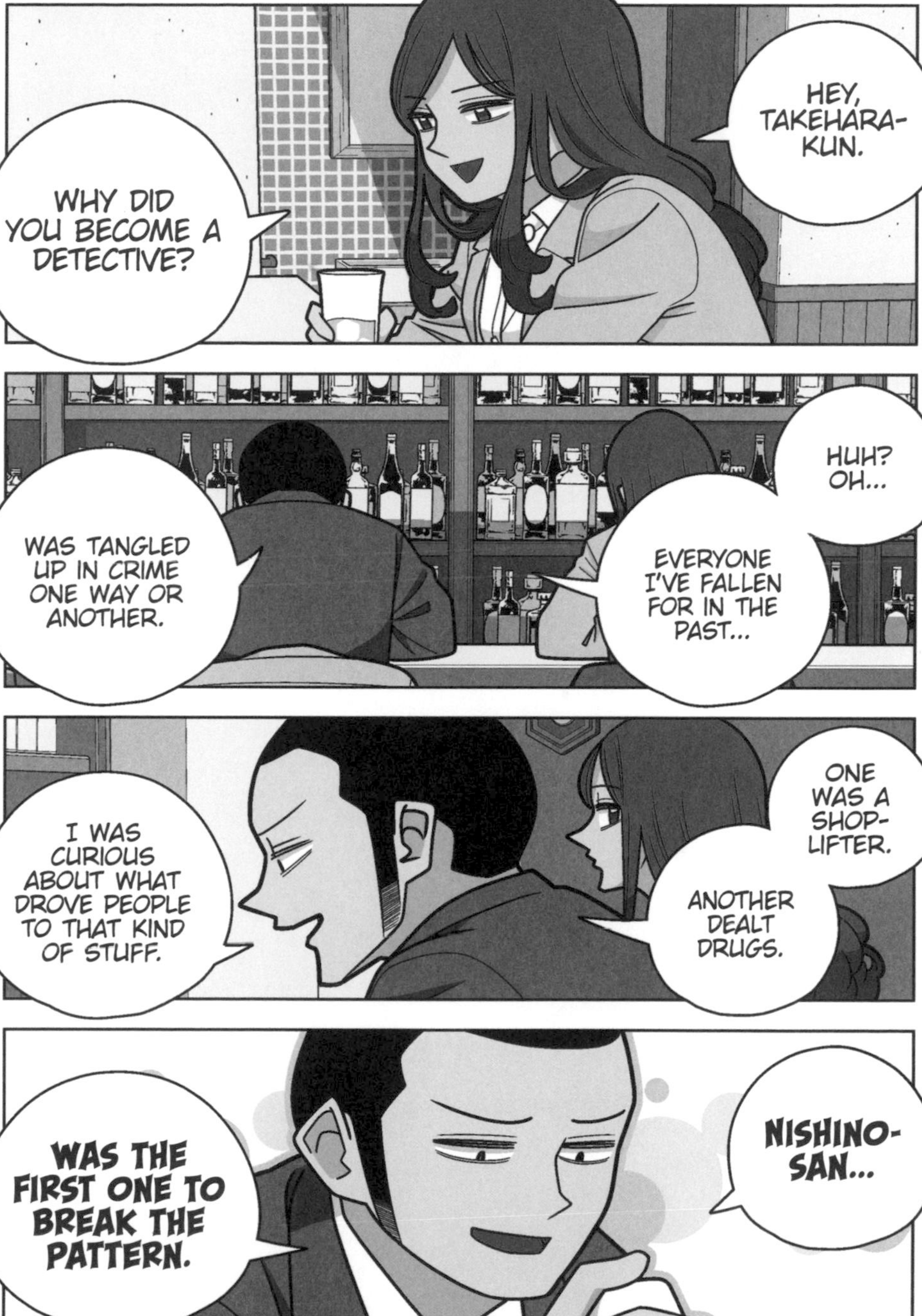
HEY, TAKEHARA-KUN.
WHY DID YOU BECOME A DETECTIVE?
HUH? OH...
EVERYONE I'VE FALLEN FOR IN THE PAST...
WAS TANGLED UP IN CRIME ONE WAY OR ANOTHER.
ONE WAS A SHOP-LIFTER.
ANOTHER DEALT DRUGS.
I WAS CURIOUS ABOUT WHAT DROVE PEOPLE TO THAT KIND OF STUFF.
NISHINO-SAN...
WAS THE FIRST ONE TO BREAK THE PATTERN.

She's probably the most dangerous one of all.——— ☆

☆ ─────────── Because I like you, you dummy.

I'm sorry. ─────────────────────────────── ★

Not your face.

080

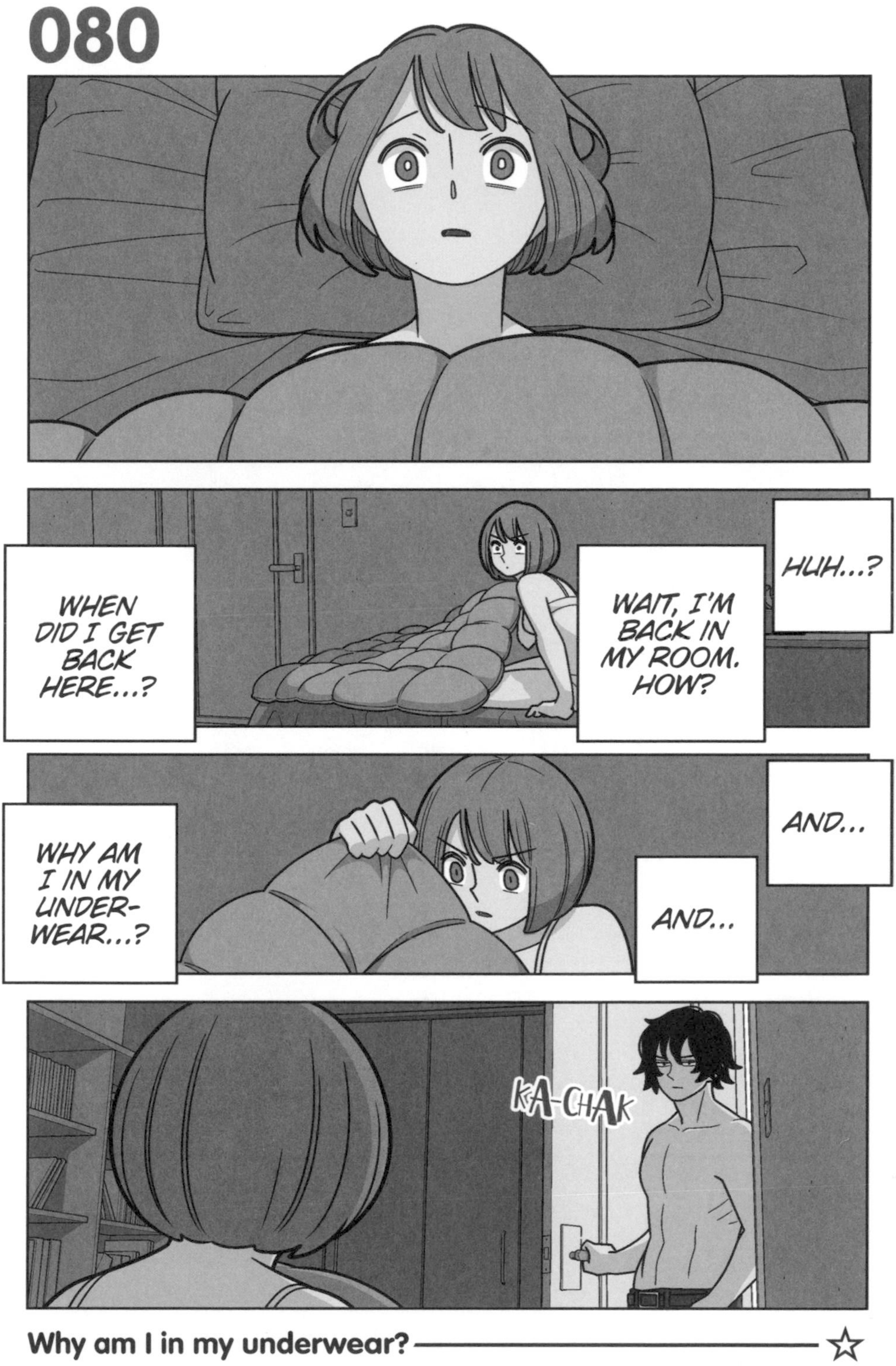
HUH...?
WAIT, I'M BACK IN MY ROOM. HOW?
WHEN DID I GET BACK HERE...?
AND...
AND...
WHY AM I IN MY UNDER-WEAR...?
KA-CHAK

Why am I in my underwear? ☆

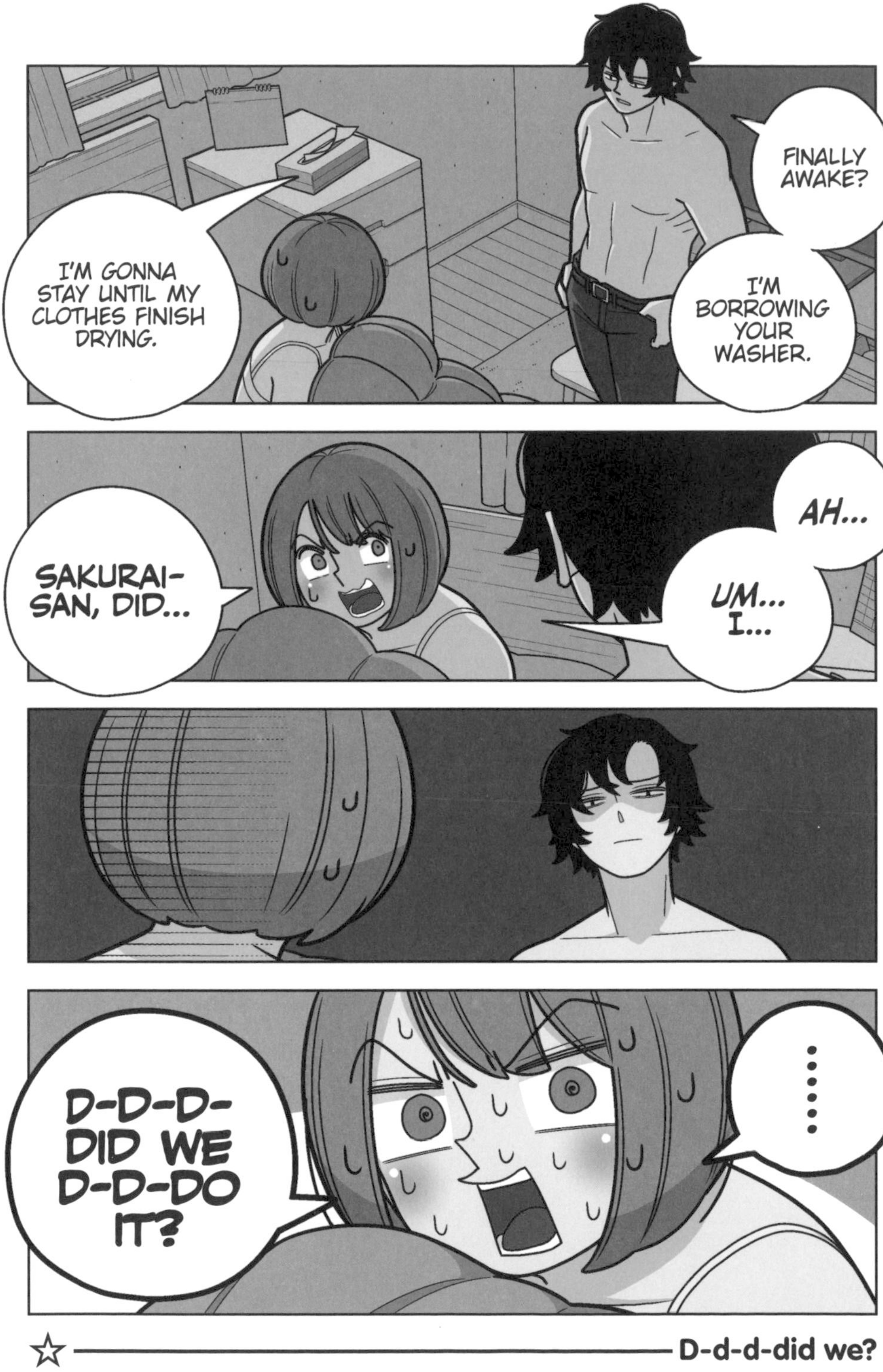
FINALLY AWAKE?
I'M BORROWING YOUR WASHER.
I'M GONNA STAY UNTIL MY CLOTHES FINISH DRYING.
AH...
UM... I...
SAKURAI-SAN, DID...
......
D-D-D-DID WE D-D-DO IT?

☆ D-d-d-did we?

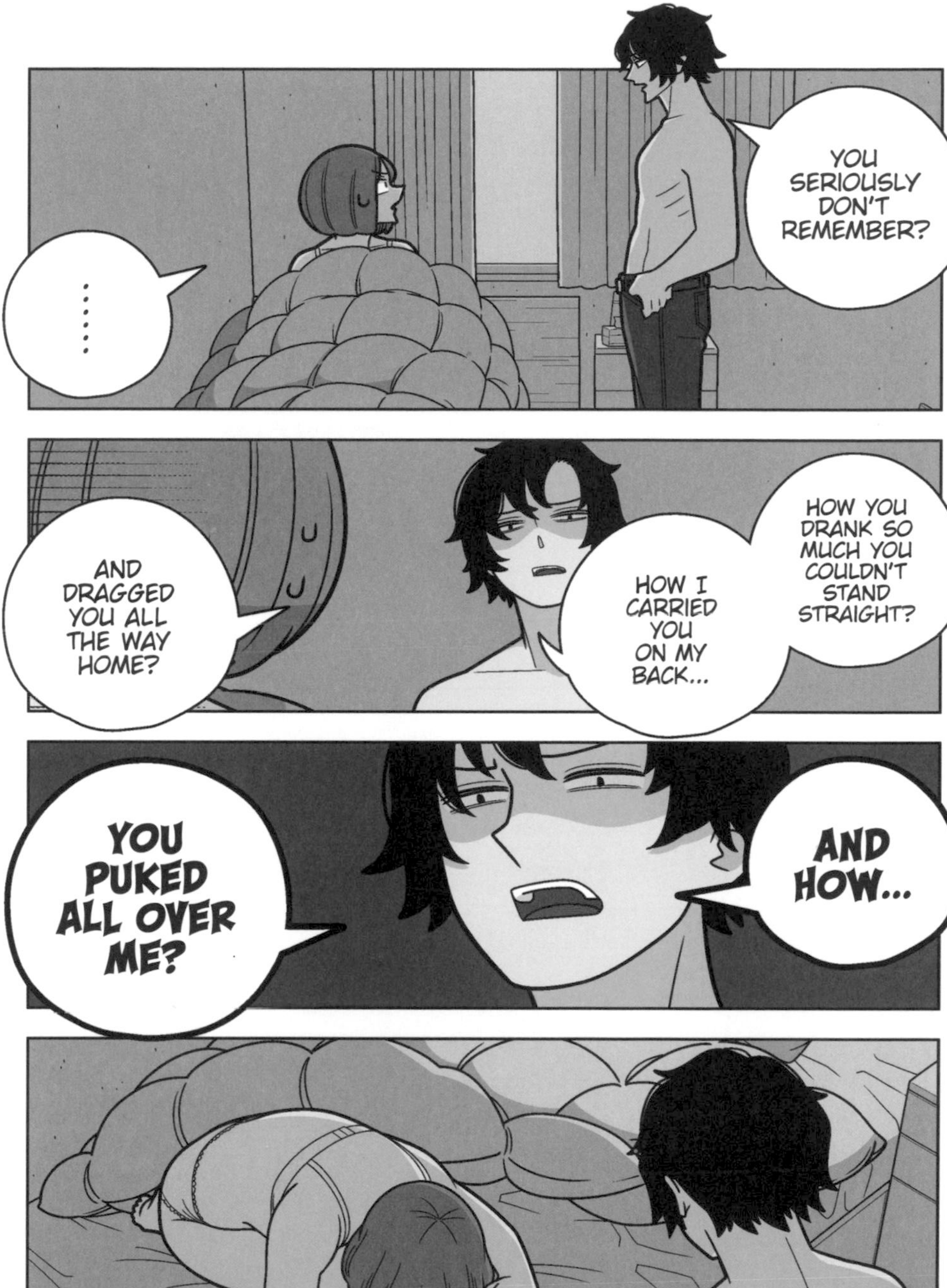
YOU SERIOUSLY DON'T REMEMBER?
......
HOW YOU DRANK SO MUCH YOU COULDN'T STAND STRAIGHT?
HOW I CARRIED YOU ON MY BACK...
AND DRAGGED YOU ALL THE WAY HOME?
AND HOW...
YOU PUKED ALL OVER ME?

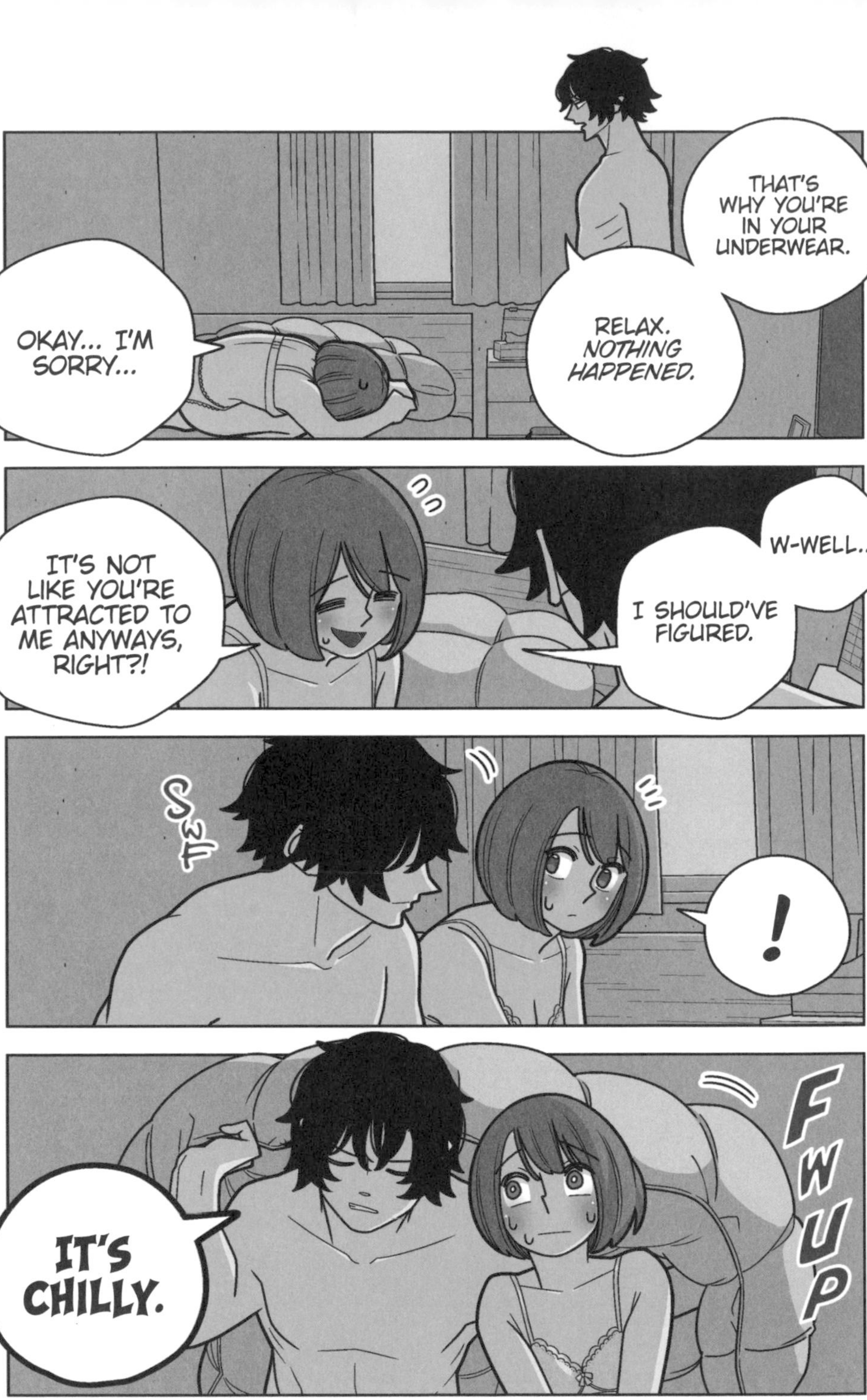
THAT'S WHY YOU'RE IN YOUR UNDERWEAR.
RELAX. NOTHING HAPPENED.
OKAY... I'M SORRY...
W-WELL...
I SHOULD'VE FIGURED.
IT'S NOT LIKE YOU'RE ATTRACTED TO ME ANYWAYS, RIGHT?!
!
FWUP
IT'S CHILLY.

☆ ———— **Not like you're attracted to me anyways, right?!**

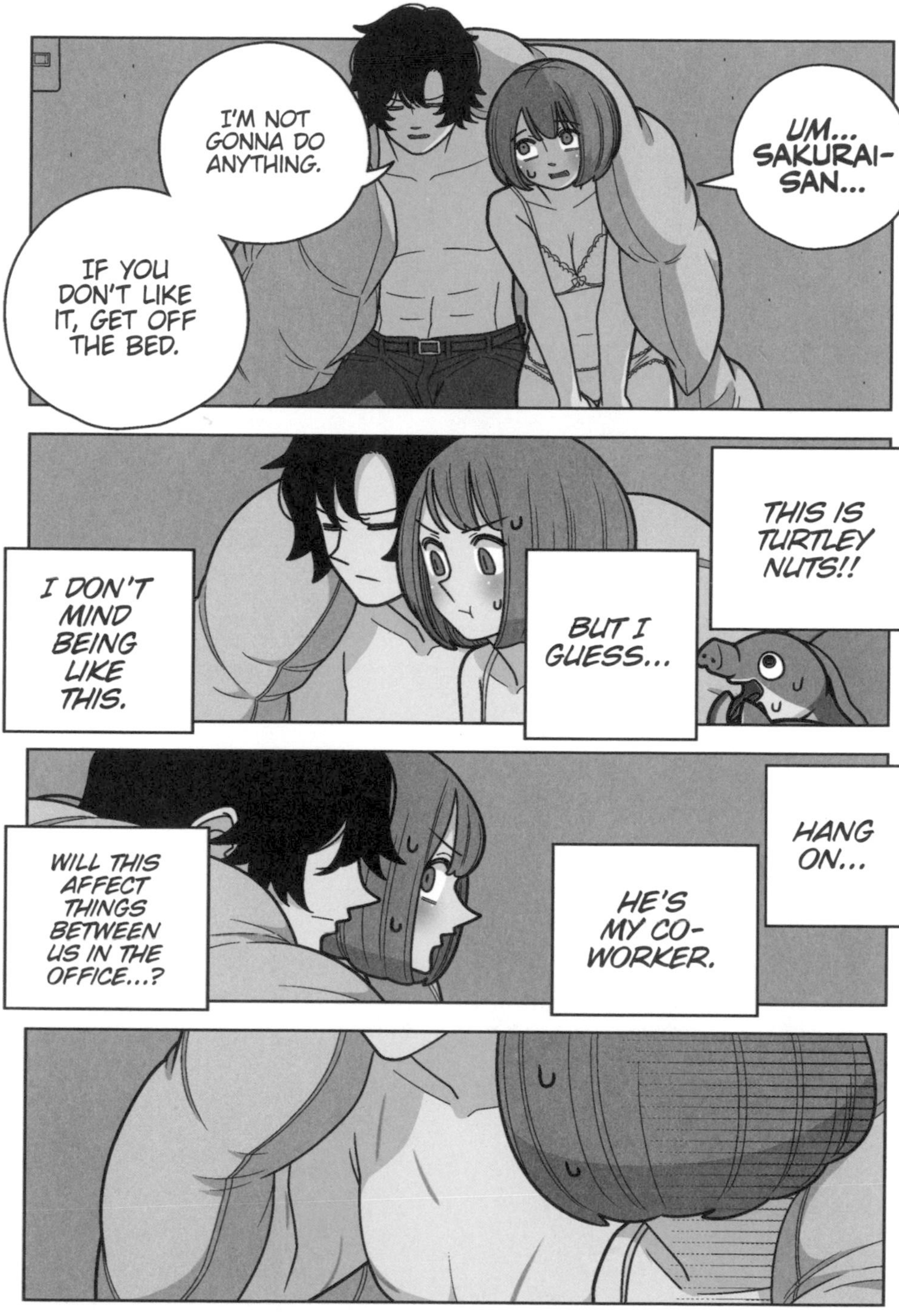
UM... SAKURAI-SAN...
I'M NOT GONNA DO ANYTHING.
IF YOU DON'T LIKE IT, GET OFF THE BED.
THIS IS TURTLEY NUTS!!
BUT I GUESS...
I DON'T MIND BEING LIKE THIS.
HANG ON...
HE'S MY CO-WORKER.
WILL THIS AFFECT THINGS BETWEEN US IN THE OFFICE...?

Will I be able to look him in the eye?——☆

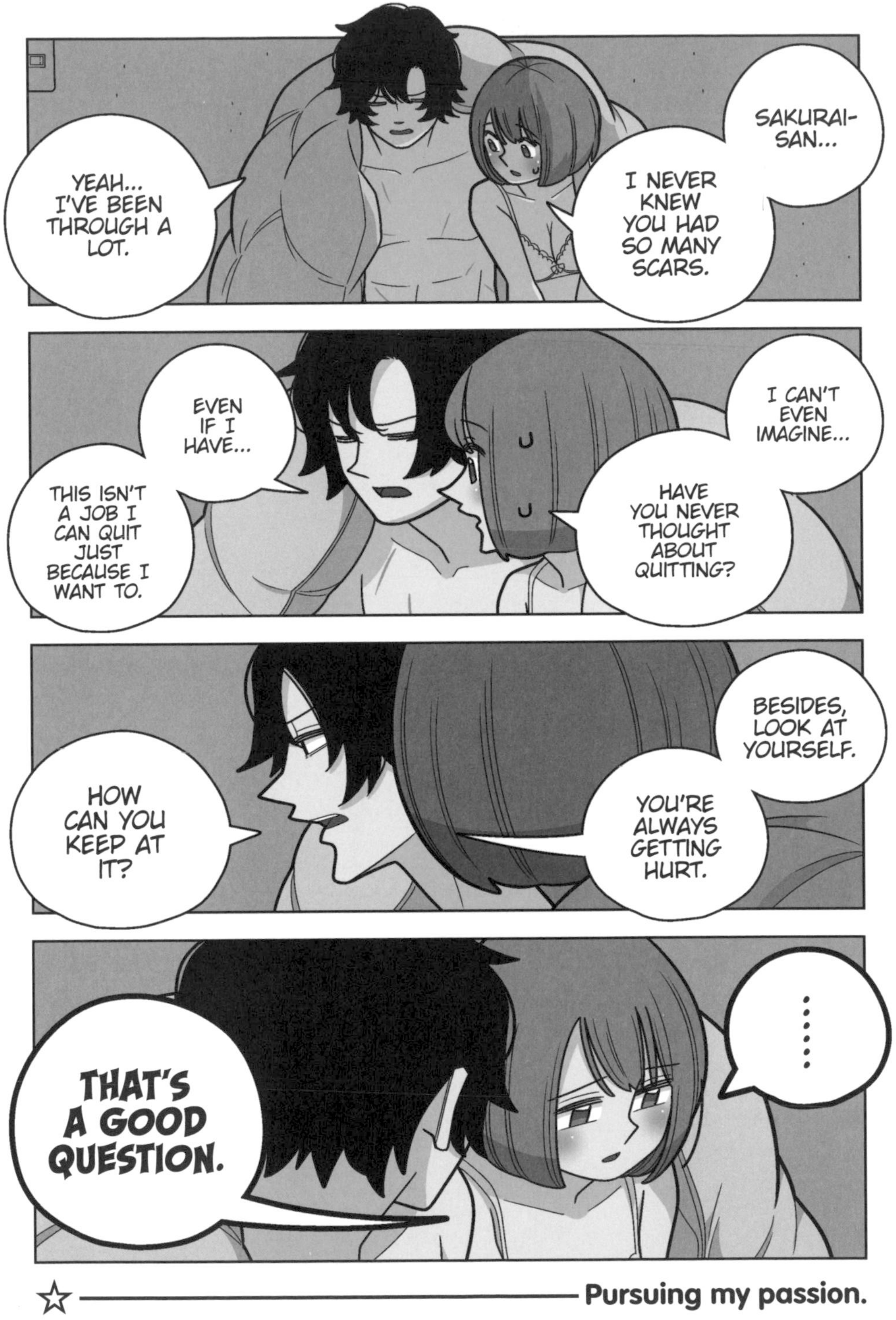
SAKURAI-SAN...
I NEVER KNEW YOU HAD SO MANY SCARS.
YEAH... I'VE BEEN THROUGH A LOT.
I CAN'T EVEN IMAGINE...
HAVE YOU NEVER THOUGHT ABOUT QUITTING?
EVEN IF I HAVE...
THIS ISN'T A JOB I CAN QUIT JUST BECAUSE I WANT TO.
BESIDES, LOOK AT YOURSELF.
YOU'RE ALWAYS GETTING HURT.
HOW CAN YOU KEEP AT IT?
......
THAT'S A GOOD QUESTION.

☆ — **Pursuing my passion.**

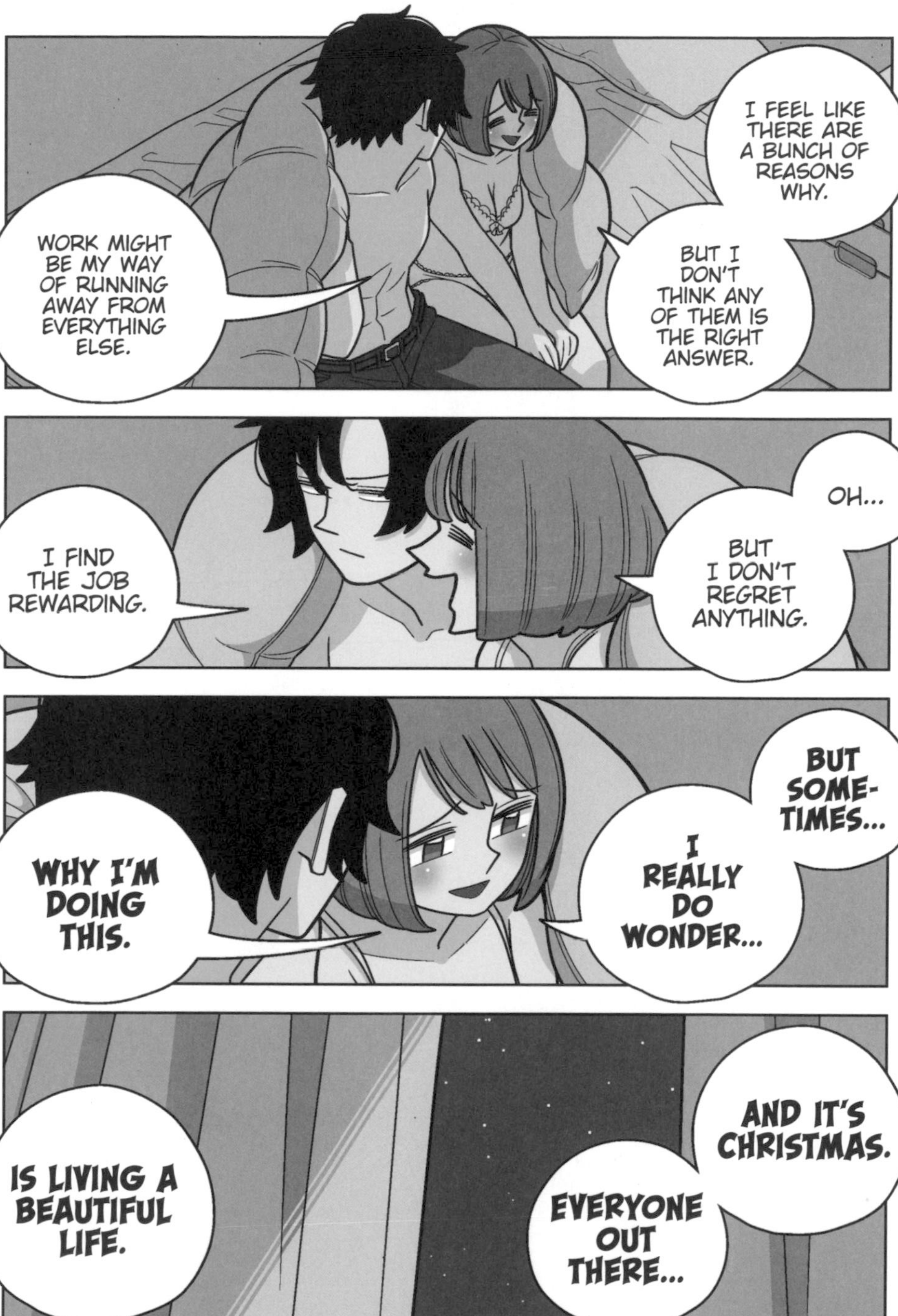
I FEEL LIKE THERE ARE A BUNCH OF REASONS WHY.
BUT I DON'T THINK ANY OF THEM IS THE RIGHT ANSWER.
WORK MIGHT BE MY WAY OF RUNNING AWAY FROM EVERYTHING ELSE.
OH...
BUT I DON'T REGRET ANYTHING.
I FIND THE JOB REWARDING.
BUT SOME-TIMES...
I REALLY DO WONDER...
WHY I'M DOING THIS.
AND IT'S CHRISTMAS.
EVERYONE OUT THERE...
IS LIVING A BEAUTIFUL LIFE.

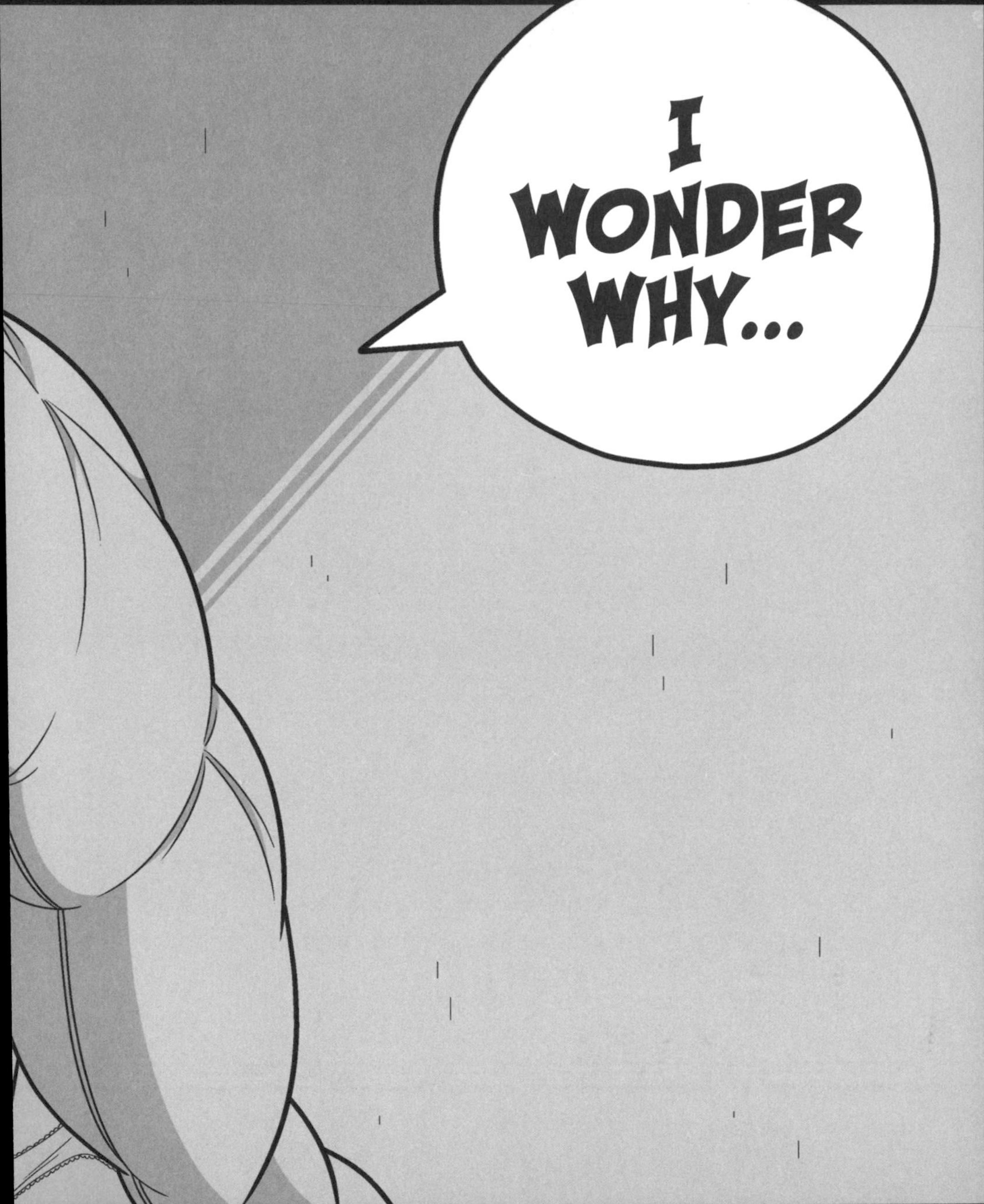
I WONDER WHY...

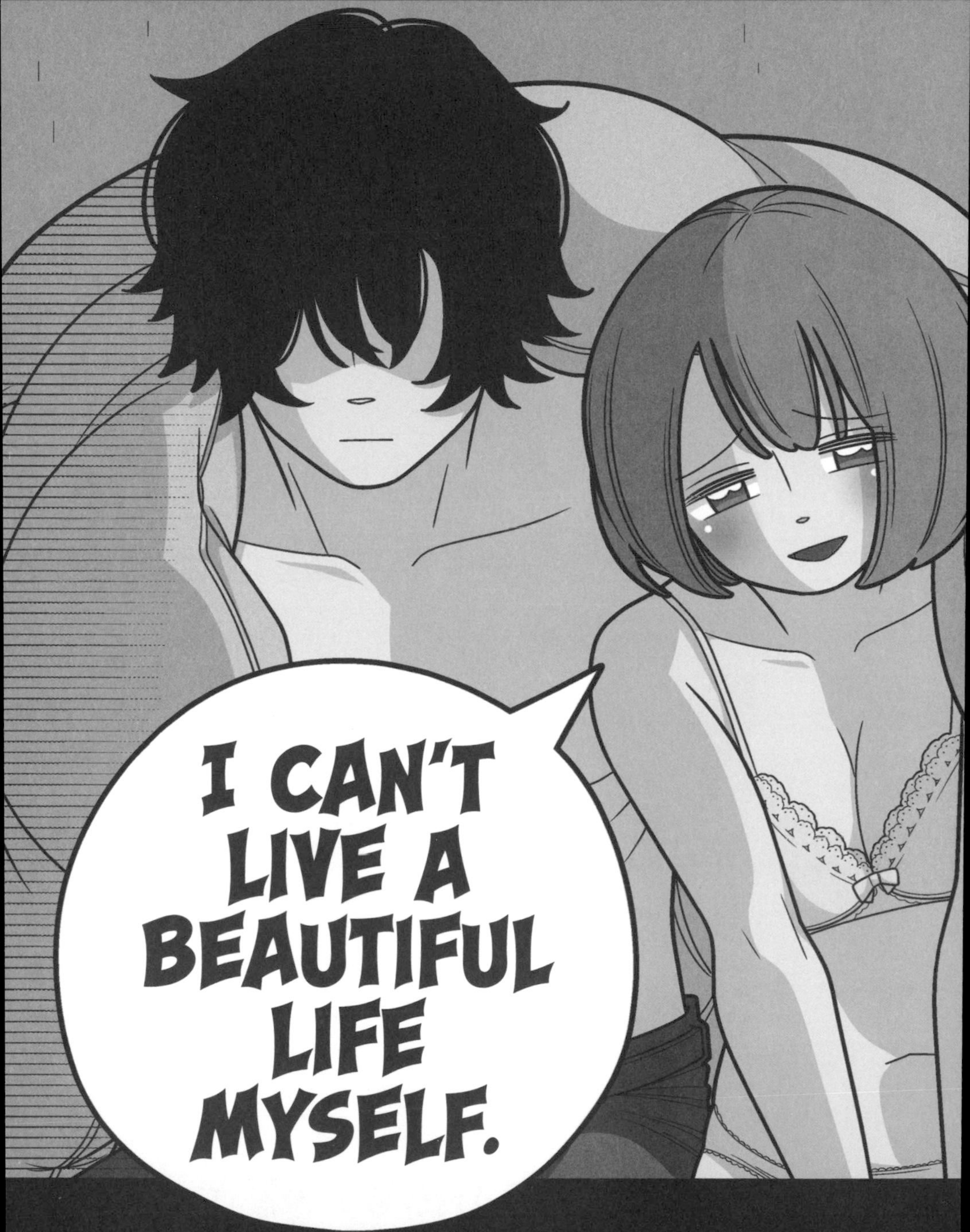
I CAN'T LIVE A BEAUTIFUL LIFE MYSELF.

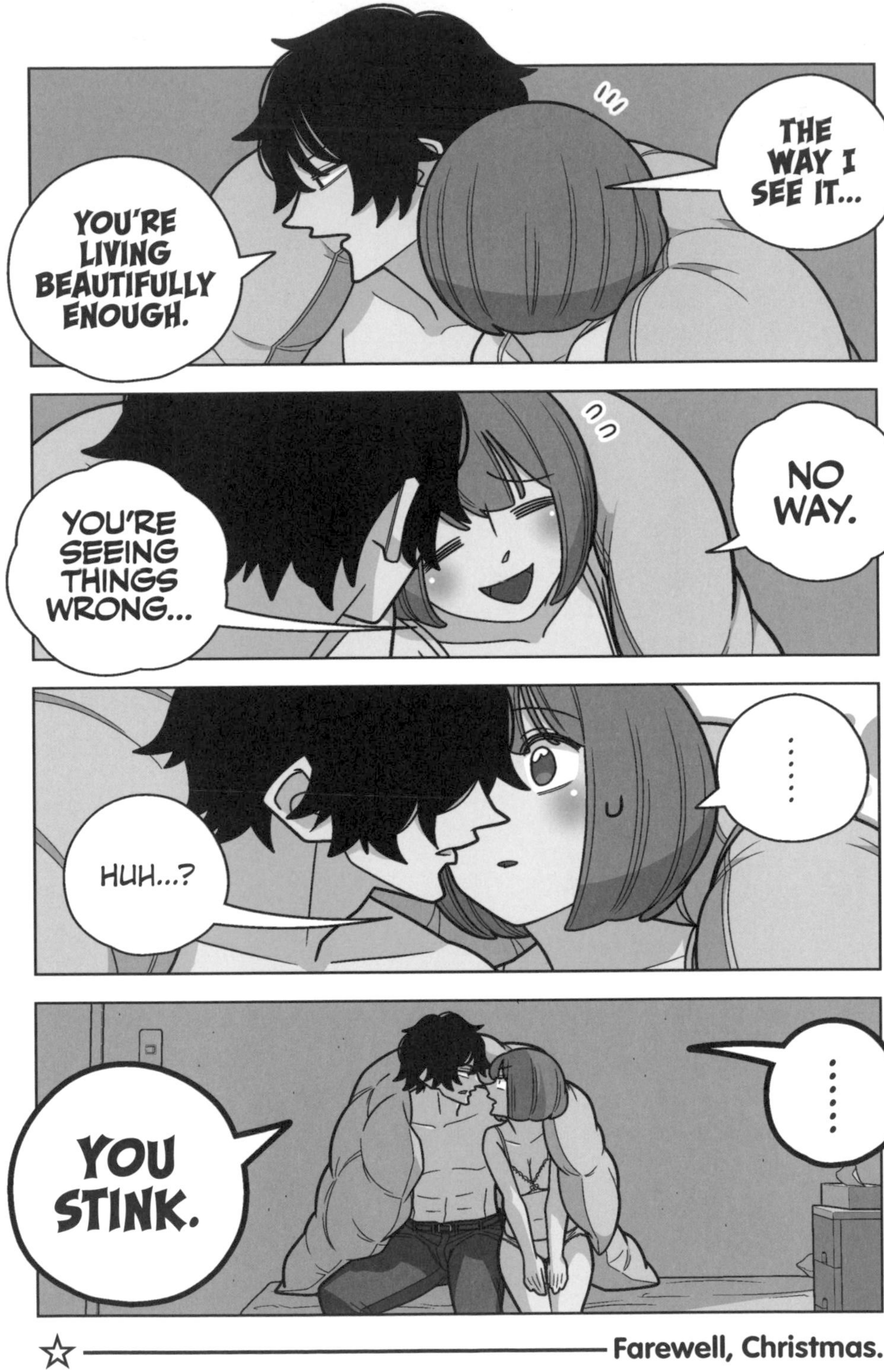
THE WAY I SEE IT...
YOU'RE LIVING BEAUTIFULLY ENOUGH.
NO WAY.
YOU'RE SEEING THINGS WRONG...
......
HUH...?
......
YOU STINK.

Bonus

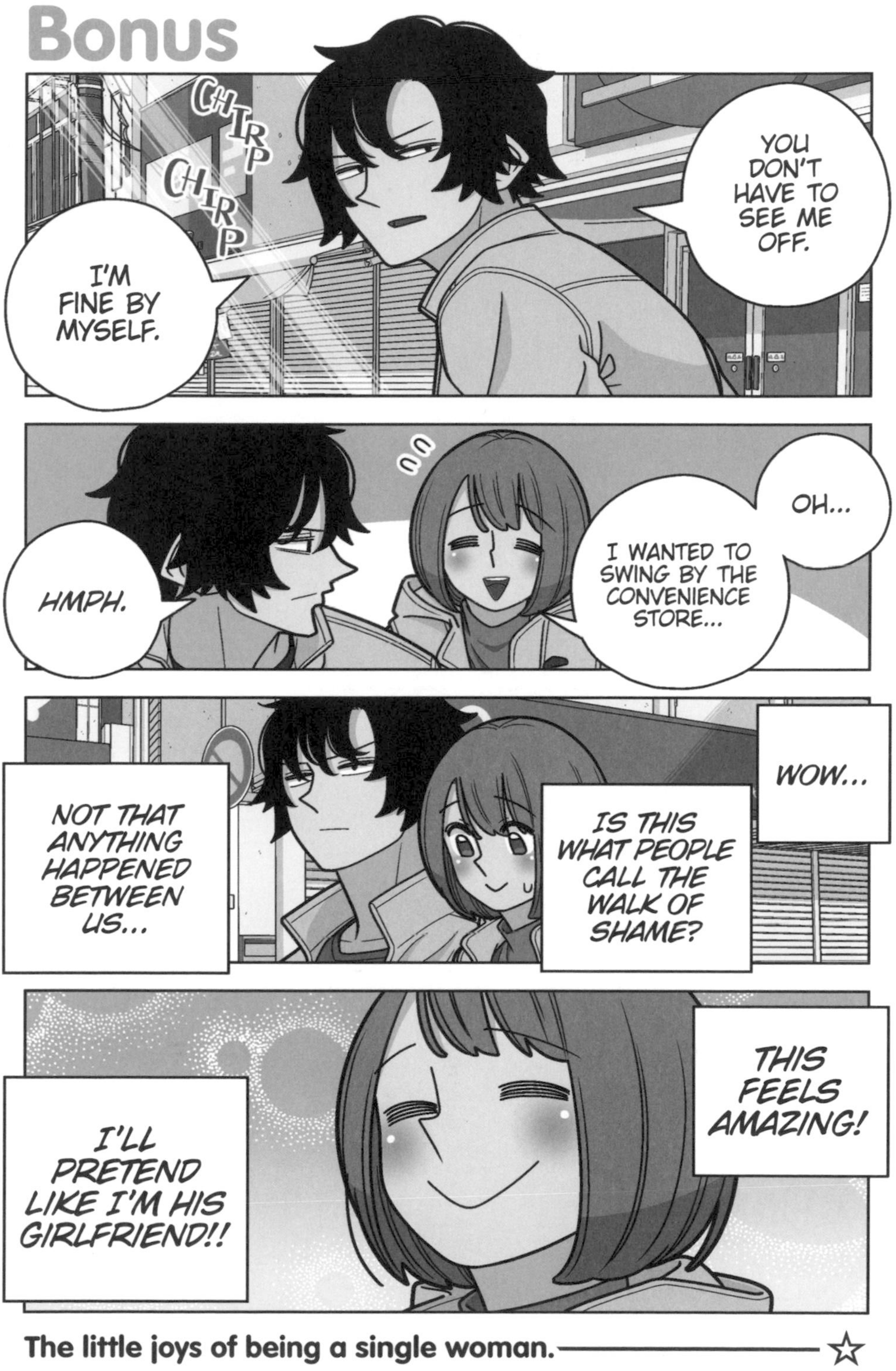
YOU DON'T HAVE TO SEE ME OFF.
CHIRP
CHIRP
I'M FINE BY MYSELF.
OH...
I WANTED TO SWING BY THE CONVENIENCE STORE...
HMPH.
WOW...
IS THIS WHAT PEOPLE CALL THE WALK OF SHAME?
NOT THAT ANYTHING HAPPENED BETWEEN US...
THIS FEELS AMAZING!
I'LL PRETEND LIKE I'M HIS GIRLFRIEND!!

The little joys of being a single woman. ☆

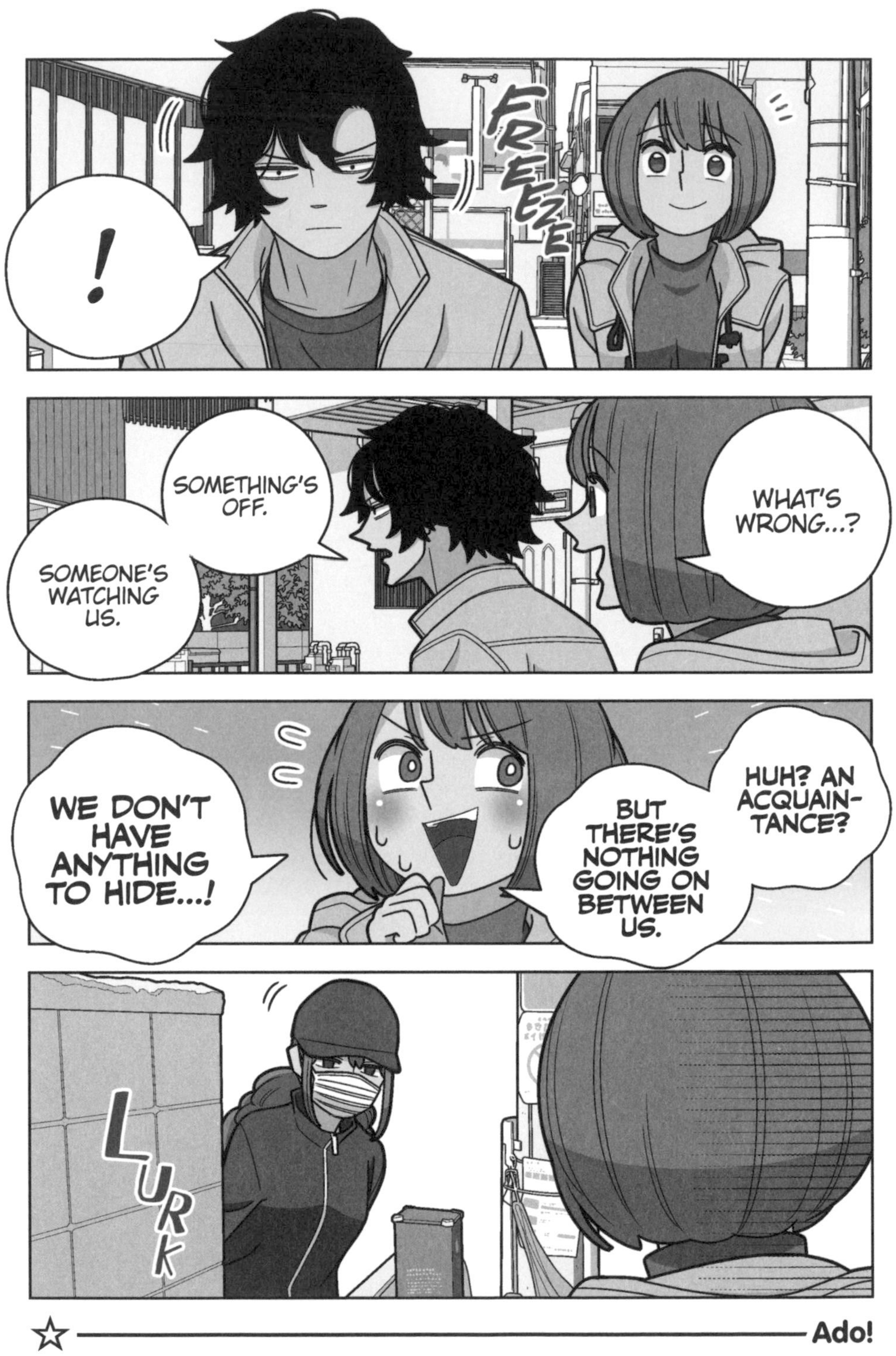
FREEZE
!
WHAT'S WRONG...?
SOMETHING'S OFF.
SOMEONE'S WATCHING US.
HUH? AN ACQUAIN-TANCE?
BUT THERE'S NOTHING GOING ON BETWEEN US.
WE DON'T HAVE ANYTHING TO HIDE...!
LURK

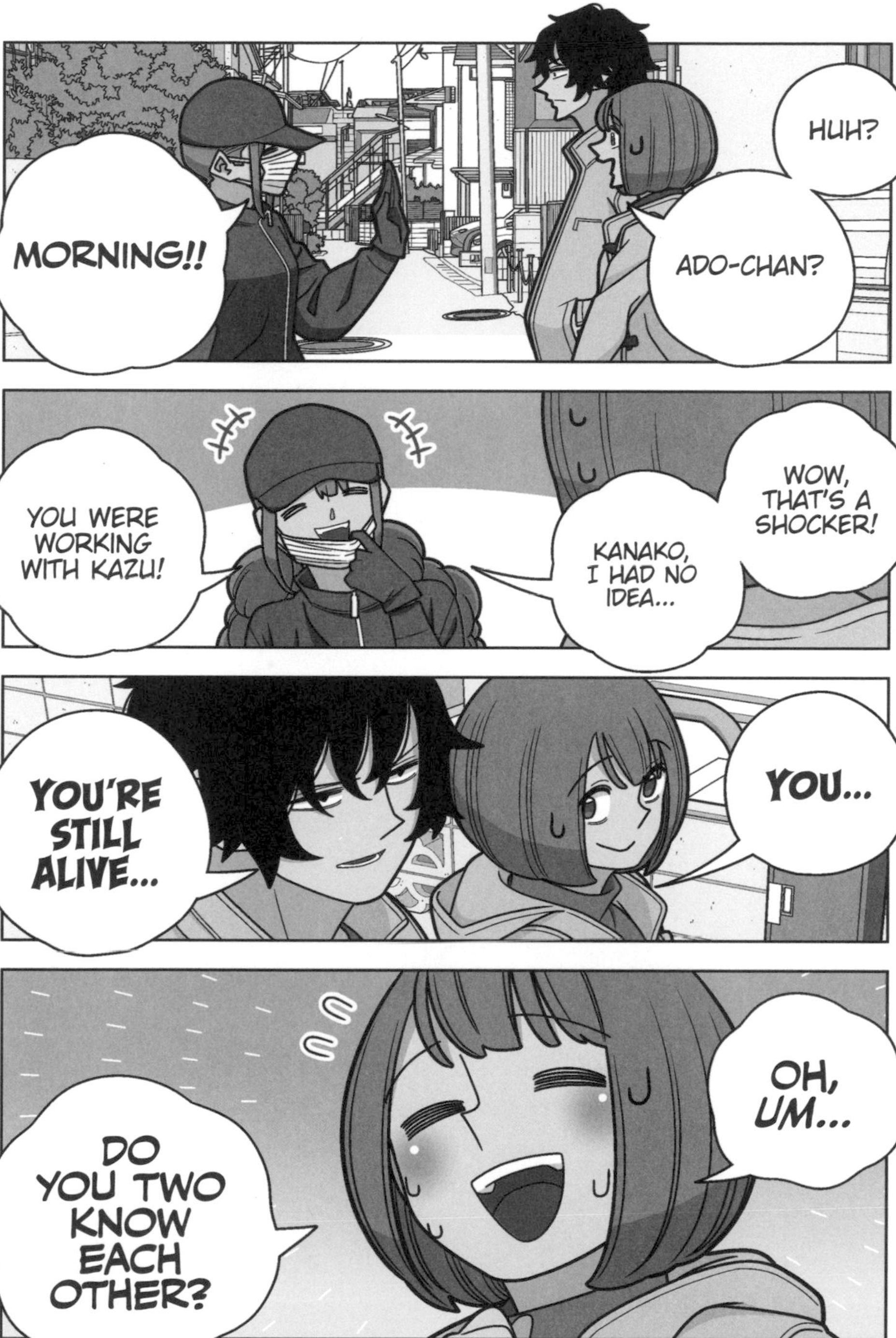
HUH?
ADO-CHAN?
MORNING!!
WOW, THAT'S A SHOCKER!
KANAKO, I HAD NO IDEA...
YOU WERE WORKING WITH KAZU!
YOU...
YOU'RE STILL ALIVE...
OH, UM...
DO YOU TWO KNOW EACH OTHER?

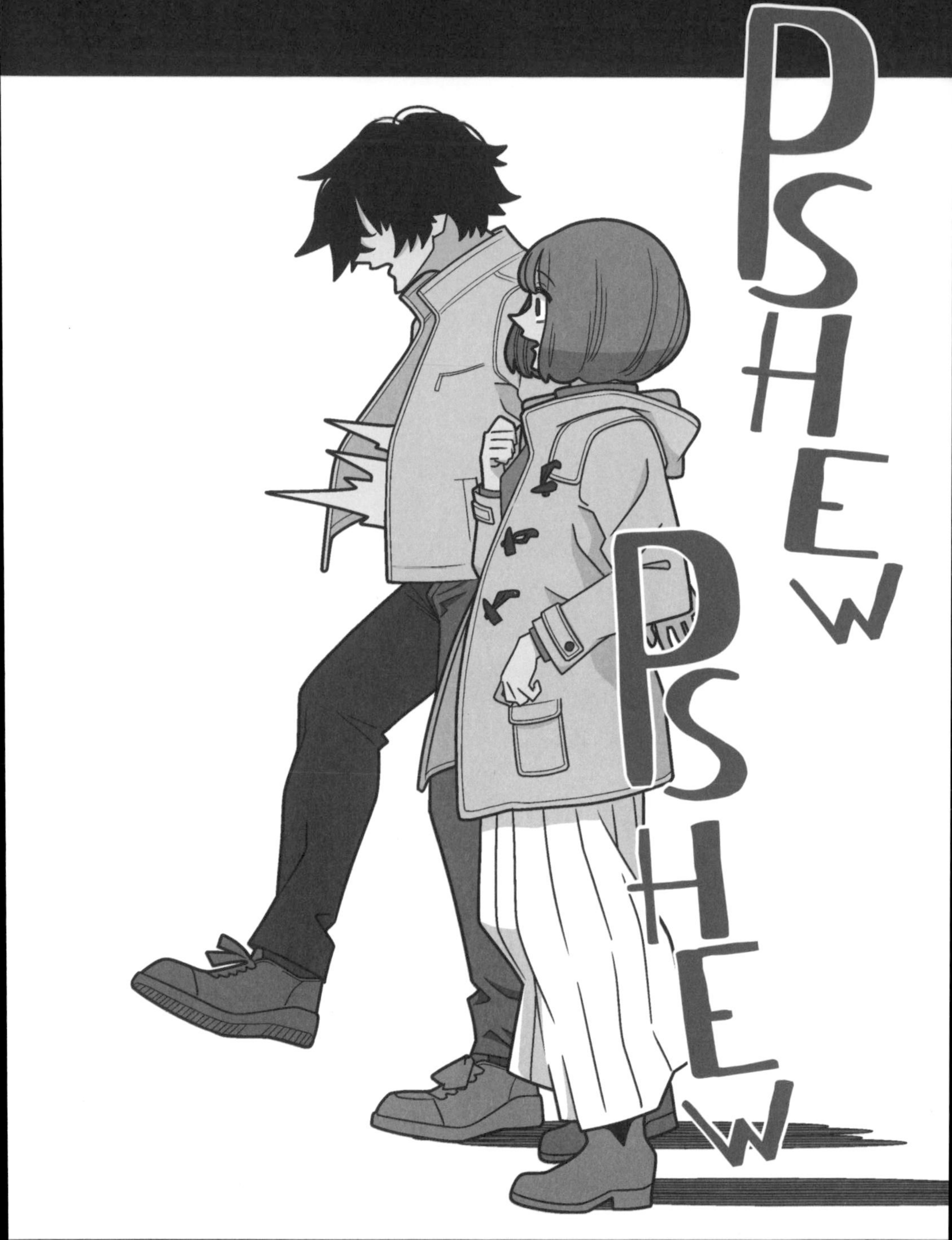
PSHEW
PSHEW

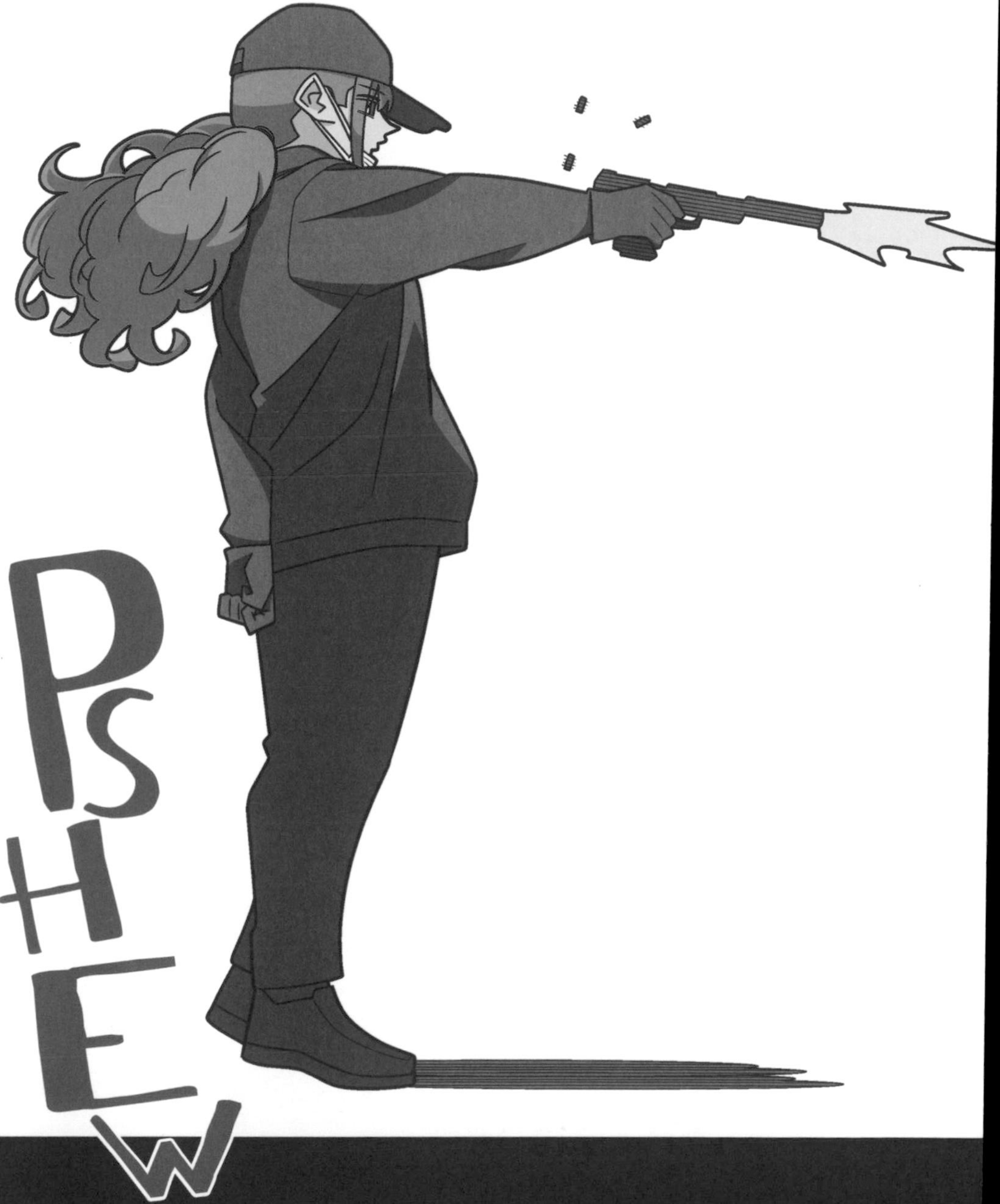
PSHEW

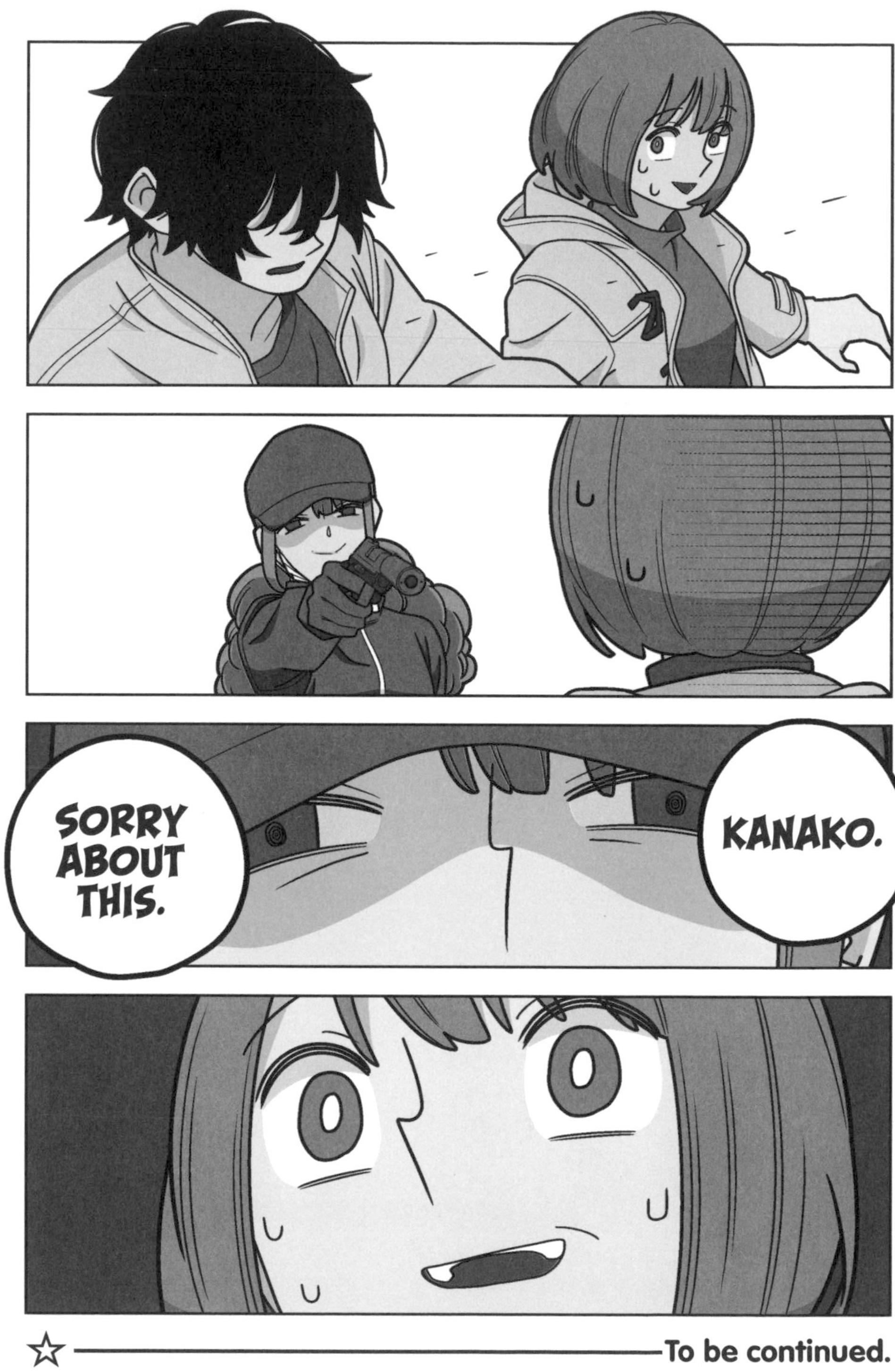
KANAKO.
SORRY ABOUT THIS.

☆ ——— To be continued.

Happy Kanako's
Killer Life

THERE'S
A LOT
GOING
ON...

Thank you for reading!! You can't always live autifully!!

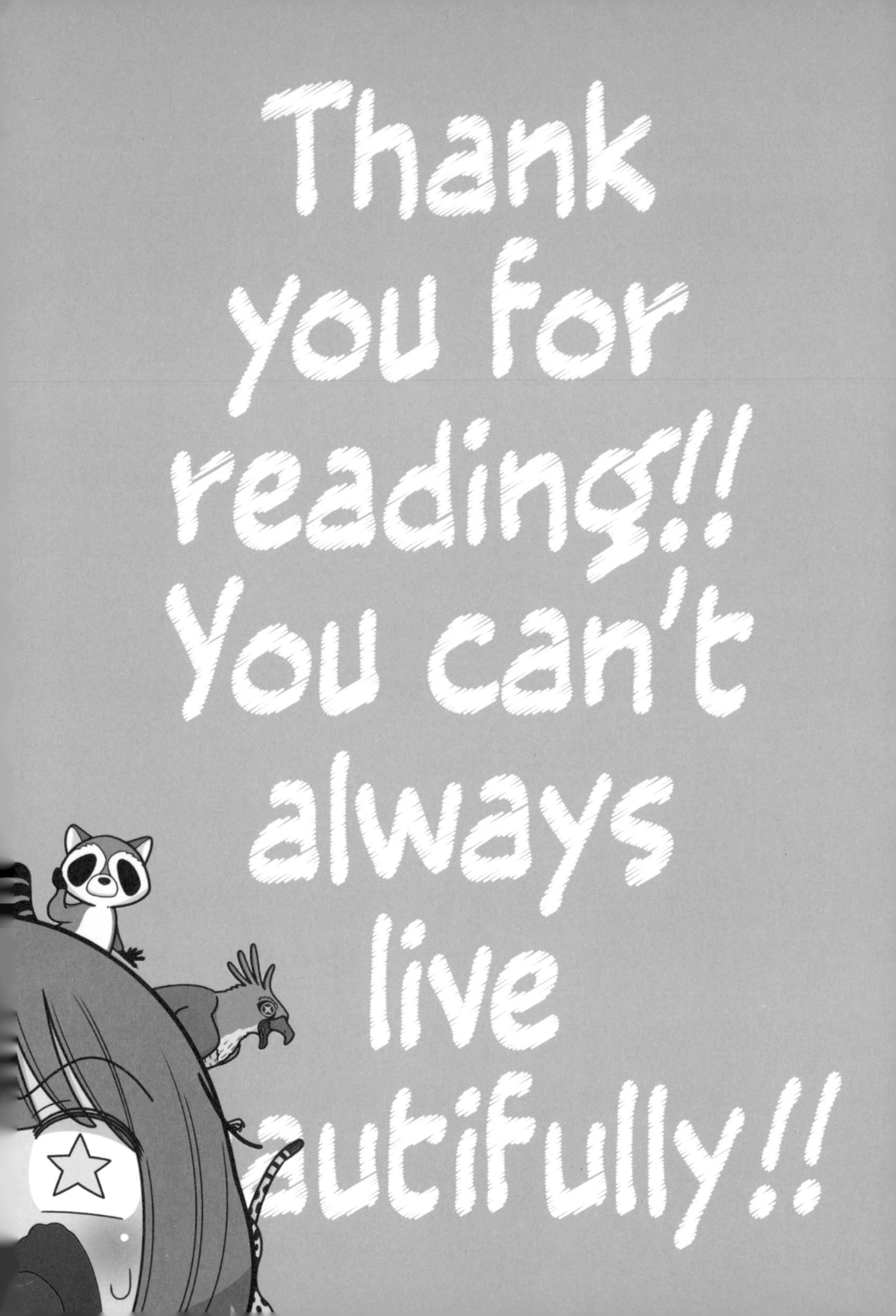

It's natural to stumble!! Still, living in itself is beautiful!! Keep on living!

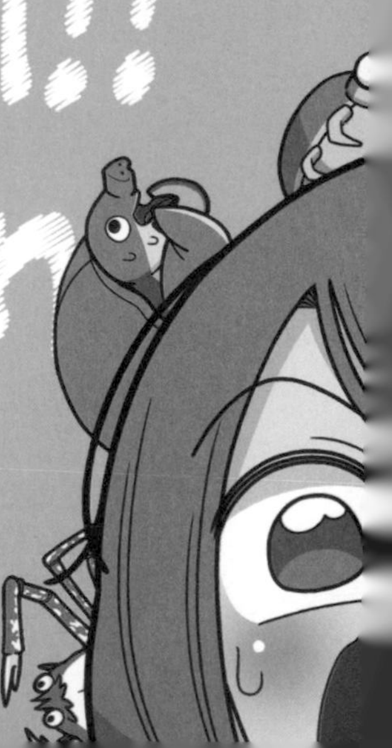

From
Toshiya Wakabayashi

SEVEN SEAS ENTERTAINMENT PRESENTS

Happy Kanako's
Killer⊙Life

story and art by TOSHIYA WAKABAYASHI   VOLUME 5

TRANSLATION
Kevin Yuan

LETTERING
Carolina Hernández Mendoza

COVER AND LOGO DESIGN
H. Qi

PROOFREADER
Kurestin Armada

SENIOR EDITOR
J.P. Sullivan

PRODUCTION MANAGER
Lissa Pattillo

PREPRESS TECHNICIAN
Melanie Ujimori

PRINT MANAGER
Rhiannon Rasmussen-Silverstein

EDITOR-IN-CHIEF
Julie Davis

ASSOCIATE PUBLISHER
Adam Arnold

PUBLISHER
Jason DeAngelis

SHIAWASE KANAKO NO KOROSHIYA SEIKATSU VOL. 5
© Toshiya Wakabayashi 2021
All rights reserved.
Original Japanese edition published by Star Seas Company.
English publishing rights arranged with Star Seas Company
through KODANSHA LTD., Tokyo.

Seven Seas press and purchase enquiries can be sent to Marketing Manager Lianne Sentar at press@gomanga.com. Information regarding the distribution and purchase of digital editions is available from Digital Manager CK Russell at digital@gomanga.com.

Seven Seas and the Seven Seas logo are trademarks of Seven Seas Entertainment. All rights reserved.

ISBN: 978-1-63858-560-2
Printed in Canada
First Printing: July 2022
10 9 8 7 6 5 4 3 2 1

▨▨▨ READING DIRECTIONS ▨▨▨

This book reads from *right to left*, Japanese style. If this is your first time reading manga, you start reading from the top right panel on each page and take it from there. If you get lost, just follow the numbered diagram here. It may seem backwards at first, but you'll get the hang of it! Have fun!!

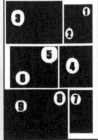

Follow us online: www.SevenSeasEntertainment.com